A Theory
of Discrimination Law

TARUNABH KHAITAN

OXFORD
UNIVERSITY PRESS

OXFORD
UNIVERSITY PRESS

Great Clarendon Street, Oxford, OX2 6DP,
United Kingdom

Oxford University Press is a department of the University of Oxford.
It furthers the University's objective of excellence in research, scholarship,
and education by publishing worldwide. Oxford is a registered trade mark of
Oxford University Press in the UK and in certain other countries

© T. Khaitan 2015

The moral rights of the author have been asserted

First published 2015
First published in paperback 2016

Published in the United States of America by Oxford University Press
198 Madison Avenue, New York, NY 10016, United States of America

British Library Cataloguing in Publication Data
Data available

Library of Congress Cataloging in Publication Data
Data available

ISBN 978–0–19–965696–7 (Hbk.)
ISBN 978–0–19–879075–4 (Pbk.)

to ma, for her instinctive even-handedness;
... and to papa, for being slow to judge

Acknowledgements

For their comments, criticisms, exhortations, and restorative cups of tea, I am very grateful to Farrah Ahmed, Shreya Atreyi, Nicholas Bamforth, Nick Barber, Pritam Baruah, Gautam Bhatia, Alan Bogg, Meghan Campbell, Marinella Capriati, Chintan Chandrachud, Hugh Collins, Julie Dickson, Ben Eidelson, Richard Ekins, Alberto Pino Emhart, Sandra Fredman, Mark Freedland, John Gardner, Leslie Green, Jeffrey Hackney, Barbara Havelková, Deborah Hellman, Nakul Krishna, Karl Laird, Christopher McConnachie, Christopher McCrudden, Dhvani Mehta, Yossi Nehushtan, Colm O'Cinneide, Thomas Pascoe, Denise Réaume, George Rutherglen, Tamas Szigeti, David Wasserman, Paul Yowell, and an anonymous reviewer. Amy Bubb and Marie Tidball helped secure permissions for the cover image, for which I am indebted to them. Many thanks to Sandy Meredith for her expert technical support. Abhishek, Gaurav, and especially Alex—your trust has been complete, your confidence unwavering, and your encouragement always at hand when most needed.

Contents

1. The Problem   1

I: SCOPE AND DEFINITION

2. The Essence of Discrimination Law   23
3. The Architecture of Discrimination Law   45

II: POINT AND PURPOSE

4. A Good Life   91
5. The Point of Discrimination Law   117

III: DESIGNING THE DUTIES

6. The Antidiscrimination Duty   143
7. The Duty-Bearers   195
8. Affirmative Action   215

IV: CONCLUSION

9. The Vindication of Discrimination Law   243

Bibliography   251
Index   261

Detailed Contents

1. The Problem   1

   1.1. The Search for a Foundation   4
   1.2. A Way Forward   9
   1.3. The Dataset   13
   1.4. The Argument   17

                    I: SCOPE AND DEFINITION

2. The Essence of Discrimination Law   23

   2.1. A Thought Experiment   25
   2.2. The Personal Grounds Condition   27
   2.3. The Cognate Groups Condition   30
   2.4. The Relative Disadvantage Condition   31
   2.5. The Eccentric Distribution Condition   38
   2.6. Conclusion   42

3. The Architecture of Discrimination Law   45

   3.1. The Protectorate   49
       3.1.1 Group Disadvantage   51
       3.1.2 Normative Irrelevance   56
       3.1.3 On Symmetry   61
   3.2. The Duty-Bearers   62
   3.3. The Duties   67
       3.3.1 Direct Discrimination   69
       3.3.2 Indirect Discrimination   73
       3.3.3 Reasonable Accommodation   76
       3.3.4 Discriminatory Harassment   79
       3.3.5 Affirmative Action   80
       3.3.6 Rights-Generating and Non-Rights-Generating Duties   86
   3.4. Conclusion   87

II: POINT AND PURPOSE

4. A Good Life   91

    4.1. Well-Being   92
    4.2. Secured Negative Freedom   98
    4.3. Secured Access to an Adequate Range
        of Valuable Opportunities   102
    4.4. Secured Self-Respect   108
    4.5. Interconnections between the Three Goods   112
    4.6. Comparative but Not Egalitarian   113
    4.7. Conclusion   115

5. The Point of Discrimination Law   117

    5.1. The Goal of Discrimination Law   117
    5.2. Justification of the Goal   121
        5.2.1 Negative Freedom   123
        5.2.2 Adequate Range of Valuable Opportunities   124
        5.2.3 Self-Respect   126
        5.2.4 Discrimination Law and the Basic Goods   128
    5.3. Debate with Egalitarians   130
    5.4. Perfectionism in Discrimination Law   134
    5.5. Conclusion   137

III: DESIGNING THE DUTIES

6. The Antidiscrimination Duty   143

    6.1. Action-Regarding Duty   146
    6.2. The Adverse Effect Clause   148
        6.2.1 Tangible and Expressive Effects   149
        6.2.2 Comparative and Non-Comparative Effects   151
        6.2.3 The Levelling-Down Objection   153
    6.3. The Group Membership Clause   154
        6.3.1 Systemic Wrongfulness   155
        6.3.2 Direct and Indirect Discrimination   156
        6.3.3 A Common Definition   159
        6.3.4 Lay and Legal Models   160
        6.3.5 Doctrinal Difficulties with the Lay Model 162
    6.4. The Correlation Clause   165
        6.4.1 Causation to Correlation   166
        6.4.2 Wrongfulness of Particular Acts   167
    6.5. The Expressive Clause   171

6.6. The Justification Clause 180
    6.6.1 Justification and Proportionality 181
    6.6.2 Permitted and Justified Discrimination 181
    6.6.3 Legislative and Judicial Determination 182
    6.6.4 Wrongfulness and Standard of Review 183
    6.6.5 Interests of the Duty-Bearer 186
    6.6.6 Interests of the Victims 191
    6.6.7 Interests of Third Parties 191
6.7. Conclusion 192

7. **The Duty-Bearers** 195
7.1. Public Character 201
7.2. Gatekeepers of Opportunities 209
7.3. Conclusion 212

8. **Affirmative Action** 215
8.1. A Definition 217
8.2. Legitimacy of Affirmative Action Measures 222
    8.2.1 Interests of the Beneficiaries 222
    8.2.2 Interests of the Administrator 225
    8.2.3 Interests of Those Adversely Affected 228
    8.2.4 Public Interest 233
8.3. Conclusion 239

IV: CONCLUSION

9. **The Vindication of Discrimination Law** 243
9.1. Significance and Implications 246
9.2. Possibilities 248

Bibliography 251
Index 261

1

The Problem

Discrimination law is controversial. It could not fail to be, given that it seldom keeps in step with society but often ends up one step ahead. Tabloid headlines decrying 'Political Correctness Gone Mad' or calling lustily for a return to 'common sense' are complaining, more often than not, about a matter somehow connected with discrimination law. In 2010, George Carey, the former Archbishop of Canterbury, waded into this controversy. He was baffled by the 'crude' 'description of religious faith in relation to sexual ethics as "discriminatory"' in law.[1] The 'descriptive word "discriminatory" is unbefitting and it is regrettable that senior members of the Judiciary feel able to make such disparaging comments', he complained.[2] In his reply to the Archbishop, Lord Justice Laws suggested that the prelate's

> mistaken suggestions arise from a misunderstanding on his part as to the meaning attributed by the law to the idea of discrimination. ... the law forbids [indirectly] discriminatory conduct not by reference to the actor's motives but by reference to the outcome of his or her acts or omissions. Acts or omissions may obviously have discriminatory effects and outcomes, as between one group or class of persons and another, whether their motivation is for good or ill ... the proposition that if conduct is accepted as discriminatory it therefore falls to be condemned as disreputable or bigoted is a non sequitur; but it is the premise of Lord Carey's position.[3]

The disagreement arises because the scope of what counts as discrimination in *law* is both wider and narrower than what the term encompasses in the *lay* understanding (readers will, I hope, forgive my labelling an Archbishop a layperson in this context). In the lay discourse,[4] discrimination is intentional, direct,

---

[1] *McFarlane v Relate* [2010] EWCA Civ 880 [16].

[2] *McFarlane v Relate* [2010] EWCA Civ 880 [16].

[3] *McFarlane v Relate* [2010] EWCA Civ 880 [18]. See also, *R (on the application of E) v Governing Body of JFS* [2009] UKSC 15 [9]: 'Nothing that I say in this judgment should be read as giving rise to criticism on moral grounds of the admissions policy of JFS in particular or the policies of Jewish faith schools in general, let alone as suggesting that these policies are "racist" as that word is generally understood.'

[4] The qualifier 'lay' is not intended to be condescending. I use it to distinguish this approach from the one that lawyers, as a set of professionals, employ. While I will disagree with many

and comparative. Attention is directed to the unreasonableness of the process of selection adopted by the discriminator. In law, discrimination may be unintended, indirect, or non-comparative. The focus is on the effect on the victim. For laypersons, discrimination entails some fault. In law, the actor may not be at fault. A college's failure to provide reading material in braille or electronic format to a blind student or an employer's administration of a facially neutral selection test which leads to the selection of fewer women than men could, under certain circumstances, constitute discrimination in the eyes of the law. It is not just that the law treats some acts as discriminatory that laypeople may not. It is also the case that, frequently, the law refuses to prohibit conduct that many non-lawyers would consider discriminatory. It applies only to a select group of duty-bearers, whereas the ordinary understanding condemns intentional discrimination in all contexts. For example, a consumer who refuses to shop at a store simply because its proprietor is Muslim has probably not violated any law, even though most people would condemn such refusal as discriminatory. The law does not require us to refrain from discriminating on the ground of race in the choice of our friends either.[5] In sum, the law treats a much wider range of conduct as discriminatory than does ordinary language, although its regulation of such conduct is restricted to a limited range of contexts.

These legal and lay approaches are, no doubt, coarse archetypes, which hide much internal dissension within the corresponding discourses. The currently dominant (if bitterly contested) legal discourse in the United States is, for example, very close to what has been presented as the lay understanding.[6] It is possible that, in some societies, the lay discourse tracks the legal model reasonably faithfully. Even so, these archetypes have sufficient traction in certain influential English-speaking liberal democratic jurisdictions to be heuristically useful *models*.[7]

For all the controversy surrounding its scope and content, discrimination law has become a mainstay of liberal democratic governance. Led by

---

features of the lay approach, these disagreements arise from its substantive content rather than the fact that it is an approach often adopted by non-lawyers.

[5] For an excellent exploration of the role of discrimination in more intimate settings, see Elizabeth Emens, 'Intimate Discrimination: The State's Role in the Accidents of Sex and Love' (2009) 122 Harvard Law Review 1307.

[6] Samuel Bagenstos, ' "Rational Discrimination", Accommodation, and the Politics of (Disability) Civil Rights' (2003) 89 Virginia Law Review 825; Bradley Areheart, 'The Anticlassification Turn in Employment Discrimination Law' (2011–12) 63 Alabama Law Review 955.

[7] The divergence between the legal and the lay models should become clearer in Chapter 3 of this book. Readers who are less familiar with the legal model may profit from reading that chapter first, before returning to this Introduction.

the 14th Amendment to the Constitution of the United States,[8] the constitutional documents of several jurisdictions, including Germany,[9] India,[10] Northern Ireland,[11] Canada,[12] and South Africa[13] contain provisions regulating discrimination. So do the European Convention on Human Rights[14] and the EU Charter of Fundamental Rights.[15] Several other instruments of international law also contain similar provisions.[16] In addition, most of the jurisdictions cited have enacted a host of legislative measures to outlaw discrimination, significantly influenced by the US Civil Rights Act of 1964.

The geographical spread of discrimination law, especially in the last six decades or so, is matched only by the expansion of the scope of its protection. Creative legislators and judges, responding to complex social problems, have crafted increasingly sophisticated tools, recognizing concepts such as direct and indirect discrimination, affirmative action, reasonable accommodation, harassment, and positive duties. Various groups, spurred on by identity politics, have successfully obtained protection of grounds such as age, disability, religion, and sexual orientation—a phenomenon that Fiss famously described as the proliferation of the protectorate.[17] The contexts in which discrimination law operates have also expanded, albeit in a limited fashion. From relatively humble beginnings (mainly) in the constitutional context, several other areas of human activities, including provisions for goods and services, employment, education, housing, and health care, now fall within its regulatory remit. Legislators and judges have moved at a remarkable speed, guided by moral intuition, political pressure, and pragmatic constraints. Like democracy, the rule of law, and human rights, a system of law regulating

---

[8] On the location of the antidiscrimination principle in the 14th Amendment, see *Brown v Board of Education* 347 US 483 (1954). See also, Christopher McCrudden, 'Introduction' in Christopher McCrudden (ed), *Anti-Discrimination Law* (Dartmouth 1991).

[9] Basic Law of the Federal Republic of Germany 1949, art 3.

[10] Constitution of the Republic of India 1950, art 15.

[11] Northern Ireland Constitution Act 1973, s 17.

[12] Canadian Charter of Rights and Freedoms, s 15, Part I of the Constitution Act, 1982, being Sch B to the Canada Act 1982 (UK), c 11.

[13] Constitution of the Republic of South Africa 1996, s 9.

[14] European Convention on Human Rights 1950, art 14, read with Protocol 12.

[15] Charter of Fundamental Rights of the European Union 2000, art 21.

[16] Universal Declaration of Human Rights 1948, art 2; International Covenant on Civil and Political Rights 1966, art 2; International Covenant on Economic, Social and Cultural Rights 1966, art 2.

[17] Owen Fiss, 'The Fate of an Idea Whose Time has Come: Anti-Discrimination Law in the Second Decade after *Brown* v. *Board of Education*' (1974) 41 University of Chicago Law Review 742, 748. See also, Christopher McCrudden, 'Introduction' in Christopher McCrudden (ed), *Anti-Discrimination Law* (Dartmouth 1991); Christopher McCrudden, 'Introduction' in Christopher McCrudden (ed), *Anti-Discrimination Law* (2nd edn, Ashgate 2004).

discrimination has become key to how some states define themselves. These features have become markers of what a 'civilized' society is.

These rapid politico-legal developments have had two (apparently contradictory) implications for the lay meaning of the term. Ordinary speech now imputes an almost exclusively pejorative sense to the term 'discrimination'—a word that once connoted shrewdness or fine taste now stands for something really quite bad. While common language has been quick to imbue the term with a strong sense of moral repugnance, it has failed to keep pace with the legal expansion of the scope of the concept. Hence the stark divergence between the scope of discrimination and the extent of its wrongfulness in legal and the lay models, reflected in the exchange between Archbishop Carey and Lord Justice Laws. This book seeks to give a theoretical account of the legal model of regulating discrimination. In doing so, it will explain what the legal conception of discrimination is, and why the legal model for regulating discrimination is justified.

1.1 The Search for a Foundation

A failure to recognize the disjuncture between the legal and lay models is responsible for many political, doctrinal, and philosophical controversies and paradoxes that beset this area of law. Our deep political disagreements are reflected in the burgeoning theoretical literature on discrimination and on discrimination law.[18] This scholarly literature is rich and increasingly

---

[18] An illustrative list follows: Charles Black, 'The Lawfulness of the Segregation Decisions' (1960) 69 The Yale Law Journal 421; Gary Becker, *The Economics of Discrimination* (2nd edn, University of Chicago Press 1971); Owen Fiss, 'The Fate of an Idea Whose Time has Come: Anti-Discrimination Law in the Second Decade after *Brown* v. *Board of Education*' (1974) 41 University of Chicago Law Review 742; Paul Brest, 'In Defense of the Antidiscrimination Principle' (1976) 90 Harvard Law Review 1; Marc Galanter, *Competing Equalities: Law and the Backward Classes in India* (University of California Press 1984); Morris Abram, 'Affirmative Action: Fair Shakers and Social Engineers' (1986) 99 Harvard Law Review 1312; Nicola Lacey, 'Legislation Against Sex Discrimination: Questions from a Feminist Perspective' (1987) 14 Journal of Law and Society 411; Richard Posner, 'An Economic Analysis of Sex Discrimination Laws' (1989) 56 University of Chicago Law Review 1311; Kimberlé Crenshaw, 'Demarginalising the Intersection of Race and Sex: A Black Feminist Critique of Antidiscrimination Doctrine, Feminist Theory and Antiracist Politics' [1989] The University of Chicago Legal Forum 139; Larry Alexander, 'What Makes Wrongful Discrimination Wrong? Biases, Preferences, Stereotypes and Proxies' (1992) 141 University of Pennsylvania Law Review 149; Richard Epstein, *Forbidden Grounds: The Case Against Employment Discrimination Laws* (Harvard University Press 1992); Cass Sunstein, 'The Anticaste Principle' (1994) 92 Michigan Law Review 2410; John Gardner, 'On the Ground of Her Sex(uality)' (1998) 18 Oxford Journal of Legal Studies 167; Sujit Choudhry, 'Distribution vs. Recognition: The Case of Anti-Discrimination Laws' (2000) 9 George Mason Law Review 145; Christine Jolls, 'Antidiscrimination and Accommodation' (2001) 115 Harvard

sophisticated, and naturally reflects the political controversy of its time: unsurprisingly, much of it originates in the United States, where the bitter political contest over the law has significantly influenced (for better and for worse) theoretical reflection.

Apart from its emphasis on the American debates, another feature of this literature deserves attention. Some of this material takes 'discrimination' as its subject matter; the rest looks at 'discrimination law'. The former is helpful to our project to the extent that there are continuities between the legal and the lay understandings of the concept.[19] It would, however, be problematic to *assume* (without argument) that the lay understanding of discrimination constitutes the 'central case' of its meaning in the legal discourse too.[20] Such assumptions may be legitimate in other areas of law. However, in our context, the divergence between the legal and the lay models is large enough to require explicit justification of the assumption. Otherwise, there is the danger that we end up converting a moral debate into a linguistic one—for, once the assumption is made, everything that

Law Review 642; Robert Post, Anthony Appiah, Judith Butler, Thomas Grey, and Reva Siegel, *Prejudicial Appearances: The Logic of American Antidiscrimination Law* (Duke University Press 2001); Hugh Collins, 'Discrimination, Equality and Social Inclusion' (2003) 66 The Modern Law Review 16; Christopher McCrudden, 'Theorising European Equality Law' in Cathryn Costello and Eilis Barry (eds), *Equality in Diversity: the New Equality Directives* (Irish Centre for European Law 2003); Denise Réaume, 'Discrimination and Dignity' (2003) 63 Louisiana Law Review 645; Nicholas Bamforth, 'Conceptions of Anti-Discrimination Law' (2004) 24 Oxford Journal of Legal Studies 693; Elisa Holmes, 'Anti-Discrimination Rights Without Equality' (2005) 68 Modern Law Review 175; Kenji Yoshino, *Covering: The Hidden Assault on our Civil Liberties* (Random House 2007); Elizabeth Emens, 'Integrating Accommodation' (2007–2008) 156 University of Pennsylvania Law Review 839; Deborah Hellman, *When is Discrimination Wrong?* (Harvard University Press 2008); John Finnis, 'Directly Discriminatory Decisions: A Missed Opportunity' (2010) 126 Law Quarterly Review 491; Sophia Moreau, 'What is Discrimination?' (2010) 38 Philosophy and Public Affairs 143; Sandra Fredman, *Discrimination Law* (2nd edn, Oxford University Press 2011); Alexander Somek, *Engineering Equality: An Essay on European Anti-Discrimination Law* (Oxford University Press 2011); Reva Siegel, 'From Colorblindness to Antibalkanization: An Emerging Ground of Decision in Race Equality Cases' (2011) 120 The Yale Law Journal 1278; Shlomi Segall, 'What's so Bad about Discrimination' (2012) 24 Utilitas 82; Kalpana Kannabiran, *Tools of Justice: Non-Discrimination and the Indian Constitution* (Routledge 2012); Deborah Hellman and Sophia Moreau (eds), *Philosophical Foundations of Discrimination Law* (Oxford University Press 2013); Joseph Fishkin, *Bottlenecks: A New Theory of Equal Opportunity* (Oxford University Press 2014); Catharine MacKinnon, 'Toward a Renewed Equal Rights Amendment: Now More than Ever' (2014) 37 Harvard Journal of Law and Gender 569; Kasper Lippert-Rasmussen, *Born Free and Equal? A Philosophical Inquiry into the Nature of Discrimination* (Oxford University Press 2014); Re'em Segev, 'Making Sense of Discrimination' (2014) 27 Ratio Juris 47.

[19] For an excellent example, see Benjamin Eidelson, 'Treating People as Individuals' in Deborah Hellman and Sophia Moreau (eds), *Philosophical Foundations of Discrimination Law* (Oxford University Press 2013).

[20] On the role of central cases in legal theory, see John Finnis, *Natural Law and Natural Rights* (Clarendon Press 1980) 9ff.

lies outside the central case must either be justified as its logical extension or stand condemned as linguistically insupportable and possibly
illegitimate. The term 'discrimination', it is true, cannot mean whatever
a whimsical legislator or theorist deems it to mean. There are semantic
limits to its carrying capacity. But the legal expansion of its meaning has
not transgressed these limits.[21] The current debate over the meaning and
scope of discrimination, and the purpose of its regulation, is essentially
normative, and not logical or linguistic. Implicit in the recognition of the
divergence between the two models is the notion that the law is not only
constructed by our moral beliefs but can (and, sometimes, should) also
refine them: the law on discrimination does not stand alone in the dock;
our unexamined moral beliefs about discrimination also await judgment.[22] This is not to say that law and morality must overlap—it is a good
thing that they don't. The point is simply that each of them is capable of
informing the other, both practically and theoretically.[23]

Caveats aside, the Holy Grail for this literature is a coherent normative
foundation upon which discrimination law can securely rest. Dismissing this
search as the fetishization of coherence will be unfair—at stake is not just
some intellectual self-satisfaction (which, even on its own, is no bad thing).
This battle of ideas has important real-world implications. The experience in
the United States in recent years should leave us in no doubt that continued
intellectual failure could incur political costs.

Despite the urgency of the challenge, theoretical consensus has so far eluded
scholars. Candidate theories can (very roughly) be classified into three broad
categories: egalitarian, liberal, and dignitarian.[24] Egalitarians believe that
equality is the, or at least the most important, value that underpins the legal
regulation of discrimination.[25] Despite the fact that many laypersons, philosophers, and even practising lawyers speak of discrimination and equality in the

---

[21] Semantically, discrimination (in the relevant sense) entails some form of relative harm. I will
show in Chapter 5 that the law respects this linguistic limit—just not in a self-evident way.

[22] Leslie Green, 'Should Law Improve Morality?' (2013) 7 Criminal Law and Philosophy 473.
See also, Jeremy Waldron, 'Dignity and Rank' in Jeremy Waldron and Meir Dan-Cohen (eds),
Dignity, Rank and Rights (Oxford University Press 2012) 13.

[23] See Bernard Williams, 'What has Philosophy to Learn from Tort Law?' in David Owen (ed),
Philosophical Foundations of Tort Law (Clarendon Press 1995).

[24] Almost no one who takes both law and philosophy seriously stands up for 'rationality' as a
foundational value anymore, although the idea did have some traction once upon a time. See generally, Donal Nolan, 'A Right to Meritorius Treatment' in Conor Gearty and Adam Tomkins (eds),
Understanding Human Rights (Pinter 1996); John Gardner, 'On the Ground of Her Sex(uality)'
(1998) 18 Oxford Journal of Legal Studies 167, 168–9.

[25] Shlomi Segall, 'What's so Bad about Discrimination' (2012) 24 Utilitas 82; Patrick Shin, 'The
Substantive Principle of Equal Treatment' (2009) 15 Legal Theory 149.

same breath,[26] no such consensus exists in the theoretical literature. Liberals think that the job of providing a normative foundation to discrimination law is best performed by some (capacious) conception of liberty, autonomy, or freedom.[27] My understanding of the liberal approaches is a broad one, and I include welfarist/utilitarian, and even some republican, approaches within this category.[28] Dignitarians locate the wrongfulness of discrimination in a violation of personal dignity (or personhood or individuality).[29]

These labels have been ascribed on the basis of emphasis, and should not detract from the intricate nuances of many of the cited works. Each of these broad approaches have their detractors. There are two common themes in the criticisms that have been levelled against each of them: one, that they lead to certain normatively unpalatable outcomes; two, that they are unable to explain certain well-established aspects of existing law. The two criticisms are related. The second, fit-related, criticism bites only because the aspect of existing law that the putative foundation cannot explain is considered morally desirable.

Detractors of equality, for example, have pointed to its essentially comparative nature and contrasted that with the legal recognition that comparisons are not essential to establish discrimination, maintaining further that they ought not to be essential either.[30] Some have highlighted the worrying

---

[26] Kasper Lippert-Rasmussen, 'Discrimination and Equality' in Andrei Marmor (ed), *Routledge Companion to Philosophy of Law* (Routledge 2012) 569: 'Conceptually, discrimination is tied to inequality. It is impossible to discriminate against someone unless there is some dimension in which the discriminator treats the discriminatee worse than those against whom she does not discriminate.'

[27] John Gardner, 'On the Ground of Her Sex(uality)' (1998) 18 Oxford Journal of Legal Studies 167; Sophia Moreau, 'What is Discrimination?' (2010) 38 Philosophy and Public Affairs 143; Kenji Yoshino, 'The New Equal Protection' (2011) 124 Harvard Law Review 747.

[28] Richard Arneson, 'Discrimination, Disparate Impact, and Theories of Justice' in Deborah Hellman and Sophia Moreau (eds), *Philosophical Foundations of Discrimination Law* (Oxford University Press 2013); Hugh Collins, 'Discrimination, Equality and Social Inclusion' (2001) 66 The Modern Law Review 16.

[29] Benjamin Eidelson, 'Treating People as Individuals' in Deborah Hellman and Sophia Moreau (eds), *Philosophical Foundations of Discrimination Law* (Oxford University Press 2013); Denise Réaume, 'Discrimination and Dignity' (2003) 63 Louisiana Law Review 645; Gay Moon and Robin Allen, 'Dignity Discourse in Discrimination Law: A Better Route to Equality?' [2006] European Human Rights Law Review 610; Deborah Hellman, *When is Discrimination Wrong?* (Harvard University Press 2008). See also, Tarunabh Khaitan, 'Dignity as an Expressive Norm: Neither Vacuous Nor a Panacea' (2012) 32 Oxford Journal of Legal Studies 1; Catherine Dupré, 'Human Dignity in Europe: A Foundational Constitutional Principle' (2013) 19 European Public Law 319.

[30] Elisa Holmes, 'Anti-Discrimination Rights Without Equality' (2005) 68 Modern Law Review 175; Denise Réaume, 'Dignity, Equality and Comparison' in Deborah Hellman and Sophia Moreau (eds), *Philosophical Foundations of Discrimination Law* (Oxford University Press 2013); Suzanne Goldberg, 'Discrimination by Comparison' (2011) 120 Yale Law Journal 728. For other concerns with equality, see Hugh Collins, 'Discrimination, Equality and Social Inclusion' (2003) 66 The Modern Law Review 16.

possibility of levelling down to meet egalitarian demands.[31] Similar complaints have been made about liberal approaches. Not all violations of discrimination law, it seems, curtail one's freedom.[32] In particular, discrimination law protects members of privileged groups too (whites, men, heterosexuals)—it is not clear how their freedom is under threat in the first place or why they are in need of liberal welfarist interventions. Dignitarians are no exception to this onslaught. Even if one could specify a concrete enough conception of dignity,[33] it is not easily apparent how some of the 'less egregious' forms of discrimination that the law prohibits violate dignity.[34]

A plausible, reasonably uncontroversial, normative foundation remains elusive.[35] Yet, when proposed normative foundations and aspects of legal practice do not fit each other, the usual demand is that the former should give way rather than the latter.[36] For all the controversy, messiness, and theoretical uncertainty that underpin it, the normative commitment to the law as it (broadly) is is surprisingly strong in the theoretical literature. The elusiveness of a clear foundation has forced some scholars to pluralism and others to despair. Pluralists have recognized that many of these ideas have something to recommend them. They illuminate important aspects of discrimination law, even as they fail to appreciate the entire picture. It must follow that discrimination law rests on multiple normative foundations.[37] The pluralists are on the right track, although fancier footwork is required. Pessimists,

---

[31] Such criticisms have often resulted in a refinement of the underlying value: Deborah Brake, 'When Equality Leaves Everyone Worse Off: The Problem of Levelling Down in Equality Law' (2004) 46 William and Mary Law Review 513.

[32] Matthew Shapiro, 'Enforcing Respect: Liberalism, Perfectionism, and Antidiscrimination Law' (DPhil thesis, University of Oxford 2012) 81–2, and ch 4; Katie Eyer, 'Marriage This Term: On Liberty and the "New Equal Protection"' (2012) 60 UCLA Law Review Discourse 2, 10ff.

[33] Tarunabh Khaitan, 'Dignity as an Expressive Norm: Neither Vacuous Nor a Panacea' (2012) 32 Oxford Journal of Legal Studies 1.

[34] Colm O'Cinneide, 'The Uncertain Foundations of Contemporary Anti-Discrimination Law' (2011) 11 International Journal of Discrimination and the Law 7, 22. See also, Rory O'Connell, 'The Role of Dignity in Equality Law: Lessons from Canada and South Africa' (2008) 6 International Journal of Constitutional Law 267; Christopher McConnachie, 'Human Dignity, "Unfair Discrimination" and Guidance' (2014) 34 Oxford Journal of Legal Studies 609; Kasper Lippert-Rasmussen, 'The Badness of Discrimination' (2006) 9 Ethical Theory and Moral Practice 167, esp 178ff; *Gosselin v Quebec* [2002] 4 SCR 429.

[35] Colm O'Cinneide, 'The Uncertain Foundations of Contemporary Anti-Discrimination Law' (2011) 11 International Journal of Discrimination and the Law 7.

[36] Matthew Shapiro, 'Enforcing Respect: Liberalism, Perfectionism, and Antidiscrimination Law' (DPhil thesis, University of Oxford 2012) ch 1.

[37] Patrick Shin, 'Is There a Unitary Concept of Discrimination?' in Deborah Hellman and Sophia Moreau (eds), *Philosophical Foundations of Discrimination Law* (Oxford University Press 2013); Re'em Segev, 'Making Sense of Discrimination' (2014) 27 Ratio Juris 47.

on the other hand, have concluded that the law must be incoherent and indefensible.[38] They have hung up their boots all too soon.

One implication of this elusive search is that a simple appeal to broad, vague, and abstract ideals will not suffice. It is true that these abstract ideals underpin most of our concrete values. It is also true that the foundation of discrimination law is probably going to entail some variation, or combination, of basic ideals such as equality, liberty, and dignity. At a generic level, appeals to at least some of these values cannot be avoided. However, when we rely upon these foundational values, they need to be concretized somewhat into a conception that we are able to grasp. Spelling out in some detail what equality or freedom or dignity entail (or ought to entail) is necessary.

1.2 A Way Forward

As is often the case in scholarship, most of these theorists are on to something important. Their work contains the seeds which can be developed to respond to the pessimistic challenge. At least some of the tension that besets the scholarship—individual versus group justice, distributive versus corrective justice, equality versus liberty, harm versus wrong models, process versus effects approaches—will melt away if we realize that different normative principles are relevant at different levels of the inquiry. Scholars have not been particularly careful in distinguishing between these different levels[39]—it is unsurprising that they end up with different answers. Let us start with an example from a different context to better understand the nature of the problem. HLA Hart, drawing upon John Rawls's seminal article on 'two conceptions of rules',[40] pointed out that while deterrence is the general justifying aim of punishment, retribution explains who should be punished and when. Rather than being alternative and incompatible justifications of punishment, both values play a role at different points in the justificatory enquiry. Hart correctly noted that:

what is most needed is not the simple admission that instead of a single value or aim ... a plurality of different values and aims should be given as a conjunctive

---

[38] George Rutherglen, 'Concrete or Abstract Conceptions of Discrimination' in Deborah Hellman and Sophia Moreau (eds), *Philosophical Foundations of Discrimination Law* (Oxford University Press 2013).

[39] See, for example, Andrew Morris, 'On the Normative Foundations of Indirect Discrimination Law: Understanding the Competing Models of Discrimination Law as Aristotelian Forms of Justice' (1995) 15 Oxford Journal of Legal Studies 199.

[40] John Rawls, 'Two Concepts of Rules' (1955) 64 The Philosophical Review 3.

answer to some *single* question concerning the justification of punishment. What is needed is the realisation that different principles … are relevant at different points in any morally acceptable account of punishment.[41]

A similar recognition in discrimination law will show that apparently incompatible theoretical explanations—drawing upon equality, autonomy, dignity, and even rationality—all have captured some essential truth about discrimination law (although none can explain everything on its own). Yet they provide responses to different questions about discrimination law. Delineating these questions and answering them separately (while recognizing, of course, their interrelationship) leads us to a value pluralism of a more sophisticated sort.

What, then, are these different questions in the context of discrimination law that the scholars have failed to differentiate from each other? As with punishment, the first of these questions demands a *purposive* inquiry into the general justifying aim of discrimination law; the second question is really a set of *distributive* sub-questions: what rights and duties does the law distribute, to whom, and when? These distributive issues are *internal* to law, and only because a regime of discrimination law exists in the first place do they arise (presumably in pursuit of its overall purpose).[42] The purposive inquiry engages with overall systemic concerns: why do we have a system of discrimination law at all? What, indeed, is the point of this area of law? This inquiry does not presuppose that every area of law has a teleological purpose—the question, simply put, is this: what type of mischief does discrimination law, taken as a whole, seek to address? The distributive questions constitute an intermediate level of inquiry, between systemic concerns and evaluation of particular disputes. At this level, one seeks to understand the different tools that the law employs: the prohibition on direct and indirect discrimination and discriminatory harassment; the role of comparators; the requirement of fault; provision for reasonable accommodation and affirmative action; and the possibility of justification.[43] Who bears the duties that these tools impose is also relevant here (the state, employers, landlords, service providers); as is

---

[41] HLA Hart, 'Prolegomenon to the Principles of Punishment' (1959–60) 60 Proceedings of the Aristotelian Society 1, 3. Emphasis in the original.

[42] Gardner makes a distinction between 'exogenous' distributive justice concerns, and 'endogenous' distributive justice concerns with respect to tort law: John Gardner, 'What is Tort Law For? Part 2: The Place of Distributive Justice' in John Oberdiek (ed), *Philosophical Foundations of the Law of Torts* (Oxford University Press 2014).

[43] See, for example, the insightful contributions by Julie Suk, Michael Selmi, and David Wasserman in Deborah Hellman and Sophia Moreau (eds), *Philosophical Foundations of Discrimination Law* (Oxford University Press 2013).

the question of who is allowed to bring a claim (men as well as women, the disabled but not the able-bodied). The background systemic concerns become manifest at this intermediate level of inquiry, albeit non-transparently.

One could say that philosophers interrogating the lay conception of discrimination have tended to focus on the distributive questions alone. This is unsurprising: law often uses the wrongfulness of an action (among other things) as a basis for distributing rights and duties, and these philosophers have mainly sought to isolate what it is that makes discrimination wrongful. Academic lawyers and legal philosophers have attended to both the distributive and the purposive questions (albeit without betraying much consciousness of the distinction between them). Although the overall purpose of discrimination law has a bearing on most of the distributive questions, there are other considerations that inform the distribution. Furthermore, the relationship between the purposive and the distributive question may or may not be a transparent one: particular distributive tools may not necessarily seek the overall systemic purpose of discrimination law directly; they may instead be designed to seek it indirectly by creating the conditions which further the said purpose. This is a strategic choice, and often a wise one.[44]

A theorist should clarify whether she is asking the purposive question or the distributive one (or a sub-question thereof). The two inquiries are, no doubt, deeply interconnected. But they remain distinct inquiries, especially in the absence of full transparency between purposive and distributive concerns. While imbibing these lessons, a successful theory would identify true, general, salient, and mutually coherent propositions about discrimination law. If its explanatory ambition includes evaluation, a theorist will also need to show why the phenomenon in question is (or is not) a good thing.[45] Because theorizing involves generalization, categorical normative claims will rarely be true: 'X is generally desirable' is likely to be more plausible than 'X is always desirable'. Generalization, essential to theoretical success, demands modesty.[46]

These success requirements, especially generality, also impose constraints on the type of dataset that will need looking into to construct a successful theory. Sometimes, theoretical insights are so closely tied to the peculiarities

---

[44] Richard Hare, 'Ethical Theory and Utilitarianism' in Hywel Lewis (ed), *Contemporary British Philosophy* (George Allen & Unwin 1976).

[45] On this point, Julie Dickson's distinction between directly and indirectly evaluative theories is helpful: Julie Dickson, *Evaluation and Legal Theory* (Hart 2001) 51ff.

[46] As Gardner notes, 'no amount of theorizing can properly eradicate the ultimate diversity of pros and cons': John Gardner, 'What is Tort Law For? Part 2: The Place of Distributive Justice' in John Oberdiek (ed), *Philosophical Foundations of the Law of Torts* (Oxford University Press 2014) 338.

of a particular jurisdiction that few generalizations are possible. Although they give valuable insights into the working of that jurisdiction, their value in illuminating the nature and purpose of discrimination law more generally is limited. The reason is not difficult to see. The interaction between practice and theory will not always be synchronized. We have already seen a few instances of theories condemned for their failures to explain certain key aspects of the practice, and can easily think of practices we find unsupportable because of our theoretical commitments. One has to be careful here—it is not always clear whether an aspect of the practice is mistaken, or whether the proposed theory is itself unsound. But it helps to spot outlying practices better if one works from a larger rather than a smaller field of data. This is the reason why it is difficult to theorize about a relatively new area of law: there is simply insufficient data to support any general theory. The best one can do is offer theoretical speculation on future developments. Similarly, if a legal phenomenon exists in several jurisdictions, a theorist would often do well to look around and gather data from many places. This is especially true if certain jurisdictions have roughly similar practice, employ similar concepts and language, explicitly or implicitly borrow from each other, and believe that they are targeting the same mischief. A theorist must, of course, be careful to look only at the same phenomenon in multiple jurisdictions, rather than different phenomena that go by the same name. She should also be aware that her own cultural, linguistic, and academic location might limit her ability to make this distinction. An eclectic, yet cautious, gathering of data, and an expectation of, rather than resistance to, exceptions to general rules make theorizing more honest.

To this, one could object that there is *no* single trans-border phenomenon called 'discrimination law'. If there is no such thing as discrimination law generally (as opposed to discrimination law in the United Kingdom or in India), no general theory is possible. The objection has its attractions, especially when we are concerned with a dynamic, unstable, contentious, and elusive area of law, with significant inter-jurisdictional differences. Even so, at least some of the common-law based, culturally conversant, liberal democratic jurisdictions employ a common vocabulary, similar structure, and comparable concepts in their practice of this area of law. Even when there are significant differences in the substantive legal position on an issue, many law-makers (legislators and judges) in these jurisdictions seem to believe that these laws respond to similar problems. This is especially evident in their readiness to borrow concepts and tools from each other and their use of more-or-less common vocabulary. These factors hint at the possibility that while law's regulation of discrimination is not quite the global phenomenon that criminal law might be, legal regimes in a smaller set of jurisdictions may be instantiations of a conspicuous beast we could call 'discrimination law'.

1.3 The Dataset

The first task for a theorist is to clearly identify the phenomenon that is under interrogation. This book's subject matter is the *practice* of discrimination law. *Practice* is intended to be used in a technical, Rawlsian, sense: 'any form of activity specified by a system of rules which defines offices, roles, moves, penalties, defenses, and so on, and which gives the activity its structure'.[47] This book's focus will remain always on the *rules* that give discrimination law its *structure*. Furthermore, we will only consider rules as they are officially published by law-makers (chiefly, legislatures and judges of appellate courts).[48] All jurisdictions have some gap between aspirational rules and their practical enforcement—without denying the importance of the latter, we will remain steadfastly concerned with the former. Here, I am interested in evaluating discrimination law in terms of its stated aspirations: examining the extent to which these aspirations are realized in practice is an important, but distinct, inquiry. Further still, we will mainly focus on specific types of rules: those that define the rights of, duties on, and licences for the various actors involved. We will, on the whole, ignore rules relating to evidence and procedure, and touch upon remedies only incidentally. In other words, we will theorize only the *normative* rules (ie rules regulating what one should or should not do). References to the *practice* of discrimination law will henceforth be limited to these rules alone.

The practice of discrimination law varies between jurisdictions. Some do not even have any area of law that may be characterized as such. In defining the subject matter of this theoretical project, the next task is to identify jurisdictions that are similar enough to be engaged in the same enterprise, yet diverse enough to give us a good spread and preclude generating too niche an account. It will also help if the developments in these jurisdictions are not too recent—this is tricky for a neoteric system like discrimination law. Roughly speaking, at least a few decades of active operation is essential for us to have sufficient data to sink our teeth into. Finally, these jurisdictions need to reflect, to some minimal degree, shared normative assumptions regarding the value

---

[47] John Rawls, 'Two Concepts of Rules' (1955) 64 The Philosophical Review 3.
[48] Rules are used broadly, and include principles, standards, norms, etc. See Joseph Raz, 'Legal Principles and the Limits of Law' (1972) 81 The Yale Law Journal 823.

of liberalism and democracy that underpin this account. Based on these factors, the picture that Part I of the book will paint will be based on discrimination law as it is practised in the following five jurisdictions: Canada, India, South Africa, the United Kingdom, and the United States. It is impossible to study the law in the United Kingdom without simultaneously looking at the law of the European Union and the Council of Europe—these European influences are part of the dataset.

Let me explain why these jurisdictions qualify. They satisfy the threshold requirement inasmuch as they are, even if compromised, liberal democracies. They satisfy the similarity condition inasmuch as they are all common-law based, English-speaking jurisdictions that are conversant with each other's cultures, including legal cultures. These factors suggest that their respective practice of discrimination law is likely to be an instance of that general phenomenon. Treading on one side of the common-law/non-common-law divide automatically checks several likeness-demanding boxes for projects seeking trans-jurisdictional similarity. Tied together by a unique colonial past, common-law jurisdictions tend to share certain basic approaches to practising and theorizing about law, legislation, adjudication, and legal scholarship. Although the similarity-inducing common-law requirement is useful, the account is saved from being too blinkered: the European Union and the Council of Europe, important non-common-law jurisdictions with developed takes on discrimination, are included in our dataset via the United Kingdom.[49] The claims in this book may well be true of other jurisdictions too—but that will require independent verification.

Colonialism transplanted not just the common law, but also the English language (at least as an 'official' language for legalese). The diversity between the jurisdictions is staggering as it is, without having to contend with translating legal concepts across languages and legal cultures. On the cultural front, the focus is on mutual intelligibility of their respective legal and political cultures—no doubt facilitated by a shared official language and a common legal approach. Cultural familiarity is important for the discourses on 'discrimination' in one regime to be understood by lawyers in other jurisdictions within our set. These features facilitate 'doctrine-swapping'—another key factor in our selection.[50] Each jurisdiction within our set has either imported

---

[49] In practice, continental jurisdictions, even within the European Union, vary. The variance is complicated further by the communist past of some of the new EU member states. See, for example, Barbara Havelková, 'Gender in Law Under and After State Socialism: The Example of the Czech Republic' (DPhil thesis, University of Oxford 2013).

[50] Transnational judicial conversations have become a key feature in human rights adjudication: Christopher McCrudden, 'A Common Law of Human Rights?: Transnational Judicial Conversations on Constitutional Rights' (2000) 20 Oxford Journal of Legal Studies 499, Arun

(usually with conscious and unconscious modifications) aspects of the doctrine from or exported them to at least one other jurisdiction in the set.[51] The United States has exported the most and imported the least, although the dissenting opinions of its judges have been at least as influential as the majority opinions. Others have given and received, to varying degrees; jurisdictions from the 'global North' (Canada, the United Kingdom, the United States) tend to bother less about developments in the 'global South' (India, South Africa) than the other way around.

These similarities allow us to safely assume that when these jurisdictions speak of discrimination law, they are referring to the same broad phenomenon. While they are similar in important respects, they are also different in a key respect: in including India and South Africa, the set does more than simply reflect the approaches adopted in the richer, 'developed', jurisdictions. Legal exchange closely tracks global power dynamics—it is important for scholarship to avoid perpetuating these power structures where possible. My selection of jurisdictions admittedly tracks the enduring legacies of the British Empire: the common-law tradition and the English language. An exclusive focus on the practice of the richer nations within this set would align our knowledge too close to power. Admittedly, South Africa and India have been influenced more than they have influenced. But their legal discourses on discrimination satisfy the requirement of sufficient similarity and adequate sophistication to merit inclusion. Their location tends to result in a more serious engagement with discriminatory disadvantage. A theory that ignores

---

Thiruvengadam, 'In Pursuit of "The Common Illumination of our House": Trans-Judicial Influence and the Origins of PIL Jurisprudence in South Asia' (2008) 2 Indian Journal of Constitutional Law 67. Insofar as at least the constitutional antidiscrimination provisions are seen as part of human rights law, they have also been affected by these judicial conversations.

[51] The UK, for example, adopted American-style prohibitions on direct and indirect discrimination in the 1970s: see the Sex Discrimination Act 1975, s 1(1)(b); the Race Relations Act 1976, s 1(1)(b). On the UK's import of US law, see Anthony Lester, 'Equality and United Kingdom Law: Past, Present and Future' [2001] Public Law 77; Bob Hepple, 'The European Legacy of *Brown v. Board of Education*' [2006] University of Illinois Law Review 605. India considered the American approach to affirmative action seriously in its landmark case: *Indra Sawhney v Union of India* AIR 1993 SC 477 [42]–[53]. On the impact of comparative law in other areas of Indian discrimination law, see Sujit Choudhry, 'How to Do Comparative Constitutional Law in India: Naz Foundation, Same Sex Rights, and Dialogical Interpretation' in Sunil Khilnani, Vikram Raghavan and Arun Thiruvengadam (eds), *Comparative Constitutionalism in South Asia* (Oxford University Press 2010). South African law was greatly influenced by the minority opinions in the Canadian jurisprudence: Christopher McConnachie, 'Human Dignity, "Unfair Discrimination" and Guidance' (2014) 34 Oxford Journal of Legal Studies 609, 613–14. Canadian law, in turn, developed in the shadow of the US discourse; even the earliest constitutional cases cited American case law: *Andrews v Law Society of British Columbia* [1989] 1 SCR 143.

serious engagements with discrimination law in poorer jurisdictions will be impoverished for that reason.

The five chosen jurisdictions are therefore sufficiently similar and importantly different to merit selection. A final factor that has played a role is their (relative) longevity. Unless a jurisdiction has had this system of laws for some time we are unlikely to find enough practical material to theorize with. Most pioneering developments in discrimination law took place in one of our chosen jurisdictions. The prohibition on direct discrimination dates back to nineteenth-century India and United States,[52] although doctrinal development did not take off until the mid-twentieth century. Indirect discrimination was first recognized in the United States.[53] The prohibition of discriminatory harassment also arose first in the United States.[54] Affirmative action measures were first adopted in India.[55] These pioneering jurisdictions are also the outlying regimes within our dataset—US law is in retreat,[56] whereas Indian law on matters other than harassment and affirmative action is still being shaped.[57] The United Kingdom, influenced deeply by early developments in the United States, seriously got into the game by the 1970s. It later influenced the development of the EU law in this regard. Canada joined in by the 1980s and South Africa in the 1990s. The fact that even an experience spanning only about two decades qualifies as sufficient time reveals just how recently the law has started taking discrimination seriously.

Each of these factors admits to degrees, and deciding whether a jurisdiction satisfies it sufficiently is undoubtedly subjective. There may well be important jurisdictions that have been left out. Perhaps Australia, Kenya, and Malaysia deserved to be included in the dataset. Despite their long

---

[52] Indian Caste Disabilities Removal Act 1850; 14th Amendment to the US Constitution 1868.

[53] *Griggs v Duke Power Co* 401 US 424 (1971).

[54] *Williams v Saxbe* 413 F Supp 654 (1976); *Meritor Savings Bank v Vinson* 477 US 57 (1986). See also, Ann Numhauser-Henning and Sylvaine Laulom, *Harassment Related to Sex and Sexual Harassment Law in 33 European Countries: Discrimination Versus Dignity* (European Commission 2012) 10: Until 'the early nineties there was no explicit regulation on sexual harassment in the then [EU] Member States. Both the UK and Ireland, however, had qualified harassment as unacceptable sex discrimination, in the U.S. tradition.'

[55] The Government of Madras framed a Grant-in-Aid Code in 1885 to regulate affirmative action for 'backward classes': Bindheshwari Mandal, Report of the Second Backward Classes Commission (First Part) (Government of India 1980) 61; Marc Galanter, 'Who are the Other Backward Classes?: An Introduction to a Constitutional Puzzle' (1978) 13 Economic and Political Weekly 1812, 1821 fn 1.

[56] See generally, Clark Cunningham, Dorsey DE Jr, Bowen J et al, 'Rethinking Equality in the Global Society' (1997) 75 Washington University Law Quarterly 1561.

[57] The starkly regressive judgment of its Supreme Court in *Koushal v Union of India* (2014) 1 SCC 1 is a huge, if reversible, setback to recent developments in Indian discrimination law. See generally, Tarunabh Khaitan, '*Koushal v Naz*: Judges Vote to Recriminalise Homosexuality' (forthcoming 2015) Modern Law Review.

standing, international law provisions regulating discrimination have also generally been excluded. Under-inclusions, if any, must be forgiven as the price paid for the viability of this project.

1.4 The Argument

Part I of the book comprises Chapters 2 and 3, which together define the subject matter of our theoretical project: the essence and the architecture of the practice of discrimination law in the selected jurisdictions. The data in our selected set pull in different directions on several issues. Even so, many of these differences are at a level of detail that is less relevant to our theoretical project. At any rate, it will be helpful to start by focussing on what they share in common between them. This invites an examination of the practice in our chosen jurisdictions at a relatively high level of abstraction, a task that I will undertake in Chapter 2. In this chapter, I will draw out the conditions that lend duty-imposing norms their identity as norms of 'discrimination law' (as opposed to, say, norms of torts law, welfare law, or criminal law). We will discover what is, at the most basic level, common to these norms that practitioners in our select jurisdictions characterize as those of discrimination law. This chapter will support our assumption that the practice in each of these jurisdictions is indeed an instance of the same phenomenon.

Having identified the essence of discrimination law, in Chapter 3 we will examine its architecture in a bit more detail. This will remain an overview rather than a street-level examination of the particularities of each system. The structure of the practice will be revealed through three organizational questions: who is protected by discrimination law (its 'protectorate'), who bears its duties, and what are these duties? Recall that this structural outline tracks the distributive questions that, we have just learnt, must be kept separate from the purposive one. The practice is more divergent at this level than it was in Chapter 2, but not as much as it might be if we were concerned with particular cases. At this intermediate level of generality, 'the legal model' of discrimination law is revealed. Differences between jurisdictions call for judgment over competing possibilities that may constitute this model. The method adopted is complicated; but very roughly, differences have been resolved in favour of the option that is popular with and stable within a greater number of jurisdictions.[58]

---

[58] See paragraph immediately preceding section 3.1 in Chapter 3 for details.

Part II of the book—made up of Chapters 4 and 5—tackles the purposive question. Chapter 4 lays down the normative groundwork for the discussion to follow by identifying four basic goods that we need to access securely to be able to lead flourishing lives: satisfaction of one's biological needs, negative freedom, an adequate range of valuable opportunities, and an appropriate level of self-respect. That we ought to have secured access to these goods is, at its core, a liberal demand; even as a textured and contextual understanding of liberty caters for some egalitarian and dignitarian concerns.

Chapter 5 builds upon our findings regarding the essence of discrimination law in Chapter 2. It shows that the general purpose of discrimination law is to reduce (and ultimately eliminate) pervasive, abiding, and substantial relative disadvantage between certain types of groups (namely groups whose membership is defined by morally irrelevant or valuable personal characteristics). Having established this, Chapter 5 then shows that this purpose is legitimate because it advances our secured access to the last three of the four basic goods we identified as essential in Chapter 4. The chapter also explains why a concern with *relative* group disadvantage is (counter-intuitively) better appreciated as a liberal rather than an egalitarian concern. The identified purpose admits that discrimination law is indeed necessarily *comparative*, but at the level of groups rather than individual victims.

Part III turns its attention to the distributive questions—what duties should the law impose, against whom, and to protect whom? Chapters 6, 7, and 8 may be seen as conceptual restatements of the doctrinal architecture of discrimination law that was outlined in Chapter 3—restatements that are informed by the overall purpose of discrimination law, and articulated in a normatively defensible form. Chapter 6 proposes and defends a general definition of the *antidiscrimination duty*. This single duty includes the doctrinal prohibitions on direct and indirect discrimination and harassment, and provisions for reasonable accommodation. The chapter argues that discrimination is a wrongful and unjustified exacerbation of relative group disadvantage. The proposed definition of discrimination identifies the scope of the protectorate too. In particular, it clarifies why the protection is sometimes 'symmetric' and at other times 'asymmetric': why an area of law primarily concerned with the well-being of disadvantaged groups (say, women) would sometimes protect their relatively advantaged cognates (men) from discrimination as well.

Chapter 7 answers the distributive concerns with respect to the selection of duty-bearers. It explains the reasons why only a select group of persons (rather than all of us) bear the antidiscrimination duty in law: the state, employers, landlords, providers of goods and services. It also defends the unidirectional application of the duty—the fact that landlords bear it but not tenants, or that retailers bear it but not consumers. The chapter further explores why the breach of the duty even by this select group is sometimes tolerated. The argument rests on two common features of persons who bear this duty—their relatively public character, and their optimal ability to facilitate access to the three basic goods that members of relatively disadvantaged groups lack.

Chapter 8 deals with affirmative action. It defines what can count as an affirmative action measure. It defends the legitimacy of affirmative action in principle, and suggests the factors that are relevant to the legitimacy and effectiveness of any particular measure. These factors are discerned by an analysis of all the relevant interests affected by affirmative action measures—those of its direct beneficiaries, the administrator of the measure, third parties, and the public. We learn that an affirmative action measure is desirable when it is legitimate and likely to be sufficiently effective at combating relative group disadvantage. These chapters, taken together, explain the legal model of regulating discrimination, and defend it normatively as necessary for protecting human freedom.

PART I

SCOPE AND DEFINITION

2

The Essence of Discrimination Law

Before we can begin to theorize about discrimination law, we need to know what we mean by the term, ie what is the scope and content of this domain of law we characterize as *discrimination law*.[1] This will be our concern in Part I of this book. This may seem to be an odd question to begin with. Theorists working on other areas of law are not usually beset by worries about what the scope of their subject matter is. We know that contract law governs a special type of agreement, company law relates to companies, labour law to employment, and land law to immovable property. Not all domains or departments of law are organized by subject matter though. Criminal law is organized primarily on the basis of a distinct legal response to certain acts (punishment), and is usually applied by a specialist set of enforcement mechanisms. The organizational basis of other legal domains is harder to discern—the uncertain scope of tort law may be an example.[2]

Discrimination law lies at the difficult end of this spectrum. It is found in constitutional Bills of Rights as well as in statutes. It applies to certain sectors (employment and health) but not others (romantic relationships). It uses a complex set of tools (direct and indirect discrimination, harassment, reasonable adjustments, affirmative action, positive duties, etc), but it is not immediately obvious how these tools are interrelated—sometimes they even seem to be in conflict with each other. To make matters worse, unlike contract, crime, or trusts, discrimination is not uniquely—perhaps not even primarily—a legal concept. As stated in Chapter 1, it is used very widely in moral, political, and popular discourses, and there is often a significant variance between its use by laypersons and by law. Some of these difficulties forced at least one theorist to suggest that: 'Upon detailed analysis, [discrimination law] may

---

[1] Most of this chapter has been previously published. See Tarunabh Khaitan, 'Prelude to a Theory of Discrimination Law' in Deborah Hellman and Sophia Moreau (eds), *Philosophical Foundations of Discrimination Law* (Oxford University Press 2013).

[2] Unsurprisingly, tort law theorists have devoted a fair amount of time and effort to understanding the nature and scope of tort law. See generally, David Owen, *Philosophical Foundations of Tort Law* (Clarendon Press 1995).

disassociate into a collection of disjointed pieces of legal doctrine that have nothing in common beyond their longstanding association together.'[3]

To add to these difficulties in finding coherence in discrimination law, it is possible to see it as a subset of several *other* domains of law rather than a domain in its own right. Constitutional and human rights lawyers can rightfully claim at least some aspects of discrimination law as belonging to their subject. Labour lawyers will be right to remind us that the historic roots of discrimination law (at least in some jurisdictions) lie in employment law. One may even argue that discrimination is really a kind of tort, and is therefore a sub-domain of tort law. It is only recently that legal practice and academy have started recognizing discrimination law as an autonomous area of law, independent of its historical forebears. The recognition continues to be hesitant and patchy. Unlike criminal law, one cannot turn to seek its identity in a unique enforcement mechanism either: parts of it are variously enforced by constitutional courts, employment tribunals, ordinary civil courts, specialist equality courts, equality or human rights commissions, etc. It is no surprise that discrimination law as an area of law continues to face a crisis of identity. A theorist of discrimination law is therefore forced to confront a preliminary question: is discrimination law even *a subject*, one that is coherent enough to be studied as such?

As we know, this book is concerned with the theory of discrimination *law*. But even within law, the term 'discrimination' is often employed loosely. When I speak of 'discrimination law' I will mainly be referring to norms that legislators often deem fit to include in a single statutory instrument (often entitled Equality Act, Antidiscrimination/Prevention of Discrimination Act, Civil Rights Act, etc), and to provisions in Bills of Rights that tend to guarantee the right against discrimination (frequently as a subset of or allied to the right to equality). At least legislators appear to think that there is something distinctive about these provisions, which justifies their being clubbed together.

This chapter is meant as a prelude to theorizing about discrimination law: along with the next one, it tells us what discrimination law *is*. I have suggested, somewhat loosely, that these chapters together answer the 'definitional' question. In this chapter, I will find the *essence* of discrimination law by inquiring into the basis on which one could determine whether any given

---

[3] George Rutherglen, 'Concrete or Abstract Conceptions of Discrimination' in Deborah Hellman and Sophia Moreau (eds), *Philosophical Foundations of Discrimination Law* (Oxford University Press 2013) 123.

norm could be characterized as a norm of discrimination law. I will therefore seek to discover the common thread that runs through all the seemingly disparate norms that constitute discrimination law. More importantly, what distinguishes these norms from other norms, especially those with which confusion is likely (eg norms regarding social welfare or socio-economic rights)? Once we have discovered this core, Chapter 3 will delve deeper into discrimination law by unearthing its architectural structure. These chapters together tell us what is salient in discrimination law for our theoretical purpose. They lay down the essential groundwork for the full-blown normative account that is to follow from Chapter 4 onwards. However, they do not fully *define* the scope of these laws in any particular jurisdiction: that exercise is not necessary for our purpose. These two chapters are definitional only in a limited sense.

In this chapter, I will show that the essence of discrimination law is to be found in four conditions that any norm must satisfy in order to be characterized as a norm of discrimination law: the *personal grounds* condition, the *cognate groups* condition, the *relative disadvantage* condition, and the *eccentric distribution* condition. Readers must excuse the use of jargon at this stage—the meaning of these terms will become clear by the end of this chapter. These four pillars dictate the purpose of discrimination law. In discovering it, this chapter provides the basis for the theoretical discussion in Part II of the book.

2.1 A Thought Experiment

Let us then begin with a thought experiment. Imagine a lawyer, reasonably familiar with the practice of discrimination law in any of the English-speaking, common-law-based, culturally conversant, liberal democratic jurisdictions. This jurisdictional selection makes it more likely that we are dealing with (more or less) the same concept when we talk of 'discrimination law'. If she is shown a duty-imposing legal norm from any of these jurisdictions and asked whether this is a norm of *discrimination* law, what theoretical resources could she draw upon to respond to this question? Would she characterize it as a norm of discrimination law only because her legal system (arbitrarily) chooses to do so? Is there really nothing distinctive about the norms that are normally characterized as norms of discrimination law?

In the following paragraphs, I will show that there are, indeed, necessary and together sufficient conditions which can help us distinguish norms of discrimination law from other legal norms. These conditions are distilled from the norms usually recognized by the practice as norms of discrimination law.

Identifying these conditions is important primarily because they provide the most fundamental theoretical insight into the nature of discrimination law. If such conditions exist, they put important constraints on other theoretical endeavours in relation to discrimination law. For example, they can help us identify whether a reform proposal or a judicial innovation is really a reform that preserves the essential features of discrimination law, or an attempt to restructure fundamentally our understanding of this area of law, or even a step towards the abolition of discrimination law as we know it. These necessary and sufficient conditions can also help us determine how plausible claims regarding the point of discrimination law really are. I may have got the precise conditions for determining whether a norm is a norm of discrimination law wrong. However, so long as we can agree that there are *some* such conditions which give these norms their distinctive identity, figuring them out will remain a fundamental explanatory quest in the philosophy of discrimination law. For those who deny the existence of any such conditions, a good starting point will be to show why plausible candidates, including the ones that follow, are unacceptable.

To find out what these conditions might be, let us ask our imaginary lawyer friend which of the following hypothetical candidate norms she would characterize as norms of discrimination law:

§1. No landlord shall refuse to let accommodation to a person on the ground of his or her race.

§2. Public employers shall take proportionate measures to enable or encourage women to participate in the workforce.

§3. No employer shall adopt a practice, policy, or criterion which has a disproportionately disadvantageous impact on persons who are overweight, unless he or she can show that the practice, policy, or criterion is objectively justifiable.

§4. Airlines shall not refuse to hire any person on the ground of his or her eye-colour.

§5. The state shall ensure that everyone has access to emergency health care.

§6. No person shall be paid wages at a rate below the national minimum wage rate.

§7. Subject to specified defences, no person shall injure another through his or her intentional, reckless, or negligent acts.

§8. Every person with a severe mobility impairment shall be paid a monthly mobility allowance by the local council.

This list should immediately clarify the nature of our inquiry. Here, we are not interested in figuring out what norms a body of discrimination law *should* (or *should not*) contain. The question we are interested in is, given certain legal norms (like those in the list above), how do we determine whether they are norms of *discrimination law*. We are not judging these norms as good or bad (yet). We are not trying to figure out what other norms should be part of this list. We are only interested in the characterization of these norms. So, the fact that §3 or §4 are not normally encountered in the practice of discrimination law does not, in itself, disqualify them from being characterized as such. The question is *if* these norms happen to exist in a jurisdiction, would we call them norms of discrimination law?

On this question our imaginary lawyer is likely to most readily characterize §1 as a norm of discrimination law. She may or may not think that §2 is a good norm, but would recognize that this mandatory affirmative action norm is connected with norms that prohibit discrimination and would locate it within the broad corpus of norms that make up 'discrimination law' with little difficulty. §3 and §4 are likely to make her uncomfortable—although the structure of the norms will be familiar, and will remind her of other prohibitions on indirect and direct discrimination respectively, there is something odd about weight and eye-colour. If pushed, our lawyer is likely to admit that designating §3 as a norm of discrimination law makes her somewhat less uncomfortable than characterizing §4 thus (assuming that these norms apply to a society not very different from our own, where people are sometimes disadvantaged because of their weight but almost never because of their eye-colour). She is unlikely to characterize §5, §6, §7, and §8 as norms of discrimination law. It may well be that our lawyer is importing the conventional nomenclature of similar rules from her own jurisdiction. But chances are she is relying on some conceptual truths about duty-imposing norms in discrimination law. Let us try to work out what these truths might be.

2.2 The Personal Grounds Condition

Let us start by asking what is it about the first four norms that make them better candidates for characterization as norms of discrimination law? What did our lawyer see in these norms that was missing from the remaining four norms? To be sure, the first four norms are messy. Some of them apply only to public bodies, others to public and private bodies alike. Some are asymmetric in that they provide for women and overweight persons but not for men or persons who are not overweight; others apply symmetrically.

Some impose positive duties, others impose negative duties. The characterization of reasonable accommodation norms—which impose positive duties—as part and parcel of 'discrimination law' has particularly bothered some scholars.[4] Of course, the structure of reasonable accommodation and affirmative action norms is different from prohibitions on direct and indirect discrimination—the former impose positive obligations, the latter impose negative ones. Furthermore, some prohibited acts are capable of being justified, while others are prohibited categorically. Therefore, the identity of the defendant, the symmetrical nature of protection, or the negative or categorical nature of the duty are unlikely to be the distinctive features of the norms of discrimination law.

What is common between the first four norms is their sensitivity to certain characteristics or attributes that persons have (usually called 'grounds'): race in §1, gender in §2, weight in §3, and eye-colour in §4. While §8 is also sensitive to a personal attribute (severe mobility impairment), the reasons why our lawyer does not characterize it as a norm of discrimination law will become apparent when we consider the eccentric distribution condition below. For now, let us focus on the first four norms. No doubt, their sensitivity to grounds manifests itself in very different ways. §1 and §4 impose a negative duty to refrain from discriminating directly on the basis of specified grounds. §3, on the other hand, prohibits indirect discrimination on the ground of weight, where the apparent ground of differentiation could be anything (eg educational qualifications, place of residence, etc). What matters is the connection between the use of the apparent criterion and the protected ground—in this case, weight. For example, it may be that a far greater number of residents of a particular neighbourhood, Bigville, are obese, in comparison to those who live in other neighbourhoods. An employer who provides commuting services to employees living in other neighbourhoods but not to those living in Bigville is indirectly discriminating on the ground of weight.[5] §2 mandates affirmative action for the benefit of women. Thus, the precise nature of the connection between the ground in question and the prohibited or mandated act or omission is not key. This connection could be causal, correlational, etc. What matters is that there is *some* connection. Direct and indirect discrimination are prohibited only if

---

[4] George Rutherglen, 'Concrete or Abstract Conceptions of Discrimination' in Deborah Hellman and Sophia Moreau (eds), *Philosophical Foundations of Discrimination Law* (Oxford University Press 2013) 121.

[5] That she may also be discriminating directly on the ground of place of residence is irrelevant for our present purpose.

they are related to certain protected grounds. A duty to make reasonable accommodation is imposed only with respect to disadvantage originating from one or more protected grounds. We only understand those measures as affirmative action measures which seek to improve the socio-economic, cultural, or political situation of a group defined by a protected ground. Even though harassment can be, and is, prohibited more generally, only the prohibition of harassment linked to personal grounds (eg sexual or racial harassment) is thought to constitute a part of discrimination law. In this light, we can identify the first necessary condition for a norm to be characterized as a norm of discrimination law:

A. *The duty-imposing norm in question must require some connection between the act or omission prohibited or mandated by the norm on the one hand and certain attributes or characteristics that persons have, called 'grounds', on the other.* [The Personal Grounds Condition]

It is important that these grounds are *personal*, in the sense that they are characteristics that persons have. Understood broadly, a *ground* for a decision is simply the reason on which a decision is based. Thus, low interest rates may be a *ground* for taking out a mortgage. Poor performance may be a *ground* for dismissal. Discrimination law does not understand grounds in this broad sense. Rather, the term is understood in a technical sense to connote only certain types of characteristics that persons have, such as race, sex, religion, weight, sexual orientation, age, disability, eye-colour, physical appearance, and marital status.[6]

The phenomenon of a ground can be said to exist in two 'orders'. In the higher *universal* order, a ground applies to all individuals. In the *particular* order, different instances of a universal ground attach to different people. So, sex is a universal order ground, while maleness is a particular order instance of sex. Persons defined by the same particular order ground constitute a 'group' (eg men). Different groups sharing the same universal order ground may be called *cognates* of each other. Thus, men and women constitute cognate groups. It may appear that certain characteristics—such as pregnancy, disability, or religion—do not have a universal order, in that it is possible not to become (even not to be able to become) pregnant or not to have any religion or disability whatsoever. However, these grounds are better expressed as religious-status, disability-status, or pregnancy-status in their universal form, so that not having a religion or not being pregnant

---

[6] For further exploration of the distinction between grounds-as-reasons versus grounds-as-characteristics, see Chapter 6, section 6.4.2.

or disabled are particular instances of this universal form. Statutory reference to 'disability' or 'pregnancy' rather than 'disability-status' or 'pregnancy-status' is simply an elliptical way of saying that the universal order grounds will be protected asymmetrically. In other words, claims can be based on one's disability or pregnancy, but not on the basis of the absence of disability or pregnancy. The imprecise use of religion instead of religious-status, on the other hand, usually calls for a further definition clarifying that religion includes the lack of religious belief or a conjunction of religion with belief. Thus, grounds are normally protected in discrimination law in their universal order, although this protection may be asymmetric—ie it does not extend to all particular order instances of this universal order.

2.3 The Cognate Groups Condition

But isn't 'personhood' itself a universal order ground? Don't the norms in §5, §6, and §7 apply to all persons? Surely they are not what our lawyer would consider norms of discrimination law. It follows, then, that the ground in question must be capable of classifying persons into two or more classes of persons. Personhood itself cannot be a protected ground. Thus, we can refine the personal grounds condition by adding a second necessary condition:

B. *A protected ground (eg sex) must be capable of classifying persons into more than one class of persons, loosely called 'groups' (eg men and women).* [The Cognate Groups Condition]

We already know that all groups defined by the same personal ground are cognates of each other: hence this condition has been labelled the 'cognate groups' condition. §§5–7 fail to satisfy the second condition. They apply to all persons and are not sensitive to grounds which classify persons into more than one group. Thus, they do not qualify as norms *of* discrimination law (although, in certain contexts, they could be in conflict with norms of discrimination law).

It may be noted that the cognate groups condition understands 'groups' loosely and should not be read to imply that the 'group' needs to possess any solidarity, coherence, sense of identity, shared history, language, or culture. Certain groups which are protected in practice, such as older people, or certain categories of disabled persons, may not possess some or all of these features. Under this loose formulation, group 'members' do not even have to be consciously aware that they belong to this group.

2.4 The Relative Disadvantage Condition

The first two conditions allow us to distinguish between §§1–4 on the one hand, and §§5–7 on the other. However, what do we make of our friend's discomfort with §3 and §4? §3 is sensitive to weight, and §4 is sensitive to eye-colour. Even though these norms satisfy the personal grounds and cognate groups conditions, they make our lawyer uncomfortable because they are unfamiliar. She is unlikely to have previously encountered norms that are sensitive to these grounds in her jurisdiction. However, the degree of discomfort caused by the two norms will be different, suggesting that she is relying on something more than mere familiarity. If we push her to examine her intuitive discomfort based on conventional practice, she is likely to tell us that she can imagine §3 being described as a norm of discrimination law, but will have graver reservations with respect to §4. The theoretical consideration she has in mind is this: she has recognized through §3 and §4 that the ground in question has to be of a certain quality—a quality that is possessed by race, religion, sex, sexual orientation, disability, etc, possibly by weight, but not by eye-colour. This quality is captured by the following condition:

C. Of all groups defined by a given universal order ground (eg race), members of at least one group (eg blacks) must be significantly more likely to suffer abiding, pervasive, and substantial disadvantage than the members of at least one other cognate group (eg whites). [The Relative Disadvantage Condition]

In our societies, black people, religious minorities, women, gay and lesbian people, and disabled persons are more likely to suffer disadvantage than white people, religious majorities, men, straight people, and non-disabled persons, respectively. For reasons that will be given in Chapter 3, I will call these relatively disadvantaged groups 'protected groups'. Furthermore, although it is quite possible for two protected groups to be cognates of each other (say, gays and bisexuals), for simplicity's sake I will mostly reserve the term 'cognate group' to refer to a *relatively advantaged* group (such as men, whites, the able-bodied, heterosexuals) which is a cognate of a protected group. Terminological clarifications aside, let us return to the argument: our lawyer was uncomfortable with §3 because similar empirical claims are not readily acknowledged in our societies with regard to weight. However, some evidence suggests that weight might satisfy the relative disadvantage condition.[7] If the evidence is robust enough,

---

[7] See generally, Elizabeth Kristen, 'Addressing the Problem of Weight Discrimination in Employment' (2002) 90 California Law Review 57.

our lawyer is likely to concede that §3 should be characterized as a norm of discrimination law.

One could argue that while relative group disadvantage is common to race, religion, sex, sexual orientation, disability, etc, it is not *the* feature that makes these grounds salient in discrimination law. Rather, it is the fact that these grounds supply (some of) their possessors with a sense of personal identity, one that they are likely to refer to when describing who they are which makes them salient.[8] This is a good objection, and responding to it is complicated by the fact that almost every instance of a ground which is sensitive to relative group disadvantage sooner or later comes to define personal identity. The reason is that relative group disadvantage is an important catalyst for political mobilization of a group, and identity politics is often the tool of choice for the group's leaders. The connection works in reverse as well, although less clearly—grounds which define personal identity often become the fault-lines along which a society's resources come to be distributed. However, personal identity does not always translate into relative group disadvantage. Take, for example, fandom of British football clubs as such, ie when it does not coincide with other personal grounds such as religion or nationality. For the fans, they do tend to provide a means (among others) of identifying themselves. This sense of identity can often be quite strongly felt. I suspect we can assume that different groups of fans do not experience abiding, pervasive, or substantive relative disadvantage. The fact that British discrimination law is unlikely to prohibit discrimination on the basis of fandom of football clubs any time soon gives us reasons to think that it is relative group disadvantage rather than personal identity which is central to discrimination law. This inference is strengthened by the inclusion of grounds such as age and disability among the grounds protected by discrimination law—barring a few exceptions, the connection of groups defined by age or disability with relative group disadvantage is much more self-evident than with personal identity. This is not to say that personal identity plays no role whatsoever—its close connection with disadvantage, just discussed, makes it highly significant. It may even play an independent role in solving particular problems in discrimination law.[9] However, as far as necessary conditions pertaining to antidiscrimination norms are concerned, the relative disadvantage condition is correct in emphasizing disadvantage rather than identity.

---

[8] Kasper Lippert-Rasmussen, *Born Free and Equal? A Philosophical Inquiry into the Nature of Discrimination* (Oxford University Press 2014) 30–6.

[9] We will see, for example, in Chapter 5, section 5.2.3 that group identity plays a critical role in its members' ability to have self-respect. Chapter 6, section 6.5 will further explore the connection between personal identity, expressive salience, and symmetric protection of certain grounds.

It may be that a given society is completely indifferent to race, where it plays no role in distributing disadvantage between groups or persons. It may also be that in this society, blue-eyed persons are much more likely to suffer disadvantage than those with any other eye-colour. In such a society, norms that outlaw discrimination on the basis of eye-colour will be our typical case, and norms dealing with racial discrimination will give rise to doubts. Our lawyer is likely to have assumed that no pattern of relative group disadvantage is discernible for persons with blue, grey, brown, green, or black eyes in her society. Let us, for the argument's sake, put aside the possibility that eye-colour has some connection with a person's race, and therefore with disadvantage, and accept her assumption to be correct. This was the reason why our lawyer felt uncomfortable with §4. This example also demonstrates that it is not the relevance of a ground to the distribution at hand which is key. Eye-colour is indeed irrelevant to most distributive decisions, and is still not protected by the practice of discrimination law. On the other hand, one could also think of specific examples where pregnancy, age, sex, and disability are actually relevant to the decision at hand, and yet reliance on these grounds is prohibited. If we accept the relative disadvantage condition, this apparent paradox is dissolved.[10]

Of course, nothing prevents a law-maker from enacting §4, even in a society where eye-colour has no connection with relative group disadvantage whatsoever. In fact, constitutional or administrative law norms which forbid the state from acting irrationally or arbitrarily will usually entail the requirement that it should not let extraneous considerations like eye-colour ground its decisions. But it will be unusual to characterize these prohibitions as prohibitions under 'discrimination law'.[11] The fact that §4 satisfies the first two conditions is what makes it look like a discrimination norm. But it does not satisfy the relative disadvantage condition. If she appreciated the lack of any connection between eye-colour and disadvantage correctly, the misgivings of our friend with regard to §4 were well founded, and her refusal to characterize it as a norm of discrimination law is justified.

[10] This is not to say that relevance of a ground plays no role in discrimination law. But the place of relevance in discrimination law is far more complex than the simplistic suggestion being disputed here. The real relevance of relevance should become apparent in Chapter 6, section 6.6.5.

[11] The structure of the 14th Amendment to the US Constitution is the main reason for confusion on this point, since that influential provision is the source of both non-arbitrariness duties (which result in rational-basis scrutiny) and antidiscrimination duties (which require heightened judicial scrutiny). The pull of this American idiosyncrasy is more than discounted by the practice in other liberal democratic jurisdictions as well as statutory protections in the United States itself, where the distinction between the two duties is more clearly understood and maintained.

This third condition is likely to be somewhat more controversial than the first two. A few clarifications will, hopefully, demonstrate that it is nonetheless a relatively thin claim which skirts the most divisive debates within discrimination law. After all, the aim of this chapter is only to identify necessary and sufficient conditions which help distinguish norms of discrimination law from other legal norms; I do not intend to resolve controversial disputes by definitional fiat. First, notice that the relative disadvantage condition says nothing about whether a ground should be protected symmetrically or asymmetrically. There is a significant amount of literature concerning the controversial issue of symmetry: should the law only protect women, blacks, or gays from sex, race, or sexual orientation discrimination respectively, or should it also protect men, whites, and straights?[12] All I am claiming here is that for a ground to be salient in discrimination law, it must define at least one group whose members are more likely to suffer disadvantage than those of another cognate group. In other words, even if the practice protects men as well as women from sex discrimination, the fact that a sexual group (women) is more likely to suffer disadvantage in our societies is a necessary trigger for sex to qualify as the type of personal attribute which could be protected.

Second, the term disadvantage has been left undefined, in order not to pre-empt debates about the kind of disadvantage that counts. It allows for disadvantage being material, political, social, cultural, etc. Nor is there any stipulation that the disadvantage in question has to be caused by past discrimination, or indeed by human agency at all. I want to leave open the possibility that it is the business of discrimination law to deal with disadvantage that has come about without the direct exercise of human agency (eg from natural disasters or biological causes). All that is stipulated is that the relevant disadvantage attaches itself to groups.

Third, the relative disadvantage condition does *not* require any comparative disadvantage to have been inflicted by a particular act or omission before *that* act or omission can be characterized as discriminatory. In other words, the third condition does not imply that the claimant needs to prove that she has suffered disadvantage relative to an appropriate comparator in any

---

[12] See generally, Owen Fiss, 'Groups and the Equal Protection Clause' (1976) 5 Philosophy and Public Affairs 107; Morris Abram, 'Affirmative Action: Fair Shakers and Social Engineers' (1986) 99 Harvard Law Review 1312; Kenji Yoshino, 'Assimilationist Bias in Equal Protection: The Visibility Presumption and the Case of "Don't Ask, Don't Tell"' (1998) 108 Yale Law Journal 485; Neil Gotanda, 'A Critique of "Our Constitution is Color-Blind"' (1991) 44 Stanford Law Review 1; Alan Freeman, 'Legitimizing Racial Discrimination Through Antidiscrimination Law: A Critical Review of Supreme Court Doctrine' (1978) 62 Minnesota Law Review 1049; Richard Fallon and Paul Weiler, '*Firefighters v. Stotts*: Conflicting Models of Racial Justice' [1984] The Supreme Court Review 1.

specific case. It is entirely consistent with a practice which does not insist upon proof of disadvantage in relation to an appropriate comparator in order to establish discrimination in particular cases.

Fourth, even in our societies, if one carefully surveys the disadvantage faced by blue-eyed persons and compares that to disadvantage faced by those with brown eyes, it is possible that one group faces slightly greater disadvantage. This may be due entirely to random chance—after all, the relative disadvantage condition does not require that the disadvantage must be *caused* by group membership. What is required is a correlation, not causation. However, note that this condition is forward-looking.[13] It asks not what the current state of disadvantage is, but what is the likelihood of disadvantage in the short-term future. Inductive reasoning is probabilistic—the greater the strength, duration, and degree of past and current disadvantage, the greater the likelihood of disadvantage in the near future. Any disadvantage that blue-eyed persons currently face in comparison to brown-eyed persons in our societies is likely to be trivial, and therefore there would be insufficient evidence to predict any likely disadvantage in the future. This forward-looking formulation also recognizes that even if there is an existing state of affairs where there is no longer any relative group disadvantage with respect to certain historically salient grounds—such as sex or religious status—such a state of affairs may be unstable. The forward-looking requirement is, of course, sensitive to present and past discrimination. But its emphasis on the future suggests that even after discrimination law achieves its objectives with regard to certain grounds, and women and religious minorities, say, are no longer disadvantaged relative to men and religious majorities respectively, there will still be good reasons to retain the protection for sex and religious status until the future stability of this state of 'no-relative-group-disadvantage' has been secured (so that sex and religious status come to have as little connection with disadvantage as eye-colour).

Finally, there are some other qualifiers in the relative disadvantage condition which are intended to confer a degree of seriousness to the likely relative disadvantage. First, the likelihood of suffering relative disadvantage must be significant. This will be the case only if the gap between the groups is more than trivial. As we have already seen, this requirement will normally rule out differences between blue-eyed and brown-eyed persons. Second, the disadvantage in question must be *abiding, pervasive*, and *substantial*. It must

---

[13] We are interested in conditions that identify discrimination *norms*, which are legislative—and, therefore, forward-looking—in nature. Adjudication to enforce these norms in particular cases, on the other hand, is temporally backward-looking. See generally, Joseph Raz, *The Authority of Law* (2nd edn, Oxford University Press 2009) 194ff.

be abiding in the sense that it must be likely to manifest itself over a certain length of time. The disadvantage must be pervasive in the sense that it should not normally be limited to a single, discrete sphere of human activity, but pervade several aspects of our lives. Usually members of disadvantaged groups suffer relative disadvantage in multiple sectors, such as employment, housing, health care, goods and services, and education simultaneously, rather than only in any one of them. Furthermore, disadvantage must be substantial in the sense that it should be likely to be more than an inconvenience.

These qualifiers are not intended to fix rigid thresholds. They are included in the condition to convey the idea that the practice of discrimination law concerns itself only with relative group disadvantage of some seriousness and pervasiveness. These are empirical judgments which admit to degrees, and are likely to be controversial. That may be so, but the *conceptual* point is an important one. An example may clarify it further. Section 137(1)(a) of the UK Trade Union and Labour Relations (Consolidation) Act 1992 says that 'It is unlawful to refuse a person employment because he is, or is not, a member of a trade union.'[14] This provision bears a striking structural similarity to provisions found in the UK Equality Act 2010. Yet, the 2010 Parliament did not think it merited a place in the consolidating legislation. There can be no doubt that when enacting the prohibition on discrimination based on trade union membership, the 1992 Parliament would have been concerned with discrimination against trade union members by their employers. Why did the 2010 Parliament then not mention trade union membership alongside protected grounds such as race, sex, religion, sexual orientation, disability, and age? The relative disadvantage condition provides a plausible explanation. Notice that the condition requires (abiding, pervasive, and substantial) relative *group disadvantage*, not *discrimination between members of different groups*. It is true that discrimination can often lead to (and, when pervasive and endemic enough, even constitute) a state of affairs where the type of disadvantage we are concerned with becomes likely. But until a ground satisfies the disadvantage test embodied in the third condition, it is unlikely to be offered the *comprehensive* protection that *discrimination law* normally affords. Notice that the 1992 provision only prohibits direct discrimination on the ground of trade union membership in the context of employment. None of the other tools available to discrimination law—including indirect discrimination, positive duties, reasonable adjustments, affirmative action—seem to be available. Nor are landlords or retailers generally prohibited from discriminating against trade union members. This is probably because, in the opinion we may attribute

---

[14] I am grateful to Alan Bogg for highlighting this example as a potential challenge to my analysis and for discussions that clarified my thinking on this point.

to the 2010 Parliament, trade union membership—or, for that matter, one's genetic make-up, credit history, or medical history—does not divide persons into groups such that one of these groups is significantly more likely to suffer abiding, pervasive, and substantial disadvantage. Needless to reiterate, the conceptual truth of the relative disadvantage condition does not turn on the possibility that this empirical judgment may be wrong.

Unsatisfied by these clarifications, a critic might mount two further challenges, and insist that this condition is over-inclusive as well as under-inclusive. These challenges would be misplaced. Let us first consider the over-inclusiveness allegation. One could point to grounds not in fact protected by discrimination law which, at least in some societies, do in fact classify persons into groups such that members of one of these groups are significantly more likely to suffer abiding, pervasive, and substantial disadvantage. It is probably true, for example, that weight or physical appearance are grounds which classify people into groups that differ significantly in terms of the relative advantage that their members enjoy. Saying that no jurisdiction actually prohibits discrimination on these grounds is not a challenge to the thin claim presented in this section. Many other considerations will go into a practical judgment about whether discrimination on a particular ground ought to be prohibited. That said, the fact that hypothetical norms prohibiting differentiation based on weight or physical appearance *would* satisfy the relative disadvantage condition offers strong, if defeasible, reasons to a legislator for actually enacting such norms. Perhaps, all things considered, these grounds should be protected by discrimination law. If this is indeed the case, it is not the condition which is over-inclusive, rather it is discrimination law which is unresponsive. Recall also that we only want to determine the set of conditions that an *existing* legal norm must satisfy in order to be characterized as a norm of discrimination law.

On the other hand, our critic could make the opposite charge that this condition is under-inclusive. He may remain unsatisfied with my argument above that differentiation on the basis of eye-colour is best understood as being irrational or arbitrary, but not discriminatory, because it does not satisfy the relative disadvantage condition. Part of the difficulty is, of course, that in ordinary language many of us would indeed characterize such differentiation as discrimination. The challenger may refuse to accept that in this particular instance, legal language adopts a technical meaning of the term 'discrimination' and diverges from its meaning in ordinary language. It does not help that legal language in this regard is not as clear as it might be (we already noticed the example of the 14th Amendment to the US Constitution, where the same guarantee of equal protection is the source for non-arbitrariness duties and antidiscrimination duties). Unconvinced, our challenger may invite us to imagine that our society has reached a stage, in part due to the success of discrimination law perhaps, when patriarchy has been dismantled and women do not suffer significant disadvantage. Even after this is achieved, and even after there is little likelihood of the state of significant relative group disadvantage making a comeback (such that sex is now akin to eye-colour), is it not possible that sex will continue to exist as a protected ground in discrimination statutes, perhaps due to legislative inertia? Doesn't this show that the relative disadvantage condition is under-inclusive?[15]

This is an interesting, but ultimately unsuccessful, challenge. The exercise we have undertaken here is to discern necessary and sufficient conditions for the characterization of a norm by analysing *existing* norms of discrimination law in comparable jurisdictions. Most, if not all, of these existing norms satisfy this condition. What our critic has done is pointed out that in a different or future legal system, there may be legal norms which do not satisfy this condition and may nonetheless be found in antidiscrimination statutes. If that is the case, there are two possibilities. It may be that this particular norm is a mistaken exception—an outlier which should not play any meaningful role in concept formation, as it is likely to lead to distortions. Legal systems are not, after all, unfamiliar with norms that have long outlived their utility and ought to be taken off the statute book. On the other hand, it is possible that norms which do not satisfy the relative disadvantage condition are pervasive in any given legal system. In that case, clearly *that* legal system has a *different* conception of discrimination than one that is proposed here. Even if the jurisdictions we are currently interested in change over time such that this condition is no longer necessary or sufficient, we will simply have to admit that our conception of discrimination law has changed. My argument, then, is that we are not there yet. Ultimately, this criticism boils down to a discomfort with the use of dynamic social phenomena (such as relative group disadvantage) in the formulation of legal concepts. This discomfort underestimates the dynamism inherent in law and its ability to respond to changing social phenomena.

2.5 The Eccentric Distribution Condition

Let us now turn our attention to §8: every person with a severe mobility impairment shall be paid a monthly mobility allowance by the local council. Our lawyer is right that it is not a norm of discrimination law. She is likely to characterize it as a provision of welfare law. Yet, it seems to make a distinction based on a personal attribute (ability to be mobile) which classifies persons into groups,

---

[15] I am grateful to Paul Yowell for making this point.

and one of those groups—persons with severe mobility impairment—is indeed likely to suffer serious disadvantage. There must be a further condition to help us distinguish norms of discrimination law from welfare provisions.

D. The duty-imposing norm must be designed such that it is likely to distribute the non-remote and tangible benefits in question to some, but not all, members of the intended beneficiary group. [The Eccentric Distribution Condition]

This condition is not satisfied by §8. It clarifies that duty-imposing norms in discrimination do not, on their own, *guarantee* access to the substantive or tangible burden or benefit whose distribution is in question to any particular individual. The duty to refrain from discriminating on the ground of disability in making hiring decisions does not entail a duty to hire every (or any) disabled applicant. Unlike a universal welfare benefit or a socio-economic right, even positive norms in discrimination law, such as affirmative action and reasonable accommodation, are not designed to tangibly benefit every member of the target group. Even programmatic welfare rights which only seek 'progressive realization' of certain socio-economic benefits do aspire to *ultimately* reach everyone (not indirectly through some trickle-down mechanism, but directly through the operation of the norm). Notice that the condition relates to the *design* of the norm—it may be that the norm is in fact utterly ineffective and benefits nobody. That does not matter for its characterization as a norm of discrimination law, so long as it is designed such that it is likely to tangibly benefit some persons protected from discrimination. What matters is that the benefits (or burdens) whose distribution is governed by the norm are not intended for distribution to everyone within the protectorate. For example, §1 deals with accommodation, while §2 with public employment, and §3 with employment generally. None of these norms guarantee the tangible benefits of accommodation or employment to anyone, let alone to everyone. It may be said that what these norms distribute is not a substantive benefit such as employment, but rather the *opportunity* to be employed. This is probably true, but we would all agree that the difference between being given a job on the one hand and the chance of getting a job on the other are significant. By non-remote and tangible benefits, I refer only to actual employment, education, or housing, and not (merely) an improved opportunity to access them: welfare norms tend to distribute the actual non-remote tangible benefits, rather than the mere chance to access them. Although not universal in scope, discrimination norms are designed such that their operation should make these tangible benefits accessible to at least *some* members of protected groups. Norms that govern certain relationships already in existence (employment, tenancy) may indeed distribute certain benefits (such as reasonable accommodation) to every existing employee/

tenant, etc in that relationship. But the prior existence of such a relationship is an essential criterion, one that only some members of the intended beneficiary group are likely to satisfy.

The final condition is eccentric not only because of its limited, non-universal, distribution. It is also eccentric in a different sense (eccentricity in this second sense is a usual feature of many antidiscrimination norms, but not an essential one, and does not inform condition D). Those members of beneficiary groups who do end up receiving the non-remote and tangible benefits of discrimination law cannot be mapped onto any discernible intra-group pattern. It is not as if those individuals who benefit are the most needy or most law-abiding or satisfy any other *general* distributive criteria. Hence the label 'eccentric distribution'.

Notice also that the distributive pattern is eccentric in this sense only with respect to individual beneficiaries. A very clear pattern emerges when we examine how groups are benefited. I will show in Chapter 3 that the benefits of discrimination law, vis-à-vis groups, are distributed largely asymmetrically, such that protected groups benefit more than their cognates. But that claim must wait. For now, the eccentric distribution condition only insists that the design of the norms must be to benefit (some) members of protected groups. Whether they also benefit members of more advantaged groups is not key to their characterization as antidiscrimination norms. So, discrimination norms that govern distribution decisions (hiring, selling, leasing) are indeed designed to ensure that at least some members of protected groups will be hired, sold to, leased to—only that there is no guarantee that all of them will be.

The eccentric distribution condition is concerned only with the *non-remote* and *tangible* benefits and burdens which are subject to distribution by the norm. §§1–3 may have several remote or expressive benefits for those who do not get these tangible benefits. These norms may set standards of behaviour and encourage non-discrimination in areas outside their immediate concern by expressing condemnation of certain discriminatory acts. §2 may create a critical mass of female employees in a public workforce, which may eventually lead to sufficient numbers of women being hired without any need for these special measures. These relatively remote benefits may have a wide reach, and in some cases, may indeed reach all members of a particular group. However, the non-remote benefits conferred because of their operation will be limited to *some* persons alone. Furthermore, even those who do not benefit tangibly may get expressive benefits—§1 may not secure a job to every black applicant, but it is likely to instil a sense of security (perhaps, even pride) in them by expressing the message that their interests are as important as those of white applicants.

The term *design* also implies a causal relationship between the norm and the distribution that results from its operation. It is not part of the design of duty-imposing norms in discrimination law that their tangible benefits may be distributed universally (ie distribution to all members of the target group). Of course, discrimination law norms can sometimes interact with other norms to result in universal distribution. Consider, for example, a norm which makes a health care scheme available to all persons except those with a mental illness (N1), or a norm which makes the legal institution of marriage accessible to all opposite-sex couples but not to any same-sex couple (N2). In these cases, an antidiscrimination norm (S) is indeed likely to operate such that all mentally ill persons get access to health care, and all same-sex couples get access to marriage. However, the resulting universal distribution is not owed, primarily, to the operation of S. Universality, in the relevant sense, is embedded in N1 and N2. Of course, these norms are not universal in the sense that they do not extend to the mentally ill and to same-sex couples, respectively. But they are universal in a different sense—they provide their benefits to *all* persons within their specified range (all persons except those with mental illness, all opposite-sex couples). Discrimination norms are not universal in this second sense. While they do provide the guarantee of non-discrimination to all, their non-remote and tangible benefits are not promised to all. When a discrimination law norm requires that health care should be available to the mentally ill and marriage to same-sex couples, all that it does is remove the discriminatory exclusion of groups protected by discrimination law from the list of groups targeted by universal norms such as N1 and N2. But the universality of application to *all* persons within the target group is a feature of N1 and N2, not of S.

The eccentric distribution condition is related to the relative disadvantage condition. As the latter clarifies, relative group disadvantage is at the heart of discrimination law. Of course, group disadvantage is connected with individual disadvantage, but disadvantage acquires a special character when it attaches itself to groups rather than when it is distributed randomly to individuals across all groups. It is true that one may be concerned about group disadvantage either for the sake of groups or for the sake of individuals. Recognizing that relative group disadvantage is distinct from individual-disadvantage-not-sensitive-to-group-membership does not entail committing oneself to any position concerning the moral worth of groups qua groups. The eccentric distribution condition simply recognizes the possibility that the nexus between group membership and disadvantage can be broken without extending a tangible benefit to all members of the group. Sensitivity to this special character of *group* disadvantage is unique to discrimination law, and absent in socio-economic entitlements and welfare benefit provisions.

2.6 Conclusion

The following picture emerges after this discussion: for a duty-imposing legal norm to be characterized as a norm of discrimination law, it must satisfy the following four necessary conditions, which, taken together, are also sufficient:

The Personal Grounds Condition: *The duty-imposing norm in question must require some connection between the act or omission prohibited or mandated by the norm on the one hand and certain attributes or characteristics that persons have, called 'grounds', on the other.*

The Cognate Groups Condition: *A protected ground must be capable of classifying persons into more than one class of persons, loosely called 'groups'.*

The Relative Disadvantage Condition: *Of all groups defined by a given universal order ground, members of at least one group must be significantly more likely to suffer abiding, pervasive, and substantial disadvantage than the members of at least one other cognate group.*

The Eccentric Distribution Condition: *The duty-imposing norm must be designed such that it is likely to distribute the non-remote tangible benefits in question to some, but not all, members of the intended beneficiary group.*

Only §§1–3 satisfy all of these conditions, and they are the only ones on our list that can therefore be characterized as norms of discrimination law. Some of these conditions may seem too obvious and perhaps uncontroversial to have merited this discussion. They are, admittedly, compatible with a wide variety of mutually inconsistent positions on what fully fleshed-out discrimination law norms should look like. Recognizing them is, nonetheless, an important step towards understanding what is distinctive about discrimination law. Personal grounds, cognate groups, relative disadvantage, and eccentric distribution of benefits are the key features that lend an identity and a degree of internal coherence to discrimination law. Discrimination law is not merely a handy label for disparate norms governing direct and indirect discrimination, discriminatory harassment, reasonable accommodation, and affirmative action, thrown together for reasons of convenience. These norms share a feature which is not shared by other legal norms, and the practice is therefore right in grouping them together. Whether these norms form a loose confederacy—like the norms of tort law—or a tight-knit family—like the law of contract—or, perhaps, something in between, will require further investigation.[16] But the notion that they are unrelated is without merit.

---

[16] These descriptions of tort law and contract law are borrowed from Peter Birks, *Unjust Enrichment* (2nd edn, Oxford University Press 2005) 16.

It is important to reiterate, to avoid unnecessary confusion, that these conditions are meant to be criteria which determine whether an *existing* legal norm ought to be characterized as a norm of discrimination law. They have not been presented as a set of criteria which help us determine which norms of discrimination law *ought* to exist (although they would, of course, be *relevant* to this question).

These conditions, if correct, provide important, if weak, constraints for suggestions of practical reform and for theoretical explanations of discrimination law. For example, while the relative disadvantage condition is compatible with symmetric protection rules which do not require proof of comparative disadvantage in an individual case, one must explain how symmetric rules governing an individual case square up with the systemic concern with relative group disadvantage. I may have got these conditions wrong: but if there are any necessary and sufficient conditions that distinguish norms of discrimination law, they are likely to provide some background constraints to the theory and practice of discrimination law. As such, they constitute an important prelude to any theory of discrimination law.

This chapter has shown that *personal grounds, cognate groups, relative disadvantage,* and *eccentric distribution* together constitute the essence of discrimination law. To draw upon an anatomical analogy, here I have identified the heart of this area of law. Chapter 3, outlining the architecture of discrimination law, will add the skeletal structure around this essential organ. These chapters are largely descriptive (and only indirectly evaluative) in their approach.[17] Because my central goal is to theorize *generally* about discrimination law, we will not put any flesh on these bones. The essence and the architecture of discrimination law will lay the foundation for the normative analysis which is to follow from Chapter 4 onwards.

---

[17] See generally, Julie Dickson, *Evaluation and Legal Theory* (Hart 2001).

3

The Architecture of Discrimination Law

> If on the road a shoe falls off my horse, and I come to a smith to have
> one put on, and the smith refuses to do it, an action will lie against
> him, because he has made profession of a trade which is for the public
> good, and has thereby exposed and vested an interest of himself in all
> the King's subjects that will employ him in the way of his trade. If an
> innkeeper refuses to entertain guests where his house is not full, an
> action will lie against him and so against a carrier, if his horses are not
> loaded, and he refuses to take a packet proper to be sent by a carrier…[1]

This is Chief Justice Holt's summary in 1701 of the English common law
duty on the providers of certain public utilities. It is perhaps one of the earliest
examples of something akin to the antidiscrimination principle in the common law tradition. Although relied upon by a famous black cricketer as late as
in 1944 to successfully challenge a London hotel's refusal to accommodate him
(because of objections made by some of its white guests),[2] it lacks the key features of contemporary discrimination law we identified in Chapter 2: it makes
no reference to personal grounds, cognate groups, or relative disadvantage.
What we now understand as discrimination law has at its core the protection
of certain definite grounds—race, sex, religion, age, disability, sexual orientation, and so on—and the groups that these classify us into. The longstanding
duty in English law protected everyone who was willing and able to pay for
the service, irrespective of the grounds on which the innkeeper (or the carrier,
etc) refused to serve. A person who was turned away because of the colour of
her eyes, or the first letter of her name, or on no ground at all, would still have

---

[1] *Lane v Cotton* [1558–1774] All ER Rep 109 KB, 114. The quotation is from a dissenting opinion, but the majority did not contest the statement of law contained therein.

[2] *Constantine v Imperial London Hotels* [1944] KB 693. See also, *Rothfield v The North British
Railway Company* [1920] SC 805; Benjamin Kline, 'The Origin of the Rule Against Unjust
Discrimination' (1917–18) 66 University of Pennsylvania Law Review 123; Benjamin Kline, 'The
Scope of the Rule Against Unjust Discrimination by Public Servants' (1919) 67 University of
Pennsylvania Law Review 109; Alfred Avins, 'What is a Place of "Public" Accommodation?' (1968)
52 Marquette Law Review 1, 1–7.

a remedy. On the other hand, contemporary discrimination law has a much wider scope inasmuch as it imposes duties on many more actors than the old common law duty on public utilities. The goal of this chapter is to describe the structure of the 'legal model' of identifying and regulating discrimination, drawing upon the practice of five chosen jurisdictions—Canada, India, South Africa, the United Kingdom (including European influences), and the United States. Recall that these jurisdictions have been chosen because, despite their differences, they seem to be engaging with the same phenomena and responding to similar concerns in their practice of discrimination law. Note also that my focus remains firmly on *doctrinal* aspects of the practice, as shaped by legislatures and appellate courts.

Rules enacted in the second half of the nineteenth century in India and the United States are much closer to what we have come to regard as discrimination law. This is hardly surprising, for these two regions have witnessed some of the most pervasive and entrenched forms of prejudice and disadvantage faced by caste and racial groups, respectively. One of the earliest provisions enacted to outlaw ground-based discrimination was the Caste Disabilities Removal Act, enacted by British India in 1850. The Act provided that:

So much of any law or usage … as inflicts on any person forfeiture of rights or property, or may be held in any way to impair or affect any right of inheritance, by reason of his or her renouncing, or having been excluded from the communion of, any religion, or being deprived of caste, shall cease to be enforced as law …

Despite this early start with outlawing certain (limited) forms of direct discrimination, contemporary Indian law's focus since the late nineteenth century has remained on affirmative action for 'low' caste groups in public education and employment.[3]

In the United States, the context for legislation prohibiting discrimination was the abolition of slavery by the 13th Amendment to the Constitution in 1865. The Civil Rights Act of 1866, passed soon after the American Civil War, extended citizenship to all persons born in the country (excluding foreign nationals and Native Americans); and provided that:

[S]uch citizens, of every race and color, without regard to any previous condition of slavery or involuntary servitude … shall have the same right … to make and

---

[3] The government of Madras framed a Grant-in-Aid Code in 1885 to regulate affirmative action for 'backward classes': Bindheshwari Mandal, *Report of the Second Backward Classes Commission (First Part)* (1980) 61; Marc Galanter, 'Who are the Other Backward Classes?: An Introduction to a Constitutional Puzzle' (1978) 13 Economic and Political Weekly 1812, 1821 fn 1. See also, Tarunabh Khaitan, 'Transcending Reservations: A Paradigm Shift in the Debate on Equality' [20 September 2008] Economic and Political Weekly 8.

enforce contracts, to sue, be parties, and give evidence, to inherit, purchase, lease, sell, hold, and convey real and personal property, and to full and equal benefit of all laws and proceedings for the security of person and property, as is enjoyed by white citizens, and shall be subject to like punishment, pains, and penalties, and to none other, any law, statute, ordinance, regulation, or custom, to the contrary notwithstanding.

The 14th Amendment, passed in 1868, gave constitutional status to the extension of citizenship to blacks and prohibited all states from denying 'to any person within its jurisdiction the equal protection of the laws'. It also conferred legislative competence upon Congress to enforce its provisions. The 15th Amendment, ratified in 1870, guaranteed that no American citizen shall be denied the right to vote 'on account of race, color, or previous condition of servitude'. What is common to all these pioneering legislative interventions is that they primarily target state action, and guarantee the enjoyment of basic civil liberties without racial discrimination.

These early developments in India and in the United States raised three enduring questions that have shaped the legal approach to discrimination. The first question relates to the beneficiaries of discrimination law. The early interventions in India and the United States protected disadvantaged caste and racial groups, respectively. Contemporary discrimination law has a much wider scope. Who is entitled to the protection of discrimination law is perhaps the most vexed question in this area of law. This question will be explored in section 3.1. Second, jurisdictions need to decide who the bearers of the burden of antidiscrimination are. The pioneering measures constrained state action alone. The unsuccessful attempt by the US Civil Rights Act of 1875 to impose antidiscrimination duties on private persons gave rise to an enduring controversy about who can be legitimately required to shoulder liability under the law. The responses of the chosen jurisdictions to this question will be presented in section 3.2. Finally, the nature and scope of the duties imposed by this law need to be determined. This discussion takes place in section 3.3. Early attempts focussed on what we would now call direct discrimination or affirmative action. But in the last few decades, new tools have been invented, and older tools have become more sophisticated. These new tools include the prohibition on indirect discrimination and ground-sensitive harassment, and provision for reasonable accommodation. The contemporary understanding of direct discrimination has also come a long way from early beginnings. These developments lie at the heart of the schism between the lay and the legal approaches to discrimination. Even affirmative action measures come in a whole range of shapes and sizes. Organizing the responses to these three questions reveals the architecture of discrimination law. They tell us how the law distributes rights, duties, and licences in practice. These responses set up the theoretical challenge that Part III of the book will meet.

These questions are interrelated rather than insular. Our answer to any of them has an impact on all the others. Different groups of potential defendants, for example, shoulder the antidiscrimination obligation to different extents. What results, therefore, is a complicated web of inter-relationships. Obviously, there are other aspects to the practice of discrimination law—mainly matters of detail—that are not captured by these questions.[4] In particular, the issue of appropriate enforcement mechanisms will be entirely overlooked.

The goal of this chapter is to present an overview of the substantive doctrinal aspects of the practice of discrimination law in the chosen juris-dictions. The hope is that, despite inter-jurisdictional differences, a com-mon, if relatively thin, structure can be discerned. One methodological assumption needs articulation. There are two important difficulties with the exercise this chapter is about to embark upon. First, there are impor-tant distinctions between the chosen jurisdictions on doctrinal matters. Second, even within each jurisdiction, the nature and scope of legal duties is sensitive to the ground in question. For example, one jurisdiction may make reasonable accommodation available only for discrimination based on disability; another only when it is based on religion or disability; and another still for discrimination on any ground. Similar diversity is seen with respect to issues such as comparators, symmetry, intersectionality, and justification. Discrimination law still remains a dynamic area of law. Its history in the last six decades or so has seen new developments arising in the context of one ground and then extended to others. The very prohibi-tion on discrimination in many jurisdictions started with an engagement with a single ground in the first instance—race in the United States, caste in India, sex in the European Union. One needs to distinguish between sta-ble differences between certain grounds from differences that arise because of the law-makers' conservative instinct to favour cautious, experimental, development of the law. My approach to making this distinction has been this: if the *same* grounds are distinguished for differential treatment in multiple jurisdictions, I have treated the distinction as a stable one. For example, most jurisdictions tend to prohibit discrimination based on race

---

[4] Nicholas Bamforth, Colm O'Cinneide, and Maleiha Malik, *Discrimination Law: Theory and Context* (Sweet & Maxwell 2008) 19–23. Other questions include the clash between antidiscrimina-tion and other rights, non-legal remedies, enforcement issues, and so on.

symmetrically but on disability asymmetrically. The consensus suggests that there is something about the difference between race and disability that dictates this differentiation. On the other hand, as I just noted, reasonable accommodation is available for different grounds in different jurisdictions (and for all grounds in at least one jurisdiction). This tells us that the specific ground in question is not essential to whether reasonable accommodation could be an available remedy. In this latter set of cases, if most jurisdictions have accepted the principle underlying a development with respect to some grounds, I have concluded that the development is part of the evolving structure of discrimination law.

3.1 The Protectorate

Discrimination law protects persons—especially groups of persons defined by certain personal characteristics that are technically called grounds. The second and the third of the four conditions that define the essence of the norms of discrimination law relate to the protectorate. Let us recall these two conditions that were discovered in Chapter 2:

> The Cognate Groups Condition: *A protected ground must be capable of classifying persons into more than one class of persons, loosely called 'groups'.*
>
> The Relative Disadvantage Condition: *Of all groups defined by a given universal order ground, members of at least one group must be significantly more likely to suffer abiding, pervasive, and substantial disadvantage than the members of at least one other cognate group.*

These conditions reveal the centrality of groups and grounds to the contemporary understanding of discrimination law. A state could prohibit harassment per se, rather than merely *sexual* or *racial harassment*. It could even distribute material goods without reference to protected grounds. These acts will not satisfy the aforementioned conditions, and therefore not qualify as measures within the scope of discrimination law. The essential findings in Chapter 2 were theoretical—now they can be substantiated and built upon with reference to practical data.

Most antidiscrimination norms prima facie refer to grounds alone, and not groups. Section 9(3) of the South African Constitution, for example, prohibits discrimination 'against anyone on one or more grounds, including race, gender, sex, pregnancy, marital status, ethnic or social origin, colour, sexual orientation, age, disability, religion, conscience, belief, culture, language and birth'.[5] Comparable provisions can be found in statutory as well as constitutional provisions in other jurisdictions.[6] Given the importance of the list of protected grounds, it is no surprise that judges and legislators have faced a growing (and often successful) clamour in the last couple of decades for expanding the list of protected grounds—candidates such as weight,[7] physical appearance,[8] and genetic identity[9] are offered as 'analogous' to the ones already listed.[10] Fiss famously called this phenomenon the 'proliferation of the protectorate'.[11] Commentators and law-makers have struggled to evolve principled criteria which can be employed to determine these claims. Judgments from jurisdictions that have an open-ended list of protected grounds are perhaps the most instructive in this regard.[12] When invited to determine whether a candidate ought to be added to this list, judges in these jurisdictions appear to be applying the following two cumulative requirements that a ground must satisfy in order to be protected by discrimination law:

(i) It must be a ground that classifies persons into groups with a significant advantage gap between them; *and*

(ii) It must either be immutable or it must constitute a fundamental choice.

The first of these requirements makes it clear that the concept of group disadvantage is central to our understanding of grounds. It is no surprise that this requirement is but a rough-and-ready version of the combination of the cognate groups and relative disadvantage conditions. We will also learn that

---

[5] Constitution of the Republic of South Africa, 1996 (Constitution of South Africa).

[6] See Canadian Charter of Fundamental Rights and Freedoms, s 15 (Canadian Charter); European Convention on Human Rights, art 14 (ECHR); Canadian Human Rights Act, RSC 1985, c H-6, s 3 (Canadian Human Rights Act); Constitution of India 1950, art 15 (Constitution of India).

[7] Elizabeth Kristen, 'Addressing the Problem of Weight Discrimination in Employment' (2002) 90 California Law Review 57.

[8] Robert Post, A Appiah, J Butler et al, *Prejudicial Appearances: the Logic of American Antidiscrimination Law* (Duke University Press 2001).

[9] Anita Silvers and Michael Stein, 'An Equality Paradigm for Preventing Genetic Discrimination' (2002) 55 Vanderbilt Law Review 1341.

[10] See generally, *Law v Canada* [1999] 1 SCR 497 [39], [62]–[75]. The US 14th Amendment is an exception, in that there are no explicitly specified grounds—all protected grounds have been determined by judicial interpretation.

[11] Owen Fiss, 'The Fate of an Idea Whose Time has Come: Anti-Discrimination Law in the Second Decade after *Brown v. Board of Education*' (1974) 41 University of Chicago Law Review 742, 748. See also, Christopher McCrudden, 'Introduction' in Christopher McCrudden (ed), *Anti-Discrimination Law* (Dartmouth 1991); Christopher McCrudden, 'Introduction' in Christopher McCrudden (ed), *Anti-Discrimination Law* (2nd edn, Ashgate 2004).

[12] For an example, see Canadian Charter, s 15(1).

group disadvantage plays a greater role than simply the gatekeeping function of identifying protected grounds: protected groups tend to get more protection than their cognates. The protectorate therefore is largely organized asymmetrically. For both these reasons, at least in law, we cannot appreciate grounds without appreciating groups. The lay model of discrimination tends not to appreciate this connection sufficiently.

The second requirement is a further hurdle that a ground must satisfy before it is protected. While the immutability requirement is a closer reflection of the lay model, it does not entail that the ground is 'irrelevant' to the purpose of the distribution at hand—a key assumption underpinning the lay approach. Instead, the second requirement is a demand for *normative* irrelevance: ie the ground in question should be morally irrelevant to the success of our lives.

3.1.1 Group Disadvantage

Let us begin with the first requirement: the ground must classify persons into groups with a significant advantage gap between them. Sex is a protected ground because there is a significant advantage gap between women and men. Recall from Chapter 2 that different groups sharing the same universal order ground are cognates of each other. Thus, men and women constitute cognate groups. However, we reserved the term 'cognate group' only for the more advantaged of these groups defined by the same ground. The less advantaged group was labelled a 'protected group'. In our example, men constitute a cognate group and women a protected group, both defined by the ground sex. We did not require a 'group' to possess any solidarity, coherence, sense of identity, shared history, language, or culture to be characterized as such. There is a theoretically relevant distinction between groups that possess some of these features (ie groups that have an 'expressive salience') and those that do not. We can, however, keep this distinction to one side until later in the book.[13]

All protected grounds divide persons into groups with a significant advantage gap between them: protected groups suffer relative disadvantage in comparison with cognate groups. Instead of adopting a blinkered view of disadvantage as merely economic, courts have usually been sophisticated in unpacking the notion of relative group disadvantage. They have recognized that disadvantage may be political, socio-cultural, material—more often, a complex combination of these different facets of disadvantage. Affluent

---

[13] See Chapter 6, section 6.5 for a discussion on expressive salience of groups.

members of racial minorities may have overcome material disadvantage, but are likely to remain saddled with political and socio-cultural disadvantage, which can be even more difficult to shake off. As Justice Wilson insisted in *Andrews*, the 'place of the group in the entire social, political and legal fabric of our society' was relevant to determining whether it should be protected.[14]

It is obvious to most of us that individuals can and do suffer disadvantage, in the absolute as well as the relative sense. But the disadvantage that groups suffer is not a simple aggregate of that suffered by its members. At least some types of disadvantages discussed below apply meaningfully only to groups—political disadvantage is one example. Other types of disadvantage, especially material disadvantage, can afflict a group as a whole, even if it does not affect all its members.

Political Disadvantage

Political disadvantage is evidenced by factors such as the numerical strength of a group as an electorate (foreigners,[15] people living with HIV/AIDS,[16] and gay and lesbian people[17] have been protected because of their numerical insignificance in the electoral process); the quantity and quality of actual representation of the group in the offices of state;[18] and the nature and the degree of attention paid by state institutions to the group in question.[19] Political disadvantage can be a cause, as well as an effect, of

---

[14] *Andrews v Law Society of British Columbia* [1989] 1 SCR 143, 152. See also, *R v Turpin* [1989] 1 SCR 1296, 1331–2; *Egan v Canada* [1995] 2 SCR 513 [172]–[180].

[15] Apart from their numerical insignificance, foreigners often do not have the right to vote. *Graham v Richardson* 403 US 365 (1971) 372. See also, *In Re Griffiths* 413 US 717; *Sugarman v Dougall* 413 US 634 (1973); *Examining Board of Engineers v Flores de Otero* 426 US 572 (1976); *Andrews v Law Society of British Columbia* [1989] 1 SCR 143, 152, 183.

[16] *Hoffmann v South African Airways* 2001 (1) SA 1 [28].

[17] *National Coalition for Gay and Lesbian Equality v Minister of Justice* 1999 (1) SA 6 [25] and fn 32.

[18] *Frontiero v Richardson* 411 US 677 (1973) 686, fn 17: although women are not a numerical minority, they 'are vastly underrepresented in this Nation's decisionmaking councils. There has never been a female President, nor a female member of this Court. Not a single woman presently sits in the United States Senate, and only 14 women hold seats in the House of Representatives. And … this underrepresentation is present throughout all levels of our State and Federal Government.' See also, *Watkins v United States Army* 875 F2d 699 (1989) 727: the 'very fact that homosexuals have historically been underrepresented in … political bodies is itself strong evidence that they lack the political power necessary to ensure fair treatment at the hands of government'.

[19] *Frontiero v Richardson* 411 US 677 (1973) 685: in the past, women could not 'hold office, serve on juries, or bring suit in their own names, and married women traditionally were denied the legal capacity to hold or convey property or to serve as legal guardians of their own children'—even the right to vote was denied to them for long. See also, *United States v Virginia* 518 US 515 (1996) 531. See generally, *United States v Carolene Products* 304 US 144 (1938) fn 4, per Justice Stone: 'prejudice against discrete and insular minorities may be a special condition, which tends seriously to curtail the operation of those political processes ordinarily to be relied upon to protect minorities, and which may call for a correspondingly more searching judicial inquiry'.

other forms of disadvantage. The socio-cultural disadvantage that women face in our societies leaves them underrepresented in and under-catered for by our public institutions. On the other hand, the important role of political power in shaping material distribution means that politically disadvantaged groups may also fail to secure fair distribution of society's resources.[20]

Socio-Cultural Disadvantage

Socio-cultural disadvantage is usually (although not exclusively) indicated by the prevalence of prejudice against and (certain) stereotypical assumptions about the members of a group.[21] Prejudice (or bias) is 'a judgment that those with a certain trait are morally less worthy than others *merely* by virtue of possessing that trait'. For example, prejudice against *dalits* signifies a belief that a person is less deserving morally because of her 'lower' caste status. This is a categorical preference against certain groups of people, simply based on who they are. A person's belief in his moral superiority can spring not just from caste—religion, sex, sexual orientation, race, and various other attributes have been, and still are, the bases for prejudice in our societies. Stereotypes (or proxies) do not entail such categorical judgments about persons.[22] Instead, they involve a judgment—rightly or wrongly—that a person with a certain trait is quite likely to possess other, relevant, traits. When the judgment is accurate, the correlation between the traits could be due to biological factors (eg a woman is likely to live longer than a man), socio-cultural factors (eg a woman is more likely to quit her job to accommodate her husband's career than the other way around), or because of the reaction of others (eg a black cop is likely to be more effective than a white cop in policing a black neighbourhood). The stronger the statistical correlation, the more accurate a stereotype will be. Often stereotypes are inaccurate, such that there is little evidence for the supposed correlation (eg the belief that the poor are lazy). Fuelled by anecdotal rather than statistically significant evidence, inaccurate stereotypes are often attempts to rationalize prejudices.[23]

---

[20] For an analysis of the institutional implications of political disadvantage, see John Ely, *Democracy and Distrust: A Theory of Judicial Review* (Harvard University Press 1980).

[21] Most of the insights in this paragraph are borrowed from Larry Alexander, 'What Makes Wrongful Discrimination Wrong? Biases, Preferences, Stereotypes and Proxies' (1992) 141 University of Pennsylvania Law Review 149.

[22] Alexandra Timmer, 'Towards an Anti-Stereotyping Approach for the European Court of Human Rights' (2011) 11 Human Rights Law Review 707.

[23] Sujit Choudhry, 'Distribution vs. Recognition: The Case of Anti-Discrimination Laws' (2000) 9 George Mason Law Review 145, 156: 'irrational proxies are so tightly linked to prejudice that discrimination relying on the former is tantamount to discrimination motivated by the latter'.

Apart from being accurate or inaccurate, stereotypes can also be positive, neutral, or negative, depending on the desirability of the correlative trait. The assumption that women are caring is a positive stereotype, and that men are violent is negative. Things get complicated because these traits may be objectively positive or negative, and still be subjectively judged differently in any given society. It may be, for example, that caring is seen as a sign of weakness, whereas a proclivity to violence is seen as strength. Furthermore, even positive stereotypes which a society correctly views as positive can have disadvantageous effects—assumptions about women's care-giving nature results in them being saddled with most of the child-rearing responsibilities while men can focus on their career advancement.

Groups against whom prejudices or subjectively negative stereotypes are widespread in a society are more clearly disadvantaged socio-culturally. They affect the members' ability to take pride in their membership of a group, especially in cases where such membership partly constitutes personal identity. Positive stereotypes that have negative effects can also contribute to social disadvantage, as also other forms of disadvantage. In fact, socio-cultural disadvantage generally has a causal relationship with other facets of disadvantage. It may result in political disadvantage for two reasons. First, political officials, as members of the society, may often share the prejudices and negative stereotypes prevalent in society, which are then reflected in official acts. The second reason is that even if public officials themselves do not hold these beliefs, the fact that they are responsible electorally to those who do gives them an incentive to act on these prejudices or stereotypes. It is for this reason that Justice O'Connor applied 'a more searching form of rational basis review' when a law was designed to harm 'a politically unpopular group'.[24] The implication seems to be that the group faces such a degree of social hostility that acting against them may accrue political dividends for public officials. Similar causal connections can sometimes be drawn between socio-cultural disadvantage and material disadvantage. The socio-cultural disadvantage of a group is often the cause of hostility and violence against, and boycotts and ghettoization of, its members—factors that render them materially disadvantaged.

Material Disadvantage

The third indicator of disadvantage is material disadvantage. While primarily determined by economic indicators like income and wealth, it can be given a broader interpretation to include access to education and employment,[25]

---

[24] *Lawrence v Texas* 539 US 558 (2003) 580.
[25] *President of RSA v Hugo* 1997 (4) SA 1 [38]: 'The result of being responsible for children makes it more difficult for women to compete in the labour market and is one of the causes of the deep

freedom from private and public violence and hostility,[26] longevity, and health, among other factors.[27] These factors indicate the socio-economic security of individuals, which in turn dictates the material status of a group composed of such individuals. Justice Marshall's opinion in *Bakke* understood material disadvantage in this wide sense, and is worth quoting in some detail:

A Negro child today has a life expectancy which is shorter by more than five years than that of a white child. The Negro child's mother is over three times more likely to die of complications in childbirth, and the infant mortality rate for Negroes is nearly twice that for whites. The median income of the Negro family is only 60% that of the median of a white family, and the percentage of Negroes who live in families with incomes below the poverty line is nearly four times greater than that of whites.

When the Negro child reaches working age, he finds that America offers him significantly less than it offers his white counterpart. For Negro adults, the unemployment rate is twice that of whites, and the unemployment rate for Negro teenagers is nearly three times that of white teenagers. A Negro male who completes four years of college can expect a median annual income of merely $110 more than a white male who has only a high school diploma. Although Negroes represent 11.5% of the population, they are only 1.2% of the lawyers, and judges, 2% of the physicians, 2.3% of the dentists, 1.1% of the engineers and 2.6% of the college and university professors.[28]

On similar lines, the criteria for 'backwardness' evolved by the Second Backward Classes Commission to determine eligibility for affirmative action programmes in India include 'social factors' ('classes considered socially backward by others', dependence on manual labour, etc), 'educational factors' (school attendance, drop-out, and matriculation rates) and 'economic factors'

---

inequalities experienced by women in employment.' *Watkins v United States Army* 875 F2d 699 (1989) 724: 'In the private sphere, homosexuals continue to face discrimination in jobs, housing and churches.' See also, *Frontiero v Richardson* 411 US 677 (1973) 686; *Harksen v Lane NO* 1998 (1) SA 300 CC [63]; *Hoffmann v South African Airways* 2001 (1) SA 1 [28].

[26] The South African Constitutional Court has taken notice of incidents of societal hostility and threats faced by aliens as evidence of their disadvantage: *Larbi-Odam v Member of the Executive Council for Education* 1998 (1) SA 745 [20]. See also, *Watkins v United States Army* 875 F2d 699 (1989) 724: 'it is indisputable that homosexuals have historically been the object of pernicious and sustained hostility' and that 'reports of violence against homosexuals have become commonplace in our society'. See further, *Egan v Canada* [1995] 2 SCR 513 [182]; *M v H* [1999] 2 SCR 3 [64], [69].

[27] Sen criticizes the focus on income as the primary focus in analysing inequality—Amartya Sen, *Inequality Reexamined* (Clarendon Press 1992) 28–30.

[28] *Regents of the University of California v Bakke* 438 US 265 (1978) 395–6 (internal footnotes omitted).

(value of assets, loans owed, and proximity to drinking water facilities).[29] Although economic factors were accorded relatively low weight, they 'were considered important as they directly flowed from social and educational backwardness. This also helped to highlight the fact that socially and educationally backward classes are economically backward also.'[30]

The disadvantage we are concerned with is relative—it is the gap between the protected and the cognate groups that counts. It may well be, of course, that a protected group is also disadvantaged in some absolute sense—it may fall below any absolute threshold of well-being necessary to live a decent life. But it seems that for judges to protect a particular ground, relative disadvantage between any two groups defined by that ground would suffice. Thus, a group need not be entirely excluded from the political process—the fact that it is a politically excluded minority will be sufficient. No doubt men bear the burden of social stereotyping too—it is enough that, on the whole, women face a significantly greater degree of social disadvantage. 'Backward classes' in India may not be poor in absolute terms—relative material disadvantage is all that is required. That said, the advantage gap between relevant groups must be significant rather than trivial. Hence our first condition that makes a ground eligible for the protection of discrimination law: it must classify persons into groups with a significant advantage gap between them. Notice that the relative disadvantage of a group (say women) makes the entire ground (sex) eligible for protection, at least in a prima facie sense. We will see in section 3.1.3 that sometimes the duties imposed by discrimination law apply asymmetrically, such that disadvantaged groups are given a greater degree of protection.

3.1.2 Normative Irrelevance

The second, additional, requirement that judges have insisted upon is that a candidate ground must either be immutable or it must constitute a fundamental choice if it is to be protected.[31] These requirements together amount to a demand that the ground be normatively irrelevant: ie our possession of these grounds should not affect how successful our lives are. Recall from Chapter 2 that the phenomenon of a ground can be said to exist in the

---

[29] Bindheshwari Mandal, *Report of the Second Backward Classes Commission* (First Part) (1980) [11.23].

[30] Bindheshwari Mandal, *Report of the Second Backward Classes Commission* (First Part) (1980) [11.24].

[31] See generally Robert Wintemute, *Sexual Orientation and Human Rights: The United States Constitution, the European Convention, and the Canadian Charter* (Clarendon Press 1995).

higher *universal* order (sex) and the *particular* order (maleness). When we speak of a person 'possessing' a ground, we usually speak of it in the particular order. Henceforth, I will rely on the context to clarify whether the term is used in the universal or the particular order.

Immutability of a characteristic has been the most frequently used rationale, especially in cases involving racial classifications. In *Korematsu*, the US Supreme Court noted that the appellant 'belongs to a race from which there is no way to resign'.[32] Courts have understood 'immutability' broadly, at least inasmuch as they include not only characteristics that cannot be changed,[33] but also those whose initial acquisition itself was not based on a choice made by the possessor.[34] Apart from race, characteristics that have been protected for immutability-based reasons include sex,[35] marital status of one's parents,[36] place of residence of young children,[37] and citizenship.[38]

---

[32] *Korematsu v United States* 323 US 214 (1944) 243. See also, *Fullilove v Klutznick* 448 US 448, 496: Justice Powell said that 'Racial classifications must be assessed under the most stringent level of review because immutable characteristics, which bear no relation to individual merit or need, are irrelevant to almost every governmental decision.' See also, *R v McKitka* [1987] BCJ No 3210 [20]. Sunstein also talks of the 'accident of birth' being irrelevant morally: Cass Sunstein, 'The Anticaste Principle' (1994) 92 Michigan Law Review 2410, 2434; likewise, Justice Murphy noted the 'accident of race or ancestry' while reluctantly concurring with the racial classification: *Hirabayashi v United States* 320 US 81.

[33] *Fullilove v Klutznick* 448 US 448 (1980) 496: 'Racial classifications must be assessed under the most stringent level of review because immutable characteristics, which bear no relation to individual merit or need, are irrelevant to almost every governmental decision.' *Andrews v Law Society of British Columbia* [1989] 1 SCR 143, 195: 'The characteristic of citizenship is one typically not within the control of the individual and, in this sense, is immutable. Citizenship is, at least temporarily, a characteristic of personhood not alterable by conscious action and in some cases not alterable except on the basis of unacceptable costs.'

[34] *R v McKitka* [1987] BCJ No 3210 [20]: 'the enumerated categories of s 15 all tend to reflect ... how, when and where we come into this world, matters over which we have no control'; *Hirabayashi v United States* 320 US 81 (1943) 111: 'The difference between their innocence and his crime would result, not from anything he did, said, or thought, different than they, but only in that he was born of different racial stock'; *Weber v Aetna Casualty & Surety Company* 406 US 164 (1972) 175: 'no child is responsible for his birth and penalizing the illegitimate child is ... unjust'.

[35] *Frontiero v Richardson* 411 US 677 (1973) 686: sex is determined 'solely by the accident of birth'.

[36] *Weber v Aetna Casualty & Surety Company* 406 US 164 (1972) 175: '[N]o child is responsible for his birth and penalizing the illegitimate child is ... unjust.' See also, *Mathews v Lucas* 427 US 495 (1976) 505; *Clark v Jeter* 486 US 456 (1988) 461; *Milne v Alberta* [1990] 5 WWR 650 [37]. In *Plyler*, a law denying educational benefits to children of unlawful immigrants was held to be 'directed against children, and imposes its discriminatory burden on the basis of a legal characteristic over which children can have little control': *Plyler v Doe* 457 US 202 (1982) 220.

[37] In *San Antonio*, the dissenting opinion of Justice Marshall held that classification 'between the schoolchildren of Texas on the basis of the taxable property wealth of the districts in which they happen to live' was a basis upon which the 'individual has no significant control': *San Antonio Independent School District v Rodriguez* 411 US 1 (1973) 96.

[38] *Larbi-Odam v Member of the Executive Council for Education* 1998 (1) SA 745 [19]. See also, *Andrews v Law Society of British Columbia* [1989] 1 SCR 143, 195.

Judicial reliance on immutability as the sole test for selecting a protected characteristic has been severely criticized.[39] It has been shown that it tends to be biased towards protecting *corporeal* grounds, ie those defined by nature, for example race, sex, etc. Non-corporeal or social grounds like religious status, linguistic identity, marital status, and sexual orientation, which are more easily hidden and (arguably) changeable, are less favourably treated.[40] These *behavioural* grounds manifest themselves to the outside world only through behaviour or conduct. In *High Tech Gays*, Judge Brunetti held that homosexuality is *behavioural*, 'hence [it] is fundamentally different from traits such as race, gender, or alienage'.[41] Thus, the argument goes, homosexuals should not be part of the protectorate. Reacting to these types of cases, Sunstein rhetorically asked if the discovery of an accessible race-altering drug could have any implication on the protection of race.[42] Feminists have also raised the same concerns, arguing that the immutability test can be (and has been) used to deny protection to pregnancy, since pregnancy is (assumed to be) within the control of a woman.[43] Furthermore, immutability is in any case a matter of degree—even one's sex can be changed, while gender is reasonably mutable (to the extent that one could distinguish between sex and gender). Even grounds such as caste and race can be hidden, if not changed.

The judicial reaction to these criticisms was two-fold. One way in which courts reacted to this problem was by distinguishing between 'strict' and 'effective' mutability:

[39] Kenji Yoshino, 'Assimilationist Bias in Equal Protection: The Visibility Presumption and the Case of "Don't Ask, Don't Tell"' (1998) 108 Yale Law Journal 485, 510–15, 530–6.

[40] Kenji Yoshino, 'Assimilationist Bias in Equal Protection: The Visibility Presumption and the Case of "Don't Ask, Don't Tell"' (1998) 108 Yale Law Journal 485, 495–8: This distinction between corporeal and social characteristics must be taken with a pinch of salt. Almost all 'corporeal' characteristics are mediated by socio-cultural norms to some extent. Clothing, contact lenses, artificial colour, high-heeled boots, and make-up are capable of masking our 'corporeal' characteristics like sex, eye-colour, hair-colour, height, and physical appearance, respectively. See also, Judith Butler, *Gender Trouble: Feminism and the Subversion of Identity* (10th anniversary edn, Routledge 1999) 10–11: 'If the immutable character of sex is contested, perhaps this construct called "sex" is as culturally constructed as gender; indeed, perhaps it was always already gender, with the consequence that the distinction between sex and gender turns out to be no distinction at all.'

[41] *High Tech Gays v Defense Industrial Security Clearance Office* 895 F2d 563 (1990) 573. See also, *Jordan v State* 2002 (6) SA 642 [17]: 'by engaging in commercial sex work prostitutes knowingly attract the stigma associated with prostitution, it can hardly be contended that female prostitutes are discriminated against on the basis of gender'. See also, *Miron v Trudel* [1995] 2 SCR 418 [28], [57]; *R v Baig* [1990] BCJ No 203; *Delisle v Attorney General of Canada* [1999] 2 SCR 989 [44].

[42] Cass Sunstein, 'The Anticaste Principle' (1994) 92 Michigan Law Review 2410, 2443.

[43] Laura Kessler, 'The Attachment Gap: Employment Discrimination Law, Women's Cultural Caregiving, and the Limits of Economic and Liberal Legal Theory' (2001) 34 University of Michigan Journal of Law Reform 371.

It is clear that by 'immutability' the Court has never meant strict immutability in the sense that members of the class must be physically unable to change or mask the trait defining their class. People can have operations to change their sex... the Supreme Court is willing to treat a trait as effectively immutable if changing it would involve great difficulty...[44]

There are other similar cases where courts have been satisfied with effective immutability, where changing the trait would impose significant personal costs.[45] Obviously, these costs are more than mere economic ones, and include psychological and social costs as well.[46]

Once this is accepted, it is easy to see how effective immutability merges with fundamental choice, for 'immutability may describe those traits that are so central to a person's identity that it would be abhorrent for government to penalize a person for refusing to change them, regardless of how easy that change might be physically'.[47] This explicit recognition of fundamental choice *alongside* immutability as an alternative basis for protection of a ground was the second judicial response to the criticisms against the immutability test. Thus, while grounds such as marital status, pregnancy, and religious status are (to an extent) a matter of choice and could be changed, such change is usually impossible without significant personal costs to the individual.[48] When judges were already protecting characteristics over which we lack *effective* control, protection for characteristics that constitute a fundamental choice merely lay further along the same spectrum, rather than in a separate category altogether. By protecting grounds constituting fundamental choice,

---

[44] *Watkins v United States Army* 875 F2d 699 (1989).

[45] Justice Mokgoro seems to have effective mutability in mind when she says that 'citizenship is a personal attribute that is difficult to change': *Larbi-Odam v Member of the Executive Council for Education* 1998 (1) SA 745 [19]. *Corbiere v Canada* [1999] 2 SCR 203 [13]: 'what these grounds have in common is the fact that they often serve as the basis for stereotypical decisions made not on the basis of merit but on the basis of a personal characteristic that is immutable or changeable only at unacceptable cost to personal identity'. See also, *Egan v Canada* [1995] 2 SCR 513 [5]: Justice La Forest considered sexual orientation to be either 'unchangeable or changeable only at unacceptable personal costs'.

[46] Dale Gibson, 'Analogous Grounds for Discrimination Under the Canadian Charter: Too Much Ado About Next to Nothing' (1991) 29 Alberta Law Review 772, 786–7.

[47] *Watkins v United States Army* 875 F2d 699 (1989) 726. See also, Kenji Yoshino, 'Covering' (2001–2002) 111 Yale Law Journal 769; *Leroux v Co-operators General Insurance Co* [1990] ILR 1-2566 [37].

[48] *Miron v Trudel* [1995] 2 SCR 418 [97]–[98]. *Watkins v United States Army* 875 F2d 699 (1989) 726: 'allowing the government to penalize the failure to change such a central aspect of individual and group identity would be abhorrent to the values animating the constitutional ideal of equal protection of the laws'. *Andrews v Law Society of British Columbia* [1989] 1 SCR 143, 174: 'Distinctions based on personal characteristics attributed to an individual solely on the basis of association with a group will rarely escape the charge of discrimination.'

discrimination law resists assimilationist demands that those carrying these grounds must convert (ie give up), pass-off (ie hide), or cover (ie not-flaunt) their chosen characteristic.[49]

To be plain, the choice in question is important because it is fundamental *to the person whose choice it is*. In *Brooks*, for example, where the issue was discrimination on the basis of pregnancy status, the defence tried to compare pregnancy with cosmetic surgery, arguing that both being matters of choice, neither should be protected. Although the court rejected this comparison, it missed the point by underscoring merely that 'pregnancy is of fundamental importance in our society'.[50] A better approach is that of Justice L'Heureux-Dubé in *Miron*, where she equates marital status to religion and citizenship: they may be matters of choice, but involve such fundamental personal judgments that legal outcomes should not depend on the failure to make a particular choice.[51] Justice O'Regan echoed the point in *Harksen*, where she held that 'the decision to enter into a permanent personal relationship with another is a momentous and defining one'.[52]

In addition to being fundamental, the choice should be valuable (or, at least, not-without-value). In *Nyquist*, for example, while rejecting the justification offered by the state that the law giving scholarships to citizens but not permanent resident aliens was intended to encourage naturalization, the majority held that resident aliens pay their full share of taxes and often provide leadership in many spheres of community life, and that the state is not harmed in providing them equal benefits.[53] Thus, the second requirement for eligibility for protection is that the ground in question must be an effectively immutable trait *or* constitute a valuable fundamental choice. Examining these alternative features—immutability and fundamental choice—through the lens of 'choice' makes them appear contradictory. We seem to be protecting grounds over the possession of which we have no choice, and also grounds that constitute a fundamental choice. But that is the wrong lens through which to examine these selection criteria.[54] It is clear that judges have used these criteria to identify grounds that are normatively irrelevant. When a ground is immutable, possessing it is not generally immoral. When a ground represents a valuable fundamental choice, it is positively valuable, rather than merely not-immoral.

---

[49] Kenji Yoshino, 'Covering' (2001–2002) 111 Yale Law Journal 769.

[50] *Brooks v Canada Safeway Ltd* [1989] 1 SCR 1219 [31].

[51] *Miron v Trudel* [1995] 2 SCR 418 [97]–[98]. See also, *Watkins v United States Army* 875 F2d 699 (1989) 726.

[52] *Harksen v Lane NO* 1998 (1) SA 300 CC [92].

[53] *Nyquist v Mauclet* 432 US 1 (1977) 12.

[54] cf John Gardner, 'On the Ground of Her Sex(uality)' (1998) 18 Oxford Journal of Legal Studies 167, 170–1.

3.1.3 On Symmetry

The shape of the protectorate of discrimination law is not symmetric. While a ground may be protected, the protection offered to all groups defined by it is not necessarily the same. The question is whether women alone are protected from sex discrimination, or also men; and, when both are protected, whether they are protected to the same degree.[55] There are three mutually incompatible positions a jurisdiction could adopt on the question of symmetrical protection of groups: (i) *completely symmetric protection*, where the cognate and the protected groups are offered exactly the same degree of protection; (ii) *completely asymmetric protection*, where only the protected group gets any protection at all; or (iii) *largely asymmetric protection*, where both groups benefit, but protected groups benefit more than cognate groups.

The prohibition on direct discrimination usually applies symmetrically for most grounds. There are, however, exceptions. The most stable exception common to all jurisdictions is the asymmetric protection of disability: only a disabled person can bring a claim of discrimination; an able-bodied person cannot claim disability discrimination.[56] Even though the actual prohibition on direct discrimination is usually symmetric, members of cognate groups who lose out because of the operation of a justified affirmative action measure are deemed not to have suffered direct discrimination.[57] Thus, all jurisdictions under study adopt the third position by providing largely asymmetric protection for most grounds, and completely asymmetric protection for some grounds (mainly disability).

In sharp contrast to the lay model, no jurisdiction under study offers completely symmetric protection. This fact alone underscores the salience of relative group disadvantage in discrimination law. Because largely asymmetric protection is the general rule, I have been referring to relatively

---

[55] See generally, Owen Fiss, 'Groups and the Equal Protection Clause' (1976) 5 Philosophy and Public Affairs 107; Alan Freeman, 'Legitimizing Racial Discrimination Through Antidiscrimination Law: A Critical Review of Supreme Court Doctrine' (1978) 62 Minnesota Law Review 1049; Richard Fallon and Paul Weiler, '*Firefighters v. Stotts*: Conflicting Models of Racial Justice' [1984] The Supreme Court Review 1; Morris Abram, 'Affirmative Action: Fair Shakers and Social Engineers' (1986) 99 Harvard Law Review 1312; Neil Gotanda, 'A Critique of "Our Constitution is Color-Blind"' (1991) 44 Stanford Law Review 1; Kenji Yoshino, 'Assimilationist Bias in Equal Protection: The Visibility Presumption and the Case of "Don't Ask, Don't Tell"' (1998) 108 Yale Law Journal 485.

[56] UK Equality Act 2010, s 13(3); Canadian Human Rights Act, s 25 (asymmetric definition of disability); South African Promotion of Equality and Prohibition of Unfair Discrimination Act 4 of 2000, s 9 (South African Equality Act); Americans with Disabilities Act, 42 USC § 12102 (asymmetric definition of disability).

[57] See section 3.3.5 below.

disadvantaged groups defined by a protected ground as *protected groups*. This is not wholly accurate as a description, since it (wrongly) implies that cognate groups are not protected at all. But I will let brevity triumph over clarity.

To summarize, the scope and shape of the protectorate of discrimination law is determined by a complex interaction between two factors: grounds and groups. Its scope is determined by two cumulative requirements for protecting a ground: that it must classify persons into groups with a significant advantage gap between them, and that it must either be immutable or constitute a fundamental choice. The shape of the protectorate is largely asymmetric, in favour of greater protection for protected groups and less so for cognate groups. This organization of the protectorate will be justified with reference to the purpose of discrimination law (in Chapter 5, section 5.4) and its distributive design (in Chapter 6, especially sections 6.3 and 6.5).

3.2 The Duty-Bearers

Having looked at the protectorate of discrimination law, it is time to examine who the bearers of its duties are. Unlike typical duties in criminal law or the law of torts, the duties of discrimination law are not borne by everyone. Instead of a universal approach, the law identifies specific types of persons to impose its burdens. In many respects, discrimination law has expanded beyond what the lay model would characterize as discriminatory. In respect to the question currently under consideration, however, the law is more restrained: it refuses to regulate conduct that laypeople would view as discriminatory unless it is the conduct of a select duty-bearer.

At the start of this chapter, we looked at the English common law duty on the providers of certain public utilities—innkeepers, blacksmiths, common-carriers—to refrain from discrimination (although this prohibition on 'discrimination' was not ground-sensitive in the contemporary sense). However, when the US Congress sought to extend legal protection to ground-sensitive discrimination by private persons in 1875, it hit a judicial roadblock. The Civil Rights Act of 1875 had declared that:

[A]ll persons within the jurisdiction of the United States shall be entitled to the full and equal enjoyment of the accommodations, advantages, facilities, and privileges of inns, public conveyances on land or water, theaters, and other places of public amusement; subject only to the conditions and limitations established by law, and applicable alike to citizens of every race and color, regardless of any previous condition of servitude.

The US Supreme Court struck it down as unconstitutional, asserting that the 14th Amendment allowed the regulation of state action alone.[58] Discrimination law has come a long way from this nineteenth-century controversy. As far as the practice of discrimination law is concerned, it is no longer contentious that antidiscrimination duties apply to public as well as private persons—ie in 'vertical' as well as 'horizontal' relationships, respectively. The debate has shifted to the determination of which private persons ought to bear the duties and what the nature and scope of these duties ought to be.

In most jurisdictions, constitutional as well as statutory provisions impose the antidiscrimination duties and license affirmative action.[59] The legal source of the duties usually has implications for who the duty-holder is. In general, duties imposed by Constitutions and Bills of Rights apply only to the 'state' or 'public authorities',[60] whereas statutory obligations tend to apply to public as well as private bodies. The two exceptions to the general rule regarding constitutional texts are South Africa[61] and the European Union[62]—constitutional texts of both these jurisdictions have provisions that are worded broadly enough to impose non-discrimination obligations not merely on public authorities but also on private bodies, although these horizontal constitutional duties are normally given effect to by statutes.

Constitutional provisions are framed vaguely, and usually guarantee a right to equality—the right against discrimination is usually understood to be an aspect of or related to this right in all jurisdictions. Judges have interpreted the duties corresponding to these rights in relation to (but not necessarily mirroring) the more specific duties imposed by statutes.[63] Although applicable usually to

---

[58] *United States v Stanley (The Civil Rights Cases)* 109 US 3 (1883).

[59] See generally, Nicholas Bamforth, 'Conceptions of Anti-Discrimination Law' (2004) 24 Oxford Journal of Legal Studies 693–701.

[60] See, for example, the 14th Amendment to the Constitution of the United States ('No state shall … deny to any person … the equal protection of the laws'); ECHR, art 14, read with Protocol 12 ('No one shall be discriminated against by any public authority …'); Constitution of India, art 15 ('The state shall not discriminate against any citizen …'); Canadian Charter, s 15 ('Every individual is equal before and under the law and has the right to the equal protection and equal benefit of the law without discrimination …'). The scope of 'public authorities' may be broad or narrow.

[61] Constitution of South Africa, s 9(4): 'No person may unfairly discriminate directly or indirectly against anyone on one or more [protected grounds]'.

[62] Charter of Fundamental Rights of the European Union, art 21(1): 'Any discrimination based on any ground … shall be prohibited.' See also, the empowering provision in the Consolidated version of the Treaty on the Functioning of the European Union, Official Journal C 115, 09/05/2008 P. 0001-0388, art 19: The European Union 'may take appropriate action to combat discrimination based on sex, racial or ethnic origin, religion or belief, disability, age or sexual orientation'.

[63] *Washington v Davis* 426 US 229 (1976).

the state, judges have sometimes given these constitutional duties 'indirect' horizontal effect (not to be confused with 'indirect discrimination'). They have done so by exercising their law-making powers to develop the common law in light of constitutional principles.[64] The Canadian Supreme Court has, for example, held that:

> Where ... private party 'A' sues private party 'B' relying on the common law and where no act of government is relied upon to support the action, the Charter [of Rights and Freedoms] will not apply ... this is a distinct issue from the question whether the judiciary ought to apply and develop the principles of the common law in a manner consistent with the fundamental values enshrined in the Constitution. The answer to this question must be in the affirmative. In this sense, then, the Charter is far from irrelevant to private litigants whose disputes fall to be decided at common law.[65]

The House of Lords relied on a constitutional right to establish a new cause of action between private parties:

> The time has come to recognise that the values enshrined in articles 8 and 10 [of the Human Rights Act] are now part of the cause of action for breach of confidence ... The values embodied in articles 8 and 10 are as much applicable in disputes between individuals or between an individual and a non-governmental body ... as they are in disputes between individuals and a public authority.[66]

Even in the context of antidiscrimination law, the House of Lords has used its interpretative power under section 3 of the Human Rights Act to give indirect horizontal effect to the right against discrimination in the context of a landlord-tenant relationship.[67] Comparably, the US Supreme Court has held that the judiciary, as an organ of the state, is constitutionally prohibited from enforcing private discriminatory contracts.[68] It appears, therefore, that a constitutional prohibition on discrimination by the state has potential implications for the antidiscrimination duties of private persons. It is better to consider the state's refusal to enforce discriminatory contractual terms as flowing from its constitutional obligations qua state, even when such refusal is mandated by statute.[69] This is because the law does not prohibit non-state

---

[64] See generally, Murray Hunt, 'The "Horizontal Effect" of the Human Rights Act' [1998] Public Law 423, 429–35; Nicholas Bamforth, 'The Application of the Human Rights Act 1998 to Public Authorities and Private Bodies' (1999) 58 Cambridge Law Journal 159, 168–70.

[65] *Retail, Wholesale and Department Store Union v Dolphin Delivery Ltd* [1986] 2 SCR 573 [39].

[66] *Campbell v MGN Ltd* [2004] UKHL 22 [17].

[67] In *Ghaidan v Godin-Mendoza* [2004] UKHL 30, a private landlord was not allowed to take possession of a flat from the surviving same-sex spouse of the deceased tenant. The House of Lords interpreted the law governing landlord-tenant relationship to protect same-sex as well as opposite-sex couples.

[68] *Shelley v Kramer* 334 US 1 (1948).

[69] See, for example, UK Equality Act 2010, s 142.

bodies from agreeing upon such terms—unlike the activities that we are going to examine shortly. It simply refuses to extend the contract enforcement services that the state normally provides to discriminatory contractual terms.

Statutory (non-constitutional) duties identify certain types of persons as the duty-bearers—usually employers,[70] landlords,[71] associations,[72] retailers,[73] service-providers,[74] educational institutions,[75] and so on. These duties apply irrespective of whether these are state institutions or non-state. So, the state—wearing its employer or service-provider hat—carries these statutory duties in addition to its constitutional antidiscrimination obligations. The duty-bearers under statutory regimes tend to be limited in three different senses. First, the *sectors* of human activity to which these duties apply are limited. Second, within these sectors, these duties apply *unidirectionally*. Finally, these statutory duties are *not comprehensive*, in that they govern some but not all activities of these duty-bearers.

The sectoral limitation essentially means that statutory duties in discrimination law operate in sectors such as employment, health care, provision for goods and services, education, etc. All these sectors are quasi-public inasmuch as they exclude deeply personal areas of human relationships—such as friendships and romantic relationships. It is, of course, possible to discriminate against protected groups in one's choice of friends or romantic partners—but the law tends not to regulate discrimination in deeply intimate and personal spheres. The state, on the other hand, must never discriminate: constitutional provisions are not limited to specified sectors as statutory regimes are (admittedly, it is difficult to think of examples of intimate and personal activities that the state could perform).

Second, statutory duties tend to be unidirectional, in the sense that they attach to employers but not employees or independent contractors,[76] to providers of goods and services but not to consumers,[77] to landlords but not tenants.[78] Another way of understanding this point is to reimagine the

---

[70] UK Equality Act 2010, s 39; US Civil Rights Act of 1964, Title VII, 42 USC § 2000e-2; Canadian Human Rights Act, s 7.

[71] UK Equality Act 2010, s 33; US Civil Rights Act of 1964, Title II, 42 USC § 2000a; Canadian Human Rights Act, s 6.

[72] UK Equality Act 2010, s 101.

[73] UK Equality Act 2010, s 29 read with s 31(2); Canadian Human Rights Act, s 5.

[74] UK Equality Act 2010, s 29; Canadian Human Rights Act, s 5.

[75] UK Equality Act 2010, ss 85, 91; US Civil Rights Act of 1964, Title IV, 42 USC § 2000c-1.

[76] It is possible for an employer to be vicariously liable for the discriminatory acts of an employee: UK Equality Act 2010, s 110.

[77] *Mingeley v Pennock* [2004] EWCA Civ 238.

[78] For a general treatment of this argument, see Christopher McCrudden, 'Institutional Discrimination' (1982) 2 Oxford Journal of Legal Studies 303, 303.

protectorate as consisting of specific groups such as consumers, employees, patients, students, tenants, citizens/subjects.[79]

Finally, unlike constitutional duties, statutory duties are not comprehensive. Constitutional duties are comprehensive in the sense that they apply to *all* state action.[80] It is not just certain functions that the state must discharge without discrimination. Instead, whatever the state does must be done while respecting its antidiscrimination duties. As Bamforth rightly notes, 'highly significant anti-discrimination issues nowadays arise in the context of the criminal law, police practice, judicial review (particularly in the context of immigration law), family law and property law'.[81] Statutory duties, on the other hand, burden the duty-holders only when they perform certain specified functions. For example, section 29 of the UK Equality Act 2010 forbids a service-provider from discriminating in providing services. This third qualification is slightly different from, and applies in addition to, the sectoral limitation we have already discussed. Employers usually carry antidiscrimination duties only when they do things in their capacity as employers—decisions about recruitment, terms of employment, pension, dismissal, etc.[82] An employer is usually free to discriminate—even on protected grounds—in choosing his friends, in determining which suppliers to buy goods from, in patronizing restaurants for workplace parties, etc.

The one exception to these differences between constitutional and statutory duties is found in the South African Promotion of Equality and Prevention of Unfair Discrimination Act 2000 (South African Equality Act). This statute prohibits all forms of unfair discrimination by all persons—public and private—in all contexts. An illustrative schedule does give examples of unfair discrimination in sectors such as employment and education—section 29, however, makes it clear that this list does not detract from 'the generality of the provisions of this Act'. Thus, none of the above differences are to be found in the South African legislation. Some, although not all, of them may work their way in through the judicial interpretation of what counts as 'unfair' discrimination. At least in so far as South Africa imposes such comprehensive antidiscrimination duties on private persons, it remains an outlier.

---

[79] Constitutional duties prohibit the state from discriminating against all citizens/subjects, even when it is a consumer of goods and services rather than the provider, and not just when it is a landlord but also when it is a tenant.

[80] See authorities cited at n 60 above.

[81] Nicholas Bamforth, 'Conceptions of Anti-Discrimination Law' (2004) 24 Oxford Journal of Legal Studies 693, 694–5.

[82] UK Equality Act 2010, s 39; Canadian Human Rights Act, ss 7, 8.

Some of these duties—say the duty to not discriminate in choosing one's friends or partners—may even be incompatible with the liberal guarantees of the South African Constitution. This legislation should therefore be treated as an anomaly—owed perhaps to the terrible history of apartheid in South Africa. It should not disturb our finding that normally antidiscrimination duties on non-state actors are sectorally limited, unidirectional, and non-comprehensive.

The scope and weight of the duties of discrimination law vary depending on who the duty-bearer is. We will see in the next section that the state generally shoulders a heavier burden of these duties than private persons—especially when it comes to affirmative action duties. But even amongst private persons, the duty is heavier on those with greater power. For example, the UK Equality Act 2010 makes exceptions for landlords with 'small premises',[83] while the South African Employment Equity Act 1998 imposes mandatory affirmative action duties only on 'designated employers'—apart from public bodies, this category includes private employers who employ more than 50 employees or have an annual turnover above a fixed threshold.[84] Title VII of the US Civil Rights Act only applies to employers who have 15 or more workers.[85] Although controversial amongst theorists, it is clear that the law is sensitive to at least some concerns relating to costs and affordability. This, and other, vexed choices that the law has made in imposing its burdens to certain types of persons will be justified in Chapter 7.

3.3 The Duties

The third step towards understanding the overall structure of discrimination law is to examine the shape and scope of the duties that it imposes. The first and the final conditions that describe the essence of discrimination law are relevant to this inquiry. Let us recall them:

The Personal Grounds Condition: *The duty-imposing norm in question must require some connection between the act or omission prohibited or mandated by the norm on the one hand and certain attributes or characteristics that persons have, called 'grounds', on the other.*

---

[83] Schedule 5, paras 3–4.

[84] South African Employment Equity Act 55 of 1998, s 13 read with s 1 (South African Employment Equity Act).

[85] 42 USC § 2000e(b).

The Eccentric Distribution Condition: *The duty-imposing norm must be designed such that it is likely to distribute the non-remote tangible benefits in question to some, but not all, members of the intended beneficiary group.*

In this section, we will see how these core conditions are fleshed out. Contemporary discrimination law prohibits direct and indirect discrimination and harassment, requires reasonable accommodation, and licenses (or mandates) affirmative action. I will explain the broad contours of each of these concepts. Before we do that, it is worth noting that there are significant differences between jurisdictions over the use of these terms—for example, reasonable 'accommodation' is reasonable 'adjustment' in British law. 'Direct' discrimination (or 'disparate treatment') was simply called discrimination, until the need to distinguish it from 'indirect' discrimination (or 'disparate impact') arose. Scholars disagree on the proper characterization of 'affirmative action'—depending on whether or not they approve of it, people characterize it as 'positive discrimination', 'positive action', 'reverse discrimination', 'compensatory discrimination', etc.[86] Based on the form it takes, specific affirmative action measures are referred to as 'quotas', 'reservations', 'preferential treatment', 'outreach', 'access programmes', 'diversity programmes', 'indirect affirmative action', 'positive duties', and such like.

We have seen that prohibition on direct discrimination and provision for affirmative action were the first tools to be devised. The 14th Amendment to the US Constitution guaranteed 'the equal protection of the laws' to all persons. Nowhere does the Amendment use the term 'discrimination'. Although it was the product of a very specific historical context, 'equal protection of the laws' was, in literal terms, a very broad guarantee. Interpreted broadly, the clause may have been capable of bearing the burden of a genuinely egalitarian redistributive programme. This was, however, not to be. In the very first case decided by the US Supreme Court on the 14th Amendment, the provision was given a firm ground-sensitive, discrimination-oriented, interpretation:

The existence of laws in the States where the newly emancipated negroes resided, which discriminated with gross injustice and hardship against them as a class, was the evil to be remedied by this clause, and by it such laws are forbidden ... We doubt very much whether any action of a State not directed by way of discrimination against the negroes as a class, or on account of their race, will ever be held to come within the purview of this provision.[87]

---

[86] Christopher McCrudden, 'A Comparative Taxonomy of "Positive Action" and "Affirmative Action" Policies' in Reiner Schulze (ed), *Non-Discrimination in European Private Law* (Mohr Siebeck 2011) 157.

[87] *Butchers Benevolent Association of New Orleans v Crescent City Slaughter-House Co (Slaughter-House cases)* 83 US 36 (1872) 81.

Even as the protected grounds expanded beyond race, the legal right to equality, in the United States and later elsewhere, came to be tied irrevocably to the right against discrimination. I will discuss the connection between equality and discrimination elsewhere.[88] For now we should focus only on the duties that discrimination law has come to impose in order to get a broad sense of the content of these duties. Several nuances and details will be glossed over at this stage, to be revisited in later chapters. It is particularly important to bear in mind though that the extent of the following duties varies depending on the ground, group, and the duty-bearer in question. The duties are more onerous in connection with some grounds than others, and for some duty-bearers (compared to others). Recall that my methodological approach treats these distinctions as stable only when they are drawn by most jurisdictions.

3.3.1 Direct Discrimination

Most non-lawyers would associate a prohibition on discrimination primarily with a prohibition on direct discrimination. Direct discrimination (or 'disparate treatment') entails unfavourable or less favourable treatment 'on the ground of' a protected characteristic (such as race, sex, religion) or, sometimes, a combination of such characteristics (to deal with intersectional or multiple ground discrimination faced by, say, black women).[89] The first thing to note is that direct discrimination characterizes some form of 'treatment'—this may be an act or an omission. In other words, the norm against direct discrimination is an action-regarding norm—it makes essential reference to something done (or the failure to do something)—as opposed to a situation-regarding norm.[90] We will see shortly that the norm against indirect discrimination is also an action-regarding norm.

Second, the treatment must be 'on the ground of' (or 'because of', 'based on', 'for a reason related to') a protected characteristic. Some causal connection between the protected ground and the treatment in question is required. Opinions diverge on whether this is an objective standard or a subjective one. In the United States, courts have held that this connection is established only if a discriminatory motive, purpose, or intention on the part of the discriminator has been proved.[91] This subjective approach probes the mental state of

---

[88] See Chapter 5, section 5.3.

[89] Canadian Human Rights Act, s 3.1; UK Equality Act 2010, s 14. See further *Corbiere v Canada* [1999] 2 SCR 203 [61].

[90] Elisa Holmes, 'Anti-Discrimination Rights Without Equality' (2005) 68 Modern Law Review 175.

[91] *Washington v Davis* 426 US 229 (1976) 240.

the perpetrator in order to determine whether the causal requirement has been satisfied. A somewhat broader subjective approach—where the causation requirement is satisfied by proof of conscious as well as sub-conscious intention—has been endorsed by Lord Nicholls in the United Kingdom.[92] On the other hand, in the landmark *James v Eastleigh Borough Council* case, Lord Goff considered that 'cases of discrimination ... can be considered by asking the simple question: would the complainant have received the same treatment ... but for his or her sex?'.[93] This objective 'but-for' formula was motivated by a desire to avoid 'complicated questions relating to concepts such as intention, motive, reason or purpose'.[94]

In *James*, there was an exact correspondence—rather than a mere correlation—between the actual ground on which the distinction was made (pensionable age) and a protected characteristic (sex). Cases where the objective test is satisfied but the more demanding subjective test is not will be rare. Notice that the required intention/purpose/motive (when it is so required) is only to use the protected ground in some way—the law does not require the intention to be malicious. A subjective intent under Lord Nicholls's standard can usually be inferred from any distinction that directly relies on a protected ground. Cases where a protected ground is not directly relied upon to make a distinction are far more likely to involve indirect discrimination rather than direct discrimination à la *James*. Even so, the objective approach has significantly altered what it means to discriminate 'on the ground of' sex: one may even question whether this is now a requirement of a mere correlation rather than causation (a question we will discuss in Chapter 6, section 6.4). This development is the primary driver of the distinction between the lay and the legal models of discrimination. The move to an objective determination of the implication of a protected ground—away from any requirement of intention or motive on the part of the discriminator—has been affirmed in subsequent cases in the United Kingdom,[95] Canada,[96] and South Africa.[97] With the Indian law on the point unclear and underdeveloped, the United States is the only jurisdiction that continues to insist on the existence of

[92] *Constable of West Yorkshire Police v Khan* [2001] UKHL 48 [29]; *Nagarajan v London Regional Transport* [2000] 1 AC 501, 511–12. See also, Samuel Bagenstos, 'Implicit Bias, "Science," and Antidiscrimination Law' (2007) 1 Harvard Law and Policy Review 477.
[93] *James v Eastleigh Borough Council* [1990] 2 AC 751, 774. See also, *Bull v Hall* [2013] UKSC 73.
[94] *James v Eastleigh Borough Council* [1990] 2 AC 751, 774.
[95] *R (on the application of E) v Governing Body of JFS* [2009] UKSC 15.
[96] *Andrews v Law Society of British Columbia* [1989] 1 SCR 143, 174–5; *Quebec v A* 2013 SCC 5 [196]. See also, *British Columbia (Public Service Employee Relations Commission) v BCGEU* [1999] 3 SCR 3 [29]: the implication of the abandonment of the distinction between direct and indirect discrimination in this case is that proof of any subjective intention to discriminate is not necessary.
[97] *Pretoria City Council v Walker* 1998 (2) SA 363 [39].

some subjective mental state as a precondition for establishing direct discrimination.[98] This move away from subjective intent is chiefly responsible for continuing anxiety over the nature of the wrong that underpins direct discrimination[99]—an anxiety that will be put to rest in Chapter 6.

Third, while discrimination law sometimes requires proof of *un*favourable treatment, at other times the claimant must show *less*-favourable treatment. In other words, sometimes the claimant has to show relative disadvantage owing to the treatment *in comparison with* a similarly situated real or hypothetical comparator. On occasion, though, non-relative disadvantage will suffice. The traditional position in most jurisdictions has been to insist upon the comparator analysis[100]—unsurprising given the assumption about the ties between discrimination and equality. Often the case turns on the choice of the appropriate comparator,[101] making the issue of comparators extremely controversial.

Apart from the difficulties in choosing the right comparator, an insistence on a comparator raises problems in cases where there is no appropriate comparator.[102] The prime example is that of discrimination based on the ground of pregnancy. In *Turley*, for example, a pregnant woman was recognized as 'a woman, as the Authorised Version of the Bible accurately puts it, with child, and there is no masculine equivalent'.[103] Other courts, in their

---

[98] Even in the US, evidential rules were tweaked to presume subjective discriminatory intent if certain objective criteria were satisfied, shifting the burden on the defendant to show that there was a genuine non-discriminatory reason for the conduct in question: *McDonnell Douglas Corp v Green* 411 US 792 (1973) 802–3. This development was effectively rolled back in *St Mary's Honor Center v Hicks* 509 US 502 (1993) 519. See also, Richard Ford, 'Bias in the Air: Rethinking Employment Discrimination Law' (2014) 66 Stanford Law Review 1381, 1393–400.

[99] *R (on the application of E) v Governing Body of JFS* [2009] UKSC 15 [9]: 'Nothing that I say in this judgment should be read as giving rise to criticism on moral grounds of the admissions policy of JFS in particular or the policies of Jewish faith schools in general, let alone as suggesting that these policies are "racist" as that word is generally understood.'

[100] UK Sex Discrimination Act 1975, s 1: 'In any circumstances relevant for the purposes of any provision of this Act, other than a provision to which subsection (2) applies, a person discriminates against a woman if—(a) on the ground of her sex he treats her less favourably than he treats or would treat a man ...'

[101] See *Auton v British Columbia* [2004] 3 SCR 657.

[102] It is also alleged that insisting on a comparator encourages assimilation of minority cultures (especially religious and queer cultures). Because the relevant comparator is invariably an idealized member of the majority community, it is claimed that such comparisons normalize majority values and make them aspirational (even when there may not be anything intrinsically wrong with minority values). See generally, Sandra Fredman, *Discrimination Law* (Oxford University Press 2002) 16: 'In practice ... the apparently abstract individual is clothed with the attributes of the dominant culture, religion or ethnicity.' See also, Nicholas Bamforth, *Sexuality, Morals and Justice* (Cassell 1997) 250–3; Kenji Yoshino, 'Assimilationist Bias in Equal Protection: The Visibility Presumption and the Case of "Don't Ask, Don't Tell"' (1998) 108 Yale Law Journal 485.

[103] *Turley v Alldders Department Stores Ltd* [1980] ICR 66, 70. See also, *Geduldig v Aiello* 417 US 484 (1974).

desperation to find a comparator, have compared pregnancy with sickness.[104] The inadequacy of such fantastical comparisons forced courts (and legislators) to seek a non-comparative approach.[105] The non-comparative approach to pregnancy discrimination has also been extended to disability discrimination,[106] and cases where multiple grounds are involved or intersectional discrimination has been claimed.[107] In other areas, although comparators are technically required, different jurisdictions place a varying degree of emphasis on this requirement. For example, in *Shamoon*, Lord Nicholls urged that:

> [T]ribunals may sometimes be able to avoid arid and confusing disputes about the identification of the appropriate comparator by concentrating primarily on why the claimant was treated as she was. Was it on the proscribed ground … or was it for some other reason?[108]

There is some recognition that the comparator analysis is only a means to determine the causation question.[109] Similar rulings expressing a general scepticism over the requirement of a comparator for proving direct discrimination have been made in Canada.[110] The South African Equality Act gives an entirely non-comparative definition of discrimination.[111] In effect, we have a situation where some jurisdictions (such as South Africa) no longer require proof of comparative adverse effect for discrimination on any ground, whereas others have made clear exceptions to the comparator rule at least with respect to some grounds

---

[104] *Hayes v Malleable Working Men's Club* [1985] ICR 703, 708: 'the proper approach is to ask whether pregnancy with its associated consequences is capable of being matched by analogous circumstances such as sickness applying to a man …'

[105] Aileen McColgan, 'Cracking the Comparator Problem: Discrimination, "Equal Treatment" and the Role of Comparisons' (2006) 6 European Human Rights Law Review 650; C-177/88 *Dekker v Stichting (VJV- Centrum) Plus* [1991] IRLR 27; C-32/93 *Webb v EMO Air Cargo* [1994] ECR I-03567 [24]–[25]. See also, Paul Lewis, 'Pregnant Workers and Sex Discrimination: The Limits of Purposive Non-Comparative Methodology' (Spring 2000) The International Journal of Comparative Labour Law and Industrial Relations 55, the United States Pregnancy Discrimination Act 1978, and the UK Equality Act 2010, s 18.

[106] UK Equality Act 2010, s 15: although this provision is entitled 'discrimination arising from disability' and treated distinctly from 'direct discrimination' in the statutory scheme, it is best understood as an instance of direct discrimination.

[107] *Hassam v Jacobs* 2009 (5) SA 572. See also, Crenshaw's seminal discussion of the problem of intersectionality: Kimberlé Crenshaw, 'Demarginalising the Intersection of Race and Sex: A Black Feminist Critique of Antidiscrimination Doctrine, Feminist Theory and Antiracist Politics' [1989] The University of Chicago Legal Forum 139.

[108] *Shamoon v Chief Constable of the Royal Ulster Constabulary* [2003] UKHL 11 [11].

[109] See generally, Denise Réaume, 'Dignity, Equality and Comparison' in Deborah Hellman and Sophia Moreau (eds), *Philosophical Foundations of Discrimination Law* (Oxford University Press 2013).

[110] *R v Kapp* [2008] 2 SCR 483 [22]; *Withler v Canada* [2011] 1 SCR 396 [2], [60].

[111] Section 1 provides: '"discrimination" means any act or omission … which directly or indirectly—(a) imposes burdens, obligations or disadvantage on; or (b) withholds benefits, opportunities or advantages from, any person on one or more prohibited grounds'.

(such as the United Kingdom). This suggests that the issue of comparators is not necessarily tied to the ground in question, and that the trend in most jurisdictions is to allow discrimination to be proved through a comparative or a non-comparative analysis, whatever the ground of discrimination.

Finally, whether and to what extent direct discrimination can be justified depends on the protected characteristic concerned and whether the norm is constitutional or statutory. There are significant jurisdictional variations too. Constitutional antidiscrimination clauses almost always permit the justification of direct discrimination, although the standard that must be met is often quite high.[112] In statutory contexts, jurisdictions differ more significantly. The US Civil Rights Act of 1964 permits limited justification of direct discrimination.[113] Canadian and South African statutes also permit the justification of direct discrimination, although the justificatory standard is quite high.[114] In the United Kingdom, direct discrimination cannot normally be justified in an adjudicative context, although there are numerous legislative exceptions to this prohibition.[115] For certain grounds, such as age, the United Kingdom allows the justification of direct as well as indirect discrimination.[116] What remains of the blanket prohibition has been criticized by some judges, who have called for some form of general justification for direct discrimination.[117] The overall consensus seems to allow limited justification of direct discrimination; it also requires that, when allowed, the standard of review for justifying direct discrimination is higher than that for justifying indirect discrimination.

3.3.2 Indirect Discrimination

Indirect discrimination (or 'disparate impact' as it is called in the United States) involves an apparently neutral practice or policy which puts persons belonging to a protected group at a particular disadvantage.[118] The concept

---

[112] In the United States, although not elsewhere, this standard is (in)famously sensitive to the protected ground involved. Race discrimination gets 'strict scrutiny', while gender gets 'intermediate scrutiny'. See generally, Suzanne Goldberg, 'Equality Without Tiers' (2004) 77 Southern California Law Review 481.

[113] 42 USC § 2000e-2(e) (2013).

[114] Canadian Human Rights Act, s 15; South African Employment Equity Act, s 6(2); South African Equality Act, s 14(3).

[115] UK Equality Act 2010, s 15, Schs 5, 7, 9, 11, 16, and 18.

[116] UK Equality Act 2010, s 13(2).

[117] *R (on the application of E) v Governing Body of JFS* [2009] UKSC 15 [9]: 'there may well be a defect in our law of discrimination. In contrast to the law in many countries, where English law forbids direct discrimination it provides no defence of justification.'

[118] See *Griggs v Duke Power Co* 401 US 424 (1971); s 703 of Title VII of the US Civil Rights Act of 1991. See also, s 19(2) of the UK Equality Act 2010: 'a provision, criterion or practice is discriminatory in relation to a relevant protected characteristic of B's if:

(a) A applies, or would apply, it to persons with whom B does not share the characteristic,

was first developed in the landmark American case *Griggs v Duke Power Company.* The US Supreme Court held that the requirement of an educational qualification which disproportionately disqualified blacks from employment would violate Title VII of the Civil Rights Act of 1964 unless the requirement could be justified on the touchstone of business necessity.[119]

Like direct discrimination, indirect discrimination is an action-regarding norm. It is triggered by some provision, policy, practice, or criterion that the alleged discriminator applies (or seeks to apply) to the complainant.[120] Of course, indirect discrimination is established if and only if a situation-regarding criterion—disproportionate impact on a group—is also satisfied. But a mere statistical disproportionality in, say, a workforce, will not amount to indirect discrimination unless it can be linked to some action, such as the adoption or enforcement of a provision or a policy.[121]

Second, the connection between the protected ground and the act in question is that the latter should have a disproportionate impact on a group defined by the protected ground. For example, in *Griggs*, the decision had a disproportionate impact on blacks, a protected group. Indirect racial discrimination in *Griggs* was direct discrimination on the ground of educational qualification. However, educational qualification is not a protected ground, race is. The claimant is not required to prove any discriminatory intention, motive, or purpose on the part of the employer. The apparent ground of discrimination could be anything whatsoever; what is moot is its connection with a protected ground in the context of a given case. Thus, the list of apparent grounds on which discrimination is prohibited is potentially limitless, for any such ground may be a proxy for a protected ground under certain circumstances. But these apparent grounds do not matter for their own sake. They matter because—and only because—they are proxies for protected grounds in these circumstances.[122]

Third, although indirect discrimination is structurally comparative, the nature of the comparator analysis is very different from that used in direct

----

(b) it puts, or would put, persons with whom B shares the characteristic at a particular disadvantage when compared with persons with whom B does not share it,

(c) it puts, or would put, B at that disadvantage, and

(d) A cannot show it to be a proportionate means of achieving a legitimate aim.'

[119] *Griggs v Duke Power Co* 401 US 424 (1971).

[120] Elisa Holmes, 'Anti-Discrimination Rights Without Equality' (2005) 68 Modern Law Review 175, 184.

[121] *Wards Cove Packing Co v Atonio* 490 US 642 (1989) 656.

[122] cf Joseph Fishkin, *Bottlenecks: A New Theory of Equal Opportunity* (Oxford University Press 2014) 246ff.

discrimination cases. The comparative analysis for indirect discrimination involves groups rather than individuals. Section 19(2)(b) of the UK Equality Act 2010 requires that the offending measure must put 'persons with whom [the claimant] shares the characteristic at a particular disadvantage when compared with persons with whom [the claimant] does not share it'. This usually avoids the need to find an *individual* 'appropriate comparator'—a search that has plagued direct discrimination jurisprudence. There are, of course, controversies surrounding comparison in indirect discrimination too—but they are of a different character. The first problem is the determination of the relevant pool within which the two comparator groups are to be identified. In the case of employment discrimination, for example, should the relevant pool be the entire population of the jurisdiction, or only the pool of persons qualified to perform the job in question, or simply the workforce of the employer? We will often arrive at different conclusions about whether a policy disproportionately excludes women in comparison to men depending on what we choose as our relevant pool. The second controversy surrounds the extent of disproportionality required for it to count as indirect discrimination. For example, section 1(1)(b)(i) of the UK Sex Discrimination Act 1975 required proof of the fact that 'the proportion of women who can comply with [the requirement or condition] is *considerably smaller* than the proportion of men who can comply with it'.[123] Following developments in EU law, the UK Equality Act 2010 has now replaced this standard by only insisting on proof of 'particular disadvantage'.[124] Related to this is the issue of whether a claimant needs to provide statistical evidence to prove disproportionate impact, or whether a rule-of-thumb assessment of likely impact will suffice.[125] The practice on many of these issues is divergent and evolving.

Fourth, indirect discrimination is almost always justifiable. The discriminator is entitled to show that the discriminatory policy is a necessary and proportionate tool to pursue a sufficiently important objective. Although the standard required to justify indirect discrimination is usually quite high, it tends to be less exacting than justifying direct discrimination. This, along with the fact that the two forms of discrimination are considered to be mutually exclusive,[126] has led to expansionary pressures on the scope of direct discrimination. The difficulties in clarifying the boundary between direct and indirect discrimination motivated the Canadian Supreme Court to reject the bifurcated approach and adopt instead a common legal response to either

---

[123] Emphasis added.   [124] UK Equality Act 2010, s 19(2)(b).
[125] *Wards Cove Packing Co v Atonio* 490 US 642 (1989); C-237/94 *O'Flynn v Adjudication Officer* [1996] 2 CMLR 103.
[126] *R (on the application of E) v Governing Body of JFS* [2009] UKSC 15 [57].

form of discrimination.[127] This strategy has not found favour in any of the other jurisdictions so far.

The usual remedy for unjustified indirect discrimination is a change in the offending rule, practice, or policy—either the abandonment of the rule in favour of a new, non-discriminatory one, or the retention of the old rule but with exceptions to accommodate the disadvantaged minority. In the absence of discriminatory intent, it is rare for damages to be awarded for indirect discrimination.[128]

3.3.3 Reasonable Accommodation

Reasonable accommodation (or 'reasonable adjustment') is yet another facet of antidiscrimination law. Section 20 of the UK Equality Act 2010 imposes three requirements that amount to 'reasonable adjustments' in the context of disability:

[A] requirement, where a provision, criterion or practice of A's puts a disabled person at a substantial disadvantage in relation to a relevant matter in comparison with persons who are not disabled, to take such steps as it is reasonable to have to take to avoid the disadvantage.

... a requirement, where a physical feature puts a disabled person at a substantial disadvantage in relation to a relevant matter in comparison with persons who are not disabled, to take such steps as it is reasonable to have to take to avoid the disadvantage.

... a requirement, where a disabled person would, but for the provision of an auxiliary aid, be put at a substantial disadvantage in relation to a relevant matter in comparison with persons who are not disabled, to take such steps as it is reasonable to have to take to provide the auxiliary aid.

'Reasonableness' must be seen as a limit to the accommodation that can be sought. The considerations that go into deciding whether an adjustment is reasonable are similar to those that determine whether an instance of indirect (or, sometimes, direct) discrimination can be justified. The right to reasonable accommodation under the Americans with Disabilities Act 1990 is available to a 'qualified individual with a disability',[129] which is defined as 'an individual with a disability who, with or without reasonable accommodation, can perform the essential functions of the employment position that such individual holds or desires'.[130] There is no logical reason why reasonable accommodation

---

[127] *British Columbia (Public Service Employee Relations Commission) v BCGEU* [1999] 3 SCR 3.
[128] UK Equality Act 2010, s 124(4) and (5); Civil Rights Act of 1991, 42 USC § 1981a.
[129] 42 USC 12112(a).
[130] 42 USC 12111(8).

should be limited to disability alone; indeed the concept was first applied in the United States with respect to religion and only later extended to disability.[131] Meenan argues that 'the reasonable accommodation approach of disability law could be applied to physiological changes associated with ageing'.[132] Although not characterized as such, flexible working hours and parental leave provisions are examples of reasonable accommodation for women, who bear the brunt of child-care duties.[133] So is a provision for flexible holidays to accommodate diverse religious festivals.[134] In fact, sections 7(e) and 8(h) of the South African Equality Act require 'steps to reasonably accommodate the needs' of persons on the basis of their race and gender, respectively. Here is an example of a development that is ground-sensitive in most jurisdictions, but one that is sensitive to different sets of grounds in each of them. Almost all jurisdictions provide for reasonable accommodation for disability discrimination. But some also allow it for religion, others for sex, and Canada and South Africa for all grounds.[135] The ground-sensitivity of reasonable accommodation does not seem to be stable, and I will therefore assume that the jurisdictions are moving towards allowing it for discrimination based on any ground.

Each of the aforementioned jurisdictions envisages the failure to provide reasonable accommodation (in certain specified contexts) as a distinct wrong in discrimination law. Conceptually, however, it is difficult to imagine a case where a failure to provide reasonable accommodation will not also amount to indirect discrimination (and, sometimes, even direct discrimination, if we follow the broader understanding of this concept as envisaged in *James v Eastleigh Borough Council*). This failure will always result in a protected group being disproportionately disadvantaged or even entirely excluded.[136] Thus, the duty to provide

---

[131] 42 USC § 2000e(j): 'The term "religion" includes all aspects of religious observance and practice, as well as belief, unless an employer demonstrates that he is unable to reasonably accommodate to an employee's or prospective employee's religious observance or practice without undue hardship on the conduct of the employer's business.' See also, Lisa Waddington, 'Reasonable Accommodation: Time to Extend the Duty to Accommodate Beyond Disability?' (2011) 36 NTM|NJCM-Bulletin 186.

[132] Helen Meenan, 'Age Discrimination—Of Cinderella and *The Golden Bough*' in Helen Meenan (ed), *Equality Law in an Enlarged European Union: Understanding the Article 13 Directives* (Cambridge University Press 2007) 278, 283.

[133] C-303/06 *Coleman v Attridge Law* [2008] 3 CMLR 27: the case relating to flexible work hours was argued as a disability discrimination case. For the connection between flexible work and sex discrimination, see Sandra Fredman, 'Women at Work: The Broken Promise of Flexicurity' (2004) 33 Industrial Law Journal 299.

[134] *Ontario Human Rights Commission v Simpsons-Sears Ltd* [1985] 2 SCR 536.

[135] Canadian Human Rights Act, s 15(2); South African Equality Act, s 14(3)(i). Also see the discussion in the following paragraph.

[136] See also, UK Equality Act 2010, s 21(2). In the words of the European Commission, 'Reasonable accommodation is not a positive action left to the discretion of public or private operators, but an obligation whose failure can constitute unfair discrimination.' *Disability Mainstreaming in the European Employment Strategy* (EMCO/11/290605, 2005) 3.

reasonable accommodation can be thought of as a possible form of remedy for discrimination—one that works by requiring exceptions to the general norm instead of a change in the norm itself (whether accomodation would be an *adequate* remedy to cure direct discrimination is, of course, another matter). Indeed, in *Simpsons-Sears*, the Canadian Supreme Court accepted that reasonable accommodation was an available remedy for all forms of indirect discrimination:

> Where direct discrimination is shown, the employer must justify the rule, if such a step is possible under the enactment in question, or it is struck down. Where there is adverse effect discrimination on account of creed, the offending order or rule will not necessarily be struck down. It will survive in most cases because its discriminatory effect is limited to one person or to one group, and it is the effect upon them rather than upon the general work force which must be considered. In such case there is no question of justification raised because the rule, if rationally connected to the employment, needs no justification; what is required is some measure of accommodation. The employer must take reasonable steps towards that end which may or may not result in full accommodation. Where such reasonable steps, however, do not fully reach the desired end, the complainant, in the absence of some accommodating steps on his own part such as an acceptance in this case of part-time work, must either sacrifice his religious principles or his employment.[137]

Read along with the abolition of the direct-indirect distinction, the conceptual difference between the Canadian approach and that of other jurisdictions boils down simply to the fact that Canada permits discrimination to be remedied by creating exceptions to the discriminatory norm in all cases where it is possible. Other jurisdictions normally require the offending rule to be replaced by a non-discriminatory rule, except where the retention of the offending rule with exceptions is specifically authorized. The difference is significant: although it is easier to create exceptions than to reformulate general rules, the former also give the impression that a certain group is getting 'special treatment' and may be more controversial for that reason. Furthermore, the availability of a separate cause of action for reasonable accommodation in jurisdictions other than Canada allows litigants to avoid having to prove the onerous requirements for establishing indirect discrimination. Further still, given the usually weighty expressive effects of direct discrimination, exception-creating accommodation measures are only rarely likely to be reasonable. These practical distinctions aside, what emerges from our discussion is the notion that the right to

---

[137] *Ontario Human Rights Commission v Simpsons-Sears Ltd* [1985] 2 SCR 536 [23]. See also, Canadian Human Rights Act, s 15(2): For any practice mentioned in paragraph (1)(a) to be considered to be based on a bona fide occupational requirement and for any practice mentioned in paragraph (1)(g) to be considered to have a bona fide justification, it must be established that accommodation of the needs of an individual or a class of individuals affected would impose undue hardship on the person who would have to accommodate those needs, considering health, safety, and cost.'

reasonable accommodation is best understood as a *secondary* right that one could become entitled to upon breach of the *primary* right against direct or indirect discrimination. Secondary rights are therefore parasitic on primary rights. This understanding also shows the poverty of the simplistic approach that divides antidiscrimination duties on the basis of whether they are negative (do not discriminate) or positive (provide reasonable accommodation), and of the concomitant discomfort with reasonable accommodation duties as if they represent a startling departure from 'traditional' antidiscrimination duties.[138]

We have seen that the duty to refrain from direct and indirect discrimination, and the duty to provide reasonable accommodation are usually subject to the *justification defence*—even though some jurisdictions do not permit this for direct discrimination. For this reason, we will fail to fully understand those duties without reference to this concept. Justification usually entails a means-end analysis, where the law tests the desirability of the objective sought to be achieved, and the proportionality and necessity of the discriminatory means employed. This is often expressed as the need to demonstrate that the protected characteristic is a necessary 'bona fide occupational qualification'.[139] The degree to which the discriminator is morally culpable, her legitimate interests, and the degree to which the victim is harmed are relevant to this analysis. The intensity of judicial scrutiny of the justification defence is sensitive to the nature of the duty infringed, the protected ground in question, and the nature of the discriminator (especially whether it is a public or a private person and the degree to which it is able to bear the cost of non-discrimination).

3.3.4 Discriminatory Harassment

Discrimination legislation also tends to prohibit harassment 'based on' a protected ground. The US Supreme Court acknowledged in 1986 that 'Nothing in Title VII suggests that a hostile environment based on discriminatory sexual harassment should not be likewise prohibited.'[140] Most jurisdictions explicitly prohibit ground-based harassment under their discrimination statutes.[141] Discriminatory harassment is usually understood in terms of its effects and not merely whether there was any intention to harass. The UK Equality Act 2010, for example, defines harassment for the purposes of discrimination law as 'unwanted conduct related to a relevant protected characteristic' which 'has the

---

[138] Pamela Karlan and George Rutherglen, 'Disabilities, Discrimination, and Reasonable Accommodation' (1996) 46 Duke Law Journal 1.

[139] 42 USC § 2000e-2(e)(1); Canadian Human Rights Act, s 15(1)(a).

[140] *Meritor Savings Bank v Vinson* 477 US 57 (1986) 66.

[141] See, for example, Canadian Human Rights Act, ss 14 and 14.1; South African Equality Act, s 11 read with s 1(1)(xiii).

purpose *or effect* of violating [the victim's] dignity, or creating an intimidating, hostile, degrading, humiliating or offensive environment for [the victim]'.[142] The definition in the South African legislation is also largely effect-based:

[H]arassment means unwanted conduct which is persistent or serious and demeans, humiliates or creates a hostile or intimidating environment or is calculated to induce submission by actual or threatened adverse consequences and which is related to

(a) sex, gender or sexual orientation; or
(b) a person's membership or presumed membership of a group identified by one or more of the prohibited grounds or a characteristic associated with such group.[143]

That said, the effect has to be sufficiently serious to suffice.[144] The harasser is not permitted to seek to justify harassment, although justification may be possible if the defendant failed to protect the claimant from harassment by a third person (for whom the defendant is legally responsible, as an employer is for the behaviour of his subordinates), especially if she can show that the harassment took place despite the reasonable steps she had taken to prevent it.[145]

In addition to regulating discriminatory harassment, jurisdictions can—and do—prohibit harassment per se. This prohibition may constitute a criminal offence, and usually requires proof of intent.[146] This harassment, which need not be ground-based, is not a part of discrimination law.

3.3.5 Affirmative Action

Finally, there is the issue of affirmative action. The term covers a wide variety of measures designed to benefit a protected group. The extent to which they actually achieve this purpose is a matter of empirical investigation and will depend on a number of contextual factors. What is essential is that their chief purpose is to benefit a group that is, in some sense, disadvantaged.[147] Section

---

[142] UK Equality Act 2010, s 26(1). Emphasis added.
[143] South African Equality Act, s 1(1)(xiii).
[144] *Meritor Savings Bank v Vinson* 477 US 57 (1986) 67: 'For sexual harassment to be actionable [as discrimination], it must be sufficiently severe or pervasive to alter the conditions of the victim's employment and create an abusive working environment.' Internal quotations and parenthesis removed.
[145] *Faragher v Boca Raton* 524 US 775 (1998).
[146] See, for example, UK Protection from Harassment Act 1997, s 1.
[147] The claim in the US context is tentative because *Gratz* and *Grutter* insist on diversity benefits for the educational institution rather than disadvantage-amelioration as the justification for the affirmative action programmes in question. While the actual argument relied upon by courts is not crucial for my reconstructive approach, it is useful to note that the judges themselves display ambivalence about the exclusive reliance on diversity: Justice O'Connor, for example, felt it important to embellish the diversity argument with the assertion that 'Access to legal education (and thus the legal profession) must be inclusive of talented and qualified individuals of every race and ethnicity, so that all members of our heterogeneous society may participate in the educational

15 of the South African Employment Equity Act, for example, requires affirmative action in favour of 'designated groups'—section 1 defines 'designated groups' to mean 'black people, women and people with disabilities'. Similarly, Article 15(4) of the Indian Constitution permits 'any special provision for the advancement of any socially and educationally backward classes of citizens'.[148] It is, of course, possible that a group is wrongly characterized as disadvantaged—this mischaracterization may even be insidious. What is important is that even in such cases, those undertaking the measure will feel compelled to insist that the beneficiary group is actually disadvantaged. No one advocates 'affirmative action' measures for groups they openly acknowledge not to be disadvantaged.

Some may object to the characterization of affirmative action as part of 'discrimination law'.[149] Admittedly, there are important distinctions between affirmative action and the other concepts examined above. What is also clear is that the practitioners—lawyers, judges, litigants, legislators—all assume that there is an essential connection between affirmative action and discrimination. Several references in the discussion that is to follow allude to antidiscrimination statutes that regulate ground-based affirmative action. At least insofar as the practice is concerned, discrimination and affirmative action seem to be inseparable. Because the practice is so unequivocal, theorists must not be too quick to deny this connection.

Remedial and Non-Remedial Measures

Affirmative action measures come in a variety of shapes and sizes.[150] In their broadest usage, they can be remedial or non-remedial. Remedial measures, understood narrowly, are those measures that benefit the same particular persons who suffered disadvantage due to past discrimination. They respond to specific acts of direct or indirect discrimination against

---

institutions that provide the training and education necessary to succeed in America.' *Grutter v Bollinger* 539 US 306 (2003) 332–3. Justice Ginsburg's dissent in *Gratz* was less generous, implying that the diversity justification was only a smoke-screen: 'The stain of generations of racial oppression is still visible in our society ... and the determination to hasten its removal remains vital ... If honesty is the best policy, surely Michigan's accurately described, fully disclosed College affirmative action program is preferable to achieving similar numbers through winks, nods, and disguises.' *Gratz v Bollinger* 539 US 244 (2003) 304–5.

[148] Also see UK Equality Act 2010, s 158 and Canadian Employment Equity Act, SC 1995, c 44, s 2 (Canadian Employment Equity Act).

[149] See Morris Abram, 'Affirmative Action: Fair Shakers and Social Engineers' (1986) 99 Harvard Law Review 1312.

[150] These distinctions are adapted, with significant modifications, from Christopher McCrudden, 'A Comparative Taxonomy of "Positive Action" and "Affirmative Action" Policies' in Reiner Schulze (ed), *Non-Discrimination in European Private Law* (Mohr Siebeck 2011) 157.

particular persons and are usually undertaken by the discriminator who caused the disadvantage in the first place. A good example is found in the facts of *Ricci v DeStefano*, where a city discarded the results of a promotional test because no black firefighter passed it, and conducted a new test.[151] The city was worried that the original test may have been indirectly discriminatory. Its cancellation and the institution of a new test was therefore meant to be a remedial affirmative action measure. The city lost the case because it failed to show that the original test would have amounted to unjustified indirect discrimination. While this ruling is controversial for several other reasons, it does not cast doubt on the fact that at least in cases where discrimination has been or can be established, affirmative measures may be taken to stop or remedy it. This category of affirmative action measures in fact concerns the question of appropriate remedies, and is likely to be less illuminating for our purposes. There are exceptions, of course. The fact that damages are usually not available for successful indirect discrimination claims, or that courts are reluctant to allow 'levelling down' remedies for direct discrimination, or that reasonable accommodation tolerates the creation of exceptions to offending rules instead of invalidating the rule itself are important features of the remedial aspects of discrimination law that a theoretical account must explain. On the other hand, the notion that discriminatory acts sometimes require affirmative action to be remedied is pedestrian.

We are mainly concerned with non-remedial affirmative action measures. These measures are not designed to remedy specific acts of discrimination against particular persons, although they may well aim to remedy past discrimination against a group generally.[152] Even so, the beneficiaries need not have suffered the past discrimination personally, and the person or body undertaking the affirmative action measure may not be responsible for this past discrimination. Subsequent references to affirmative action measures will refer only to measures of the non-remedial type.

Non-remedial measures can be classified into three sets on the basis of different aspects of their regulatory design. In the first set, affirmative action measures can be divided on the basis of the tools employed. In the second overlapping set, we can classify these measures based on the degree of their sensitivity to protected grounds. In the final set, we can organize measures based on whether they are voluntary, contractual, or mandatory. These sets are overlapping rather than discrete.

---

[151] *Ricci v DeStefano* 557 US 557 (2009).
[152] See *Canadian National Railway v Canadian Human Rights Commission* [1987] 1 SCR 1114.

Facilitative and Distributive Measures

Based on the tools they employ, affirmative action measures can be divided into facilitative or distributive measures. Facilitative measures seek to enable the access to certain goods to the intended beneficiaries. Distributive measures seek to supply these goods directly to them. Measures that seek to increase transparency or to influence the behaviour of the intended beneficiaries are typically facilitative. Facilitative measures tend to be less controversial than distributive measures. Measures that seek to influence the behaviour of persons who control access to the scarce resource whose distribution is in question (usually employment or education), or to influence the behaviour of policy-makers may be facilitative or distributive.

Let us look at a few types of facilitative measures. Transparency measures aim to publicize the degree of access that disadvantaged groups have to scarce resources. This is often done by requiring employers and universities to disclose information such as the racial, religious, or gender make-up of their application pool and work-force, or any pay gap between men and women.[153] It may seem a bit stretched to characterize transparency measures as affirmative action, but this is justified because they are often motivated by the need to secure, and result in, greater representation of previously excluded groups. Transparency may lead to further investigation and uncovering of underlying discrimination. Certain types of information may also trigger other mandatory affirmative action obligations or shame the resource-controller into adopting one. As such, these measures are typically facilitative.

Measures that seek to influence the behaviour of the intended beneficiaries are also typically facilitative. This category includes advertising, scholarships, training, and outreach targeted at members of disadvantaged groups to increase the likelihood that more of them will seek access to the scarce resource.

Measures that regulate the behaviour of the employer, the university, and other controllers of scarce resources, who may be public or private bodies, are usually distributive. They include rules resolving ties in favour of intended beneficiaries, preferential treatment, quotas, and the redefinition of eligibility criteria so that more intended beneficiaries qualify.[154] Tie-break rules are weakly distributive, whereas quotas are examples of strong distributive measures.

---

[153] UK Equality Act 2010, s 78; Canadian Employment Equity Act, s 9.

[154] See generally, Christopher McCrudden, 'A Comparative Taxonomy of "Positive Action" and "Affirmative Action" Policies' in Reiner Schulze (ed), *Non-Discrimination in European Private Law* (Mohr Siebeck 2011) 157, 163–5.

Finally, certain affirmative action measures seek to influence the behaviour of public bodies in their capacity as policy-makers, rather than as controllers of access to scarce resources. 'Mainstreaming' measures that bring the goals of discrimination law to bear upon all policy decisions made by public bodies tend to be facilitative. Section 149 of the UK Equality Act 2010, for example, requires public authorities to 'have due regard to the need to eliminate discrimination, ... advance equality of opportunity between persons who share a relevant characteristic and persons who do not share it [and] foster good relations between [them]'.[155] Strong distributive versions of such measures include quotas for women and minorities in legislative bodies.[156]

Direct and Indirect Measures

In the second set of our overlapping classification scheme, affirmative action measures can be divided on the basis of their sensitivity to protected grounds. Direct affirmative action measures are, as the name suggests, directly sensitive to a prohibited ground. In this respect, they correspond to directly discriminatory acts. For example, quotas for 'lower' caste groups in public employment in India are directly sensitive to caste, and therefore constitute a direct affirmative action measure. Indirect affirmative action measures do not distribute benefits based on protected grounds, but they are nonetheless designed to have a disproportionately beneficial impact on protected groups. A good example of such measures is the Texan 'Top Ten Percent Law'. In 1996, the US Court of Appeal Fifth Circuit had declared direct affirmative action programmes for racial minorities unconstitutional.[157] Following this ruling, Texas enacted the Top Ten Percent Law, requiring that 'each general academic teaching institution shall admit an applicant for admission to the institution as an undergraduate student if the applicant graduated with a grade point average in the top 10 percent of the student's high school graduating class'.[158] Increasing the intake of underrepresented minorities was the announced target of this measure, and it did succeed in increasing the number of racial minorities being admitted to Texan universities.[159] Thus, a facially neutral policy relied on the lack of racial diversity in the high school system to increase the access of racial minorities to higher education. It is an

---

[155] See Colm O'Cinneide, 'Positive Duties and Gender Equality' (2005) 8 International Journal of Discrimination and the Law 91; Sandra Fredman, 'Equality: A New Generation?' (2001) 30 Industrial Law Journal 145.
[156] Constitution of India, art 330 reserves certain seats for scheduled castes and tribes in the House of the People.
[157] *Hopwood v Texas* 78 F 3d 932 (1996).   [158] Texas Education Code §51.803 (1997).
[159] *Fisher v University of Texas at Austin* 631 F 3d 213 (2011) 224.

indirect affirmative action measure because it does not rely upon race directly in order to achieve its intended objective, which is to disproportionately benefit racial minorities.[160]

Voluntary or Mandatory Measures

In the final set, affirmative action measures can be classified based on whether they are voluntary, contractual, or mandatory. Voluntary affirmative action measures are undertaken by the person who controls access to the scarce resource without any legal or contractual duty to do so. When not required to do so, private persons are almost always allowed to undertake justified voluntary affirmative action.[161] This permission usually takes the form of an exemption from direct discrimination liability for affirmative action. Most constitutional frameworks also tend to permit affirmative action by public bodies, although subject to prescribed limits.[162] A legal permission to private persons to engage in affirmative action is compatible with affirmative action being morally required (because law does not enforce all our moral obligations), morally permitted, or even morally repugnant (for we do, sometimes, have the right to do wrong).[163]

Contractual affirmative action measures are undertaken in fulfilment of obligations usually imposed by public sector procurement contracts. Contracts entered into by US government contracting agencies must specify that the 'contractor will take affirmative action to ensure that applicants are employed, and that employees are treated during employment, without regard to their race, color, religion, sex or national origin'.[164] McCrudden has documented that the imposition of affirmative action duties through government contracts—ie through the state's dominium (power of the purse) rather than its imperium (power of sanction)—has been used extensively in jurisdictions as diverse as the United States, Malaysia, the EU, Canada, and South Africa.[165] At least some states, however, also use their imperium to impose mandatory (albeit facilitative or weakly distributive) affirmative action duties on private persons. Canada,[166]

---

[160] On indirect affirmative action, see generally, Daniel Sabbagh, 'The Rise of Indirect Affirmative Action: Converging Strategies for Promoting "Diversity" in Selective Institutions of Higher Education in the United States and France' (2011) 63 World Politics 470.

[161] UK Equality Act 2010, s 158; South African Employment Equity Act, s 14; *United Steelworkers of America v Weber* 443 US 193 (1979).

[162] Canadian Charter, s 15(2); Constitution of India, art 15(3)–(5); Constitution of South Africa, s 8(3); *Gratz v Bollinger* 539 US 244 (2003).

[163] Jeremy Waldron, 'A Right to Do Wrong' (1981) 92 Ethics 21.

[164] US Executive Order 11246 (1965), s 202(1).

[165] Christopher McCrudden, *Buying Social Justice: Equality, Government Procurement, and Legal Change* (Oxford University Press 2007) 2.

[166] Canadian Employment Equity Act, ss 5, 9, and 10.

South Africa,[167] and the United Kingdom[168] have enacted limited provisions to this end. Contractual and mandatory affirmative action measures give rise to affirmative action *duties* in law. Even where the law is only permissive, as many constitutional provisions with respect to public bodies are, it is best to read this permission simply as law's unwillingness to specify the precise shape and form that affirmative action measures should take. After all, these permissive provisions are often drafted with the hope that the power to undertake affirmative action will be exercised—they simply leave more room to policy-makers to determine and modify the details of any affirmative action measure. The development of mandatory procedural measures—for example, the 'positive duties' in section 149 of the UK Equality Act 2010—may be an attempt to avoid the possibility that permissive measures may not be used, while retaining the necessary flexibility to allow for context-dependent designs.

3.3.6 Rights-Generating and Non-Rights-Generating Duties

We can now see the entire range of duties imposed by discrimination law—duties to refrain from direct and indirect discrimination and harassment, duties to provide reasonable accommodation, and duties (or licenses) to undertake positive action. These duties do not, in themselves, require the conferment of a substantive benefit (such as education, housing, employment, etc) to all members of a protected group. They control the manner in which certain allocative decisions can be made. As a result of their operation, some, but not all, members of protected groups will get access to these scarce substantive benefits.

Many theorists are tempted to classify these duties on the basis of whether they impose positive or negative obligations. We have already seen that, at least in the context of reasonable accommodation, this dichotomy is misleading: it fails to illuminate the fact that, conceptually, reasonable accommodation is a secondary right that becomes available on the breach of the primary right against discrimination. In other words, reasonable accommodation is more akin to the prohibition on discrimination than to provision for affirmative action.[169] The negative duty versus positive duty dichotomy also fails to acknowledge that the performance of negative duties

---

[167] South African Equality Act, ss 24–28; South African Employment Equity Act, s 15.

[168] Fair Employment and Treatment (Northern Ireland) Order 1998, arts 55, 56, 72. See also, Christopher McCrudden, Raya Muttarak, Heather Hamill, and Anthony Heath, 'Affirmative Action Without Quotas in Northern Ireland' (2009) 4 The Equal Rights Review 7.

[169] Christine Jolls, 'Antidiscrimination and Accommodation' (2001) 115 Harvard Law Review 642.

in discrimination law can also impose significant financial costs on the duty-bearer—the possibility of justification is a means to keep these costs manageable. This divide also fails to account for what is really distinctive about affirmative action duties.

Affirmative action duties—whether imposed mandatorily or through contract—are different from the duty to refrain from direct and indirect discrimination and from harassment, and even from the duty to provide reasonable accommodation. The breach of these non-affirmative action duties in discrimination law vest *particular* persons with correlative private rights. In Kelsen's terms, the duty to refrain from discrimination and the anti-harassment duty are accompanied by 'reflex rights'—when these duties are breached, their intended beneficiaries have correlative individualized claims against the breach.[170] We can call them rights-generating duties. Not all duties are rights-generating. Kelsen gives the example of the duty to perform military service, which is not accompanied by any reflex right in any person.[171] Affirmative action duties do not usually generate rights. The intended beneficiaries of affirmative action measures tend to be non-specific members of disadvantaged groups, and particular individuals usually cannot claim to have the right to a specific affirmative action measure. Of course, the contracting party or the state or even a private body (through a public interest claim) can complain about the breach of an affirmative action duty. Of these claimants, only the contracting party can claim to have a 'private' right to the duty being performed, but this private right is not in the capacity of a direct beneficiary of the measure. Affirmative action duties, therefore, do not create any individualized private right in their intended beneficiaries; other duties in discrimination law do. Together, these duties (and licenses) determine the scope of the protection of antidiscrimination law.

3.4 Conclusion

This chapter and its predecessor should have made it clear that discrimination law is unusual and complex. It protects all of us, but to varying degrees depending on the context. In particular, its protection depends on the sensitivity of the impugned act or omission to certain personal characteristics

---

[170] Hans Kelsen, *The Pure Theory of Law* (Max Knight tr, University of California Press 1967) 127–8.
[171] Hans Kelsen, *The Pure Theory of Law* (Max Knight tr, University of California Press 1967) 128.

called grounds, and on our membership of a protected group. This sensitivity to grounds is what distinguishes discrimination law from other welfare measures such as legal guarantees to food, health care, housing. Any theory of discrimination law must account for this ground sensitivity generally, and explain the basis on which the protected grounds are selected. It must also justify the role that relative group disadvantage plays in determining the largely asymmetric protection afforded.

Antidiscrimination duties are imposed not on members of advantaged groups, but on certain categories of persons which primarily include the state, employers, and providers of goods and services. These duties are imposed unidirectionally—on the employer but not the employee, on the service-provider but not the consumer, etc. Again, the scope of the duties vary depending on who the duty-holder is (especially whether it is a public or a private body) and the context where the duty is applicable. Theoretical explanations must help us understand these peculiarities.

Finally, the duties that discrimination law imposes do not guarantee access to any non-remote and tangible benefits that flow from the sectors it regulates, including employment, health care, education, housing, etc. A theoretical account must tell us what interest it is, then, that discrimination law protects, and why its infringement can sometimes be justified. Some of these duties give rise to concomitant rights, others don't. An intention to discriminate is relevant for evidential or remedial reasons, but is generally not essential to prove discrimination. The role of comparators, at least in the context of direct discrimination, is settling into a similar arrangement.

These are some of the central features of the practice of discrimination law in the chosen democratic, culturally conversant, English-speaking, doctrine-swapping, common-law jurisdictions. These features gloss over important matters of detail, where the practice in these jurisdictions is significantly divergent. Even with respect to these core features, there are issues on which a chosen jurisdiction is an outlier. But there is remarkable consensus on most of the core issues identified in this chapter, even in the atypical jurisdictions.

PART II

POINT AND PURPOSE

4

A Good Life

The first three chapters of this book set the scene for a full-blown theoretical explanation and defence of discrimination law. In the introductory chapter, we saw that the deficiencies of the existing theories of discrimination law were down to the inability of most theorists to separate the definitional, purposive, and distributive questions around which the practice is organized. Part I explored the definitional question. In Chapter 2, we saw that at the heart of discrimination law lay the concepts of personal grounds, cognate groups, relative disadvantage, and eccentric distribution of benefits. In Chapter 3, we added some structure to this essence. We surveyed the nature of the protectorate of discrimination law, the persons on whom its duties are imposed, and the nature of the duties the law imposes (including the licenses it grants). Together, these chapters tell us what is salient in discrimination law. They outline the structure and limits of this area of law at a level of abstraction which is neither too close to, nor too removed from, the practice.

Having dealt with the definitional question in Part I, Part II will explore the purposive question. In this chapter, I will lay the normative groundwork for the exploration of the purposive question in Chapter 5: what is the *point* of discrimination law, ie what is its general justifying aim? Recall that this question is prior to, and distinct from, the *distributive* questions: what is it that discrimination law distributes? From whom? To whom? How? But I am getting ahead of myself. Chapter 5 will argue that the general justifying aim—the point or purpose, if you may—of discrimination law is to secure an aspect of the well-being of persons by reducing the abiding, pervasive, and substantial relative disadvantage faced by members of protected groups. Such disadvantage, it will be argued, prevents a person from securely accessing three basic goods necessary to live a good life. These goods are negative freedom, an adequate range of valuable opportunities, and self-respect. Before we can understand the connection between discrimination law and these basic goods, however, we need to understand what these goods are and how they interrelate. To do this, this chapter will take a detour of sorts. We will leave discrimination law aside (only briefly) and understand the nature of these three basic goods. We will also learn that the ideal of securing these goods to all persons can broadly be understood as securing the freedom to pursue a good life unhindered by certain unjustified constraints which affect our well-being adversely.

I will show that this freedom cannot be secured without some regard to the relative well-being of groups. This is not, strictly speaking, an *egalitarian* concern. But the need to incorporate comparative well-being into a theory of discrimination law explains why so many people (wrongly, in my view) continue to think that antidiscrimination and equality are interchangeable. My account has a place for relative disadvantage, but only because we cannot truly be free if our groups suffer certain egregious forms of relative disadvantage. The general justifying aim of discrimination law, in my view, is to secure an aspect of freedom rather than equality.[1]

It is worth reiterating that this general justifying aim does not fully dictate the manner in which benefits and burdens are distributed to particular individuals: to put the point more technically, the purposive and the distributive concerns in discrimination law are not fully transparent. What we want to achieve and how we should go about achieving it are related, but ultimately distinct, questions. The fact that reducing the relative disadvantage faced by members of protected groups is the point of discrimination law does not fully settle distributive questions concerning symmetry or comparators or the identity of the duty-bearers. We need to ask the purposive question only with regard to the overall practice of discrimination law. Demanding that distributive decisions in every particular case should *directly* pursue this purpose may seem intuitive, but could in fact be counterproductive to achieving the overall purpose. Furthermore, there may be other constraints which limit a transparent pursuit of this general justifying aim—reducing relative group disadvantage is not the only role of a state; it is not even the most important one. Part III will explore these distributive issues in some detail. For now, let us lay down the normative groundwork for answering the purposive question in Chapter 5.

4.1 Well-Being

The *point* of discrimination law is to promote (an aspect of) personal well-being. Well-being is a measure of how *successful* one's life is. A successful life is one spent pursuing (through valuable means) valuable—moral,

---

[1] I have mostly used 'freedom' and 'liberty' interchangeably in the book.

worthwhile—personal goals,[2] nurturing valuable relationships, making valuable choices, living virtuously.[3] For a life to be successful, the pursuit of at least some personal goals should have a positive result. While a modest degree of failure in our pursuit of valuable goals may not affect our well-being, consistent failure at most of our pursuits will. Thus, the success of one's life depends not only on the availability of certain goods and on personal effort, but—at least to some measure—on luck. In requiring that our pursuits be 'valuable', what is being presented is a 'perfectionist' understanding of human flourishing, one that is based on an objective account of the human good.[4] It differs from anti-perfectionist accounts which seek a connection between well-being and the subjective satisfaction of one's preferences and desires, or the pleasure one may derive from such satisfaction.[5] It insists that our well-being is not served by the pursuit of valueless goals: well-being has a decidedly moral character. Despite the label, a perfectionist account need not require a life to be 'perfect' in order to be successful. At least the version being endorsed here only insists that whether a life has been successful can only be determined objectively.[6]

The perfectionism of this account of well-being is tempered by several assumptions. First, this account assumes the truth of value pluralism—the idea that 'there are various forms and styles of life which exemplify different virtues and which are incompatible'.[7] There are innumerable and mutually incompatible ways of living a successful life, but no one life can, even in theory, achieve total perfection. The life of a farmer is valuable not only because it is the life of a person—who is intrinsically valuable—but also because it is

---

[2] These goals are *personal* in two different senses. In the first sense, they are personal because in order to be valuable—at least in the context of modern industrial societies—personal goals must be freely *chosen by the person* whose goals they are. In the second sense, these goals are personal because they must largely be *pursued by the person* whose goals they are in order to contribute to her well-being. Joseph Raz, *The Morality of Freedom* (Clarendon Press 1986) 306: 'a large proportion of a person's goals are agency goals. They are normally goals others can help him reach ... But they cannot reach them for him.'

[3] I am using terms like value and morality in a critical, objective, non-relativist sense, and naturally assume the possibility of objectively true moral propositions. See generally, Herbert Hart, *Law, Liberty and Morality* (Oxford University Press 1963) 20.

[4] Perfectionism has a long philosophical lineage, going back at least to Aristotle. See Aristotle, *The Nicomachean Ethics* (David Ross tr, Oxford University Press 2009) 1.5.

[5] Given the human capacity to evaluate their first-order desires and preferences and possess second-order desires about whether one wants to have a particular first-order desire, any preference-satisfaction account of well-being will have to provide an account of what counts as a person's real preference or desire. See Gerald Dworkin, *The Theory and Practice of Autonomy* (Cambridge University Press 1998) 20.

[6] This version borrows extensively from Joseph Raz's account of well-being, albeit with some modifications: Joseph Raz, *The Morality of Freedom* (Clarendon Press 1986) ch 12.

[7] Joseph Raz, *The Morality of Freedom* (Clarendon Press 1986) 395.

spent pursuing a productive activity: farming. The same is true for the life of a philosopher, a dancer, a parent, and an ascetic monk living in the woods. No one life can embody all, or even more than a few, of these and numerous other valuable but incompatible pursuits.

Second, an unrestrained perfectionist may argue that even though there are innumerable ways of living a good life, for a particular person—given their particular talents and tastes—there is one, or only a few, best ways of living. So, for example, a person with a particular facility for music should, one may say, become a musician of some sort to fully realize her potential. But, on my account, even if she does not become a musician, her life may yet be successful. A successful life need not be one that is fully self-realized in this sense. As long as the life is characterized by value, it is sufficiently successful.

Third, as Aristotle puts it, we must examine 'a complete life. For one swallow does not make a summer, nor does one day; and so too one day, or a short time does not make a man blessed and happy.'[8] A life's overall success is to be judged across its entire span, and not in relation to a particular moment in time or in the context of any particular event(s).

Fourth, the success of a life is to be judged holistically from the point of view of the person whose life it is, in light of the resources and opportunities available to her.[9] The life of a poor woman who, against great odds, ensured that her children were well fed and educated is not necessarily less successful than that of a rich philanthropist whose charity has helped hundreds of other lives. Having said that, without at least a minimum access to the basic goods we are about to consider, a successful life does become impossible.

Finally, the goals, relationships, choices, and so on that contribute to the success of our lives are themselves to be evaluated holistically. A choice—say the choice to follow a particular religion—must be judged based on whether following that religion, on the whole, constitutes a valuable choice. Often, choices such as those about faith, come as a packaged deal. Some aspects of the package may be very unattractive. The question to be considered is whether, these ugly aspects notwithstanding, the choice of following that religion is—on the whole—a valuable one. The issue will turn on how bad those particularly ugly aspects are, and how central they are to the practice of that religion. This is not an argument for the toleration of immoral aspects of religion—often manifested in patriarchal, casteist, or homophobic practices. Instead, it is an argument for not condemning the choice of that religion as

---

[8] Aristotle, *The Nicomachean Ethics* (David Ross tr, Oxford University Press 2009) I.7, 1098a18–19. See also, Gerald Dworkin, *The Theory and Practice of Autonomy* (Cambridge University Press 1998) 16.

[9] Joseph Raz, *The Morality of Freedom* (Clarendon Press 1986) 299.

immoral without first considering whether it has redeeming qualities which make it, on balance, a valuable choice.

These caveats remind us that one should be slow to evaluate people's lives and pursuits, and do so with due caution, mindful of the context and in light of the resources, opportunities, and possibilities. But they retain the original insistence that our well-being is not served merely through the satisfaction of our desires and preferences. The moral value of our pursuits is relevant to the success of our lives, and therefore to our well-being.

To be able to live successful lives, individuals need secured access to at least four basic goods.[10] Before I give an account of these goods, it must be admitted that the necessity of these freedom-securing basic goods can be—and has been—defended on non-perfectionist grounds as well.[11] While a normative defence of a perfectionist account of well-being over anti-perfectionist ones is beyond the scope of this book,[12] I will show in Chapter 5 that the general justifying aim of discrimination law must be perfectionist (in the qualified sense I have just explained).

The basic goods necessary for well-being secure certain freedoms to all persons and therefore make a good life possible. One can, of course, fail to live a good life despite having secured access to all of them. *Secured* access means that not only should an individual have access to these goods, she should also be free from a reasonable fear of losing access to any of these goods.[13] The first three goods are external to the individual: (a) a set of goods which will adequately satisfy one's biological needs; (b) negative freedom,

---

[10] Although the following account of the basic goods necessary for well-being primarily draws upon aspects of Raz's liberal-perfectionist suggestions about the conditions that make us autonomous (Joseph Raz, *The Morality of Freedom* (Clarendon Press 1986) ch 14), it includes compatible insights from political liberalism (especially as theorized by John Rawls) and the republican tradition (in particular, from Philip Pettit).

[11] See John Rawls's famous account of a morally neutral preference-based list of prerequisite 'primary goods'—'things which it is supposed a rational man wants whatever else he wants ... With more of these goods men can generally be assured of greater success in carrying out their intentions and in advancing their ends, whatever these ends may be.' He lists rights and liberties, opportunities and powers, income and wealth, and self-respect as primary goods. John Rawls, *A Theory of Justice* (Oxford University Press 1999) 92. Nussbaum developed this Rawlsian idea into what she calls the 'capabilities approach': Martha Nussbaum, *Women and Human Development: The Capabilities Approach* (Cambridge University Press 2000).

[12] Any such defence will have to respond to the arguments made in Martha Nussbaum, 'Perfectionist Liberalism and Political Liberalism' (2011) 39 Philosophy and Public Affairs 3.

[13] Henry Shue understands 'security' as a social guarantee (of a right, etc) against standard threats. See generally Henry Shue, *Basic Rights: Subsistence, Affluence, and US Foreign Policy* (Princeton University Press 1980) 13. The contemporary notion of security resonates with the value of freedom from disturbance (ataraxia) that was emphasized by many Hellenistic philosophical traditions, including the cynics, the Epicureans, and the skeptics.

ie freedom from unjustified interference by others in one's person, projects, possessions, relationships, and affairs;[14] and (c) an adequate range of valuable opportunities to choose from.[15] The last remaining basic good is internal to a person, although it may be influenced by external factors: (d) an appropriate level of self-respect.[16] Together, these goods constitute necessary (although not sufficient) preconditions for a person's well-being. Because all of us have a fundamental interest in our well-being, we also have a fundamental interest in having secured access to these basic goods that facilitate our well-being.

It should be obvious that having secured access to these basic goods is not sufficient to lead a good life. It depends on what we do with these goods. This chapter does not provide a full account of what human well-being is. It is limited to an account of certain basic goods that the state must strive to secure for us and thus enable us to lead flourishing lives. It is a defining feature of modern liberal states that they do not coerce their citizens to lead a good life. We have already noticed that a project is valuable only if it is *personal*—ie freely chosen and pursued by the person whose project it is. The state cannot choose our goals for us. Unlike libertarians, however, contemporary liberals believe that it is appropriate for the state to strive to secure for its people certain basic prerequisites of a good life. I share this belief, although for its defence one must look elsewhere.[17] What suffices for our purposes is that there is broad liberal consensus that, subject to other considerations, the state has a prima facie duty to secure at least some aspects of these basic goods to its citizens. A theory of discrimination law in liberal democracies which locates its general justifying goal within this general academic and political consensus must be attractive, in part, for that reason.

What follows in this chapter is a brief discussion of the last three basic goods that have a direct connection to discrimination law. Before we move on, however, four overarching features of these goods may be noticed. First, as I have already pointed out, these goods must be possessed securely. It is not enough that one currently enjoys these basic goods. One must, in addition, be free from reasonable fear of losing access to any of these goods (except, of course, the anticipation of inevitable natural death). This

---

[14] See generally, John Mill, *On Liberty* (JW Parker & Son 1859); Isaiah Berlin, *Liberty: Incorporating Four Essays on Liberty* (Henry Hardy ed, Oxford University Press 2002).

[15] Joseph Raz argued that a liberal state must strive to make us autonomous in order to facilitate our well-being, which requires the availability of an adequate range of valuable *options* to all of us. Joseph Raz, *The Morality of Freedom* (Clarendon Press 1986) ch 14.

[16] See John Rawls, *A Theory of Justice* (Oxford University Press 1999) 440ff.

[17] This belief is shared by perfectionist and anti-perfectionist liberals. See generally John Rawls, *Political Liberalism* (Columbia University Press 1993); Joseph Raz, *The Morality of Freedom* (Clarendon Press 1986).

insistence that access to these basic goods be 'secured' is inspired by the republican insight that a person in a relationship of dominance is not free, even if her benign master does not in fact violate her negative freedom by actually interfering with her pursuit of her projects. The mere *possibility* that he has the power to do so at whim is antithetical to her freedom, and therefore to her well-being.[18]

Second, with the exception of negative freedom, the level of access that one requires to these goods is optimal rather than maximal or equal. One only needs adequate satisfaction of one's biological needs. One does not need to be able to choose from all possible valuable goals in order to live a good life—so long as an adequate range is available, it will suffice. Likewise, self-respect has a tendency to morph into pride and egoism if we have too much of it. We need enough of these goods, rather than as much as possible or even as much as everyone else. That said, I will show that what amounts to an adequate range of valuable opportunities and our ability to have adequate self-respect depend considerably on the range of valuable goods available to others and to the respect shown to us by others, respectively. Furthermore, the adequacy threshold is not fixed for all places at all times—it depends instead on the kind of societies we live in at a given historical moment. We will explore these comparative and contingent dimensions later in this chapter.[19]

Third, the last three basic goods are relational, ie they make sense only with respect to social, communal beings like humans. Freedom from interference by others is self-evidently relational—our secure enjoyment of negative freedom depends on the relative power that we wield vis-à-vis others. We will see later in this chapter that a good number of opportunities available in a society depend on the complex web of social practices of that society. Our self-respect is influenced by the respect or disrespect that others express towards us and also by how we evaluate the success of our life, often in comparison to that of others. A list of basic goods drawn up for the well-being of asocial individualistic beings would look very different.

Finally, a person's access to these goods must be evaluated holistically, taking her life as a whole, and not at any particular moment in time or with respect to particular events. Since we are interested in one's well-being in the

---

[18] Philip Pettit, 'Freedom as Antipower' (1996) 106 Ethics 576.

[19] The 'adequacy' requirement is a nod to the principle of sufficiency. See generally, Harry Frankfurt, 'Equality as a Moral Ideal' (1987) 98 Ethics 21. The recognition that the adequacy threshold depends on comparative well-being incorporates prioritarian concerns into a fundamentally sufficientarian principle. On prioritarianism, see Derek Parfit, 'Equality and Priority' (1997) 10 Ratio 202. On a plausible combination of prioritarian and sufficientarian concerns, see Roger Crisp, 'Equality, Priority and Compassion' (2003) 113 Ethics 745.

context of their life as a whole rather than at any particular moment, we need
to evaluate whether a person's life, on the whole, has secured access to these
basic goods. In this sense, these goods are essentially person-regarding rather
than act-regarding.

The importance of the first basic good is probably most self-evident. Even
Henry David Thoreau, seeking to escape a life of acquisitiveness and debt,
acknowledged that:

> The necessaries of life for man, in this climate may, accurately enough, be distrib-
> uted under the several heads of Food, Shelter, Clothing, and Fuel; for not till we
> have secured these are we prepared to entertain the true problems of life with free-
> dom and a prospect of success.[20]

It is in the remaining three basic goods that our interest mainly lies,[21]
although it is true that a lack of access to the first basic good could point
to particularly egregious forms of discrimination. The next three sections
will briefly examine each of these goods. Then we will turn our attention in
Chapter 5 to the establishment of the connection between these goods on the
one hand and discrimination law on the other. The breathless treatment that
follows hardly does justice to the complexity of issues involved. My focus will
be limited only to emphasizing those aspects that are particularly relevant to
the task at hand.

4.2 Secured Negative Freedom

Classical liberals understood freedom to be the absence of interference by
others. Following the eighteenth-century tradition, Isaiah Berlin explained
that 'If I am prevented by others from doing what I could otherwise do, I am
to that degree unfree.'[22] Interference can be coercive or manipulative, and is
designed to worsen the agent's range of opportunities, either by reducing that
range, or by making some opportunities seem less attractive by altering the
expected payoffs of choosing these opportunities, or by changing the actual
payoffs of opportunities already chosen.[23] As Raz explains:

[20] Henry Thoreau, *Walden and Other Writings* (Bantam Books 1981) 114.
[21] We will learn that the last three basic goods have a comparative dimension. The first good
does not, *intrinsically*, have this comparative dimension.
[22] Isaiah Berlin, *Liberty: Incorporating Four Essays on Liberty* (Henry Hardy ed, Oxford
University Press 2002) 122.
[23] Philip Pettit, *Republicanism: A Theory of Freedom and Government* (Oxford University Press
1999) 53.

Coercion and manipulation subject the will of one person to that of another. That violates his independence and is inconsistent with his autonomy. This explains why coercion and manipulation are intentional actions: they would not amount to a subjecting of the will of another person if they were not.[24]

Interference is therefore intentional, although it need not always be direct. Direct interference with another's will, without any mitigating factor, is often a criminal or a tortious act in most legal systems. But interference can take many other forms and a person can be coerced in many ways. Raz tells us that:

> A person is forced to act in a certain way if (1) he regrets the fact that he is in the circumstances he believes himself to be in and which are his reasons for acting as he does, and (2) his action is justified or excused ... The coerced person is forced to act as he did. Hence his action is either justified or excused.[25]

To understand this conception of interference, let us consider the example of an atheist, Fatima, who is well qualified for and very keen on a particular teaching position advertised by the local school. Fatima finds out that most members of the selection committee are religious and also prejudiced against non-believers. Let us assume, to avoid unnecessary distraction, that the teacher's religious status is wholly irrelevant for the satisfactory performance of this job. Now, Fatima has four (among other) 'choices' in relation to this job: (i) she can change her religious status, become a follower of a religion, and apply for the job (*conversion*); (ii) she can try and hide the fact that she is a non-believer, without actually converting, and apply for the job (*passing*); (iii) she can decide neither to convert nor pass, but instead to not 'flaunt' her atheism, and apply for the job (*covering*); or (iv) she can refuse to do any of the above (*non-assimilation*).[26] Which, if any, of the first three assimilationist strategies—conversion, passing, covering—will suffice to get her the job will depend on the strength of the prejudice that the members of the selection committee hold against atheists.[27] For our purposes, however, let us assume that Fatima 'chooses' option (iv), ie fails to convert, pass, or cover. She certainly regrets the fact that the selectors for this job are a prejudiced bunch, and this fact is also the reason for her not to apply (or apply

---

[24] Joseph Raz, *The Morality of Freedom* (Clarendon Press 1986) 378.

[25] Joseph Raz, *The Morality of Freedom* (Clarendon Press 1986) 151–2.

[26] This description of assimilationist techniques of conversion, passing, and covering are borrowed from Kenji Yoshino, *Covering: The Hidden Assault on Our Civil Liberties* (Random House 2007).

[27] Kenji Yoshino, 'Covering' (2001–2002) 111 Yale Law Journal 769, 774–5.

without any reasonable prospect of getting the job).[28] If Fatima's action is justified or excused, she will have been coerced to act as she did. Since there is nothing wrong with being an atheist, Fatima's choice of non-assimilation is justified. Under the circumstances, Fatima's will has been interfered with, albeit indirectly—it is irrelevant that she 'chose' option (iv).

A capacious understanding of what interference is is not the only precondition for a full appreciation of this basic good. We also need to understand that one could lack negative freedom even if there is no actual interference by others. The idea is closely related to that of power, which Weber defined as 'the chance of a man or of a number of men to realize their own will in a communal action even against the resistance of others who are participating in the action'.[29] Dominance is a particular form of power relation. Republican philosophers have pointed out that freedom requires that one is free from *dominance*, so that no one has the power to interfere in my choices systematically and pervasively.[30] The exemplary case of a relationship of dominance is provided by the relationship between a slave and a master: a master is able to constrain the slave's actions and enforce his will over the will of the slave. The slave is in the master's power: the master can exercise such a power, and enforce his own will; or he might not do so, because, for example, he does not need to or want to. Yet, the slave is bound by a relationship of dominance even if the master is benign, perhaps doting—she remains unfree. These relationships of dominance need not necessarily be interpersonal. We will see in Chapter 5 that grotesque power imbalances between different groups in a society can also result in one group dominating the other politically, socially, or economically.

I emphasize secured negative freedom because the mere existence of relationships of dominance is problematic for a person's freedom. Insecurity about the enjoyment of one's negative freedom may arise from many sources—being in a relationship of dominance is only one of them. Frequent coercive interferences with a person's property by burglars not only infringes the victim's negative freedom but also makes her insecure about her freedom—this will

---

[28] It is wholly immaterial for our example that Fatima found out about the prejudiced selection committee before applying and therefore refused to apply. Supposing that she would have applied for the job without hiding her religious status, irrespective of any prior knowledge of the selection committee's attitude to atheism, and was denied the job because of her religious status nonetheless, the 'choice' was made for her by someone else. If anything, this may amount to a greater degree of coercion, certainly not less.

[29] Max Weber, *From Max Weber: Essays in Sociology* (HH Gerth and Wright Mills trs, Routledge & Kegan Paul Ltd 1970) 180.

[30] Philip Pettit, *Republicanism: A Theory of Freedom and Government* (Oxford University Press 1999) 52.

be the case even if these interferences are by different burglars acting independently, where none of them is in a relationship of dominance with the victim. What is key is that a person should not live in fear of a reasonable possibility that her negative freedom will be infringed. With this fear haunting our lives, we will be unfree. Thus, even if the powerful group in a given society does not actually oppress members of the weaker group, the mere likelihood of such domination may be sufficient to threaten the secured enjoyment of negative freedom by such members.

This need for security explains why negative freedom is valuable even if the interference will make very little difference to the range of opportunities available to a rich victim, and even if the loot is used to benefit the poor, whose needs are greater. Robin Hood makes one's enjoyment of negative freedom insecure in a manner which a progressive tax coercively collected by a rule of law abiding state does not.[31] In both cases, the persons coerced are the rich, who can afford to part with some of their wealth, and those benefited are (hopefully) the poor. The difference in the case of coercion by the state is that it allows the person being taxed to predict the amount of her liability and the time when it must be paid, enabling her to plan her life around it.[32] Her negative freedom remains on surer footing.

A person's access to secured negative freedom is compromised only when the (actual or potential) interferences are unjustified.[33] We have just seen that a fair system of progressive taxation does not deny secured negative freedom to a person. A full account of when an interference might be justified is far beyond the scope of this book. In general, we can say that an interference is more likely to be justified when it is not arbitrary, concerns a harmful activity, does not ignore the legitimate interests of the person being interfered with, proportionately serves an appropriately weighty objective, does not infringe upon one's moral rights, etc. This understanding of secured negative freedom as the absence of actual or potential *unjustified* interference captures the intuition that life in a political community does not, as some libertarians might claim, constitute a constraint on freedom.[34]

[31] This is not to say that a Robin Hood robbery can never be justified or excused. Secured negative freedom is one of many goods, and may, exceptionally, be sacrificed for other, weightier, goods (say, in order to save the life of a child).

[32] See generally, Joseph Raz, 'The Rule of Law and its Virtue' (1977) 93 The Law Quarterly Review 195.

[33] Note that here the term 'unjustified' qualifies the actions of the perpetrator; unlike in Fatima's case, where it was used in the context of the actions of the person whose freedom was compromised.

[34] Philip Pettit, *Republicanism: A Theory of Freedom and Government* (Oxford University Press 1999) 35. However, negative liberty does not require that one has to actively participate in the political life of her community in order to be free. That is a feature of what Berlin called 'positive freedom'.

Furthermore, although isolated acts of unjustified interference may decrease one's access to this basic good, they may not constitute its complete negation. Recall that the basic goods are person-regarding rather than action-regarding and that one can have more or less of them. We need to judge whether a person has access to secured negative freedom holistically—sometimes a dozen minor interferences may not make her unfree, at other times one significant interference may result in loss of secured freedom. Of course, the more secure we can be from unjustified interferences in our lives, the better our lives will be.

If the state is to secure the negative freedom of a person, it must not only refrain from infringing it but also facilitate its enjoyment by ensuring that it is not infringed by others. Negative freedom therefore makes negative as well as positive demands on the state. But unlike the other basic goods, secured negative freedom is, at least in aspiration, maximal. There is no optimal adequacy threshold—we should have as much of it as we can.

4.3 Secured Access to an Adequate Range of Valuable Opportunities

The next basic good entails having a secured access to an adequate range of valuable opportunities.[35] These opportunities should enable a person to 'exercise all capacities human beings have an innate drive to exercise'—the drive, for example, to move around, stimulate our senses, nurture relationships, have an occupation—'as well as to decline to develop any of them'.[36]

These opportunities should allow us to pursue long-term pervasive goals as well as (relatively) short-term and trivial goals.[37] Our long-term and pervasive

---

[35] This basic good draws upon Raz's understanding of autonomy, although my account is crucially different in several respects. See generally, Joseph Raz, *The Morality of Freedom* (Clarendon Press 1986) ch 14. In particular, unlike Raz, I use the term 'opportunities' rather than 'options'. Option-talk is susceptible to the criticism that what is valuable is that one has chosen *well*, and not that one has chosen *between valuable options*. See Oran Doyle, 'Direct Discrimination, Indirect Discrimination and Autonomy' (2007) 27 Oxford Journal of Legal Studies 537, 552.

[36] Joseph Raz, *The Morality of Freedom* (Clarendon Press 1986) 375.

[37] Joseph Raz, *The Morality of Freedom* (Clarendon Press 1986) 374. To further explain the concept of adequacy of options, Raz gives two examples. The first example involves a man in the pit, whose only options are whether to eat now or later, whether to sleep now or later. Since all his options are trivial ones, he does not have an adequate range of valuable options. In the second example, a hounded woman on a desert island is perennially trying to save her life from a dangerous animal. She has no trivial options available to her—she cannot choose to listen to music or read a book, or indeed do anything but try and save her life. She too lacks an adequate range of valuable options: 373–4.

goals chiefly concern our employment, education, domicile, relationships, and other aspects of life which have a significant impact on many facets of our well-being. Trivial goals—usually relating to what you want to do in the short-term—are also essential. They include things like listening to music, shaving one's head, going on a holiday, chatting with a friend, playing football, getting tattooed, dancing, etc. Trivial goals are important intrinsically because our innate human drives concern not only goals with pervasive consequences but also those with little, short-term, or no consequences. They are also important instrumentally because experimenting with trivial goals helps us determine our talents and level of enthusiasm for more pervasive ones. Pursuing relatively trivial goals may also be a necessary prerequisite that determines our ability to choose a more pervasive goal: personal goals are 'nested' within hierarchical structures; immediate goals (learning to speak Italian) may be adopted in service of a larger goal (to retire in Italy).[38] For one to have the opportunity to retire in Italy, one would probably also need to have the opportunity to learn to speak Italian.

These opportunities are, to a large extent, dependent on the *social forms* that exist in a particular culture. Raz describes social forms as widespread and complex social practices which define activities and relationships, for example marriage, the practice of medicine or law, bird-watching, friendship, etc. In a society without the social form of bird-watching, for example, tracking and noting different types of birds will not have the same significance to the well-being of an individual that it will have in a society which does.[39] Valuable social forms are *collective* goods, and accessing them can be essential for a person's well-being, although Raz is quick to clarify that individual experimentation and innovation with social forms, eg 'open' marriages, are not ruled out. The dependence of comprehensive goals on social forms underscores the anti-individualistic nature of this basic good. Our opportunities are shaped in the context of the society we live in. Existing social forms provide one such context. The vision offered here is that of a flourishing individual, embedded in (but not oppressed by) her culture's social forms.

Only the pursuit of *valuable* opportunities enhances a person's well-being—it contributes to the value of a life. Immoral opportunities, on the other hand, diminish our well-being. We should, of course, understand value

---

[38] Joseph Raz, *The Morality of Freedom* (Clarendon Press 1986) 292.
[39] Joseph Raz, *The Morality of Freedom* (Clarendon Press 1986) 307f. See also, Joseph Raz, 'Facing Up: A Reply' (1989) 62 Southern California Law Review 1153, 1218: 'our historical knowledge sets the limits on the imaginable, and ... our own practices set the limits to what is feasible for us'.

(and the implied perfectionism) in light of the qualifications explained earlier in this chapter.[40]

Moreover, what is required is access to a *range* of valuable opportunities. There must be a good spread between the opportunities and they should be sufficiently differentiated. Valuable opportunities can be categorized into broad families of opportunities—relational, recreational, occupational, expressive, associational—affecting diverse spheres of human activity, such as work, education, politics, culture, and society. One must have access to a range of opportunities within each family, especially within those families of opportunities which are particularly important for a person's well-being because they relate to life's pervasive goals.[41] If, however, there exists in a given society only one way to pursue a pervasive long-term goal, that particular opportunity must be universally available. Furthermore, if a previously available valuable opportunity has already been pursued, in the sense that a person has already committed herself to it and invested time, effort, and emotions into pursuing it, then the second basic good (secured negative freedom) requires that her continued access to this opportunity is protected.

Further still, if one is to lead a flourishing life, what is essential is that the range of opportunities available to her be *adequate* in a given context—rather than maximal (ie having all the opportunities there are to have) or equal (ie as much as anyone else). Adequate opportunities—ie a sufficient number of opportunities of sufficient quality—are all we need for our well-being.[42] Having all the opportunities there are, or even aspiring to do so, is certainly not essential to our well-being. Some may say, probably with some justification, that it may even be bad for our well-being. Allocating opportunities equally is not essential for a person's well-being either, although the pursuit of equal opportunities may sometimes be justified by other instrumental goals.[43]

That said, a determination of what range of opportunities is adequate is sensitive to the relative differences between the ranges of opportunities available to and exploited by different persons. Take, for example, an opportunity that has become key to our well-being in industrial societies—access to

---

[40] See section 4.1 above.

[41] Hugh Collins, 'Discrimination, Equality and Social Inclusion' (2003) 66 The Modern Law Review 16, 23–4.

[42] For a defence of the principle of sufficiency, see Harry Frankfurt, 'Equality as a Moral Ideal' (1987) 98 Ethics 21.

[43] See, for example, Richard Wilkinson and Kate Pickett, *The Spirit Level: Why Equality is Better for Everyone* (Penguin 2010).

electricity. Discounting (for the sake of the argument) the environmental costs of electricity production and transmission, and assuming that access to an uninterrupted, reliable, safe, and affordable supply of electricity is significantly superior as an opportunity to all available alternatives in contributing to our interest in staying warm/cool/well-lit/mechanized, we can say that people who have such access are better off than people who do not. This is true not only for comparisons over space (eg between people living in Cambodia and in Canada), but also over time—our lives today, with access to electricity, are better than those living four centuries ago who lacked it *in this respect.*

The fact that there is a reliable supply of electricity to most Canadian homes tells us what is *possible* in terms of accessing electricity. Any adequacy threshold must be determined in the context of what is possible. What is adequate access to electricity for a Cambodian today is sensitive to how much electricity a Canadian is normally able to access. This sensitivity is owed not to any egalitarian impulse, but to the fact that the amount of electricity normally available to any person or group (here, Canadians) recalibrates the range of possibility against which the adequacy threshold for everyone must be judged. The same is true of our access to clean water, clothes, entertainment, information, etc. The range of possibilities with respect to these and many other opportunities has vastly increased over time. We must judge what is adequate access to any of them on the basis of what is possible in our time. Those with the best access to these opportunities today show us the limits of what is possible. How much is adequate for each person depends on this possibility and on our need (which can itself depend on what is possible).

If human technological progress continues forever, the world of possible opportunities may forever expand or, it may be, that the quality and supply of certain opportunities deteriorates over time. At any rate, we must peg adequacy *at least* in relation to the level of access that is currently possible for a person to enjoy. This account is therefore comparative, but not egalitarian.

Some opportunities that are *deeply* conditioned by social forms, however, are an exception to this sensitivity to comparison.[44] Recall that social forms are widespread and complex practices that underpin activities and

---

[44] I do not mean to suggest that even opportunities like electricity are totally independent of social forms. The difference, albeit an important one, between access to electricity and (say) to marriage, in terms of their dependence on social forms, may be one of degree rather than kind.

relationships in a given society. Let us assume that marriage—at least in the form of a consensual, (more or less) equal, aspirationally permanent (but dissoluble), romantic relationship between adults protected by law and (if the parties so choose) sanctified by religion—is a valuable social form existing in a given society X. Let us also assume a different society, Y, where the institution of marriage does not exist. In Y, couples enter into relationship contracts where they specify the terms which will govern their relationship. The state restricts itself to enforcing the contractual terms, subject to the condition that they are not unfair to either party and protect the interests of any dependent children. Let us assume further that there are no institutions other than marriage in X and relationship contracts in Y which can facilitate stable, nurturing, long-term romantic relationships. Under these circumstances, it will be essential for the well-being of X-landers to be able to marry, and for Y-ites to have the opportunity to enter into relationship contracts. But it is not essential for the well-being of Y-ites to be able to marry or for X-landers to be able to enter into relationship contracts. This is because these social forms do not exist in the respective societies. As long as any existing social form(s) provide(s) adequate means to pursue valuable goals in each family of options, there is no moral obligation to encourage the creation of new social forms. Only when this is not the case—say, if Y did not have any institution which could support long-term romantic relationships—may there be reasons which require the creation of new social forms.

Let us now suppose that because of cultural exchange with X, some Y-ites start getting married and over time marriage comes to be established as a social form in Y alongside relationship contracts. Under these circumstances, whether each Y-ite needs to have access to both marriage and relationship contracts or at least one of them will depend on whether access to one of these forms is adequate for their well-being (the judgment will have to be contextual, and we will need a lot more information to be able to make it). However, even if accessing either of the two social forms will be adequate, the need to secure other basic goods—negative freedom and self-respect— may forbid certain types of denials of either social form to some citizens of Y. Opportunities conditioned by social forms, such as access to marriage, bird-watching, and the practice of medicine, tend not to be subject to the constraints imposed by resource limitations in the same way that opportunities like access to electricity, water, and housing are. The fact that a valuable and relatively resource-indifferent social form exists in a society is usually enough reason for allowing anyone (with the capacity to engage valuably with that social form) to access it. If a Y-ite is not allowed to marry, she may continue to have adequate access to an opportunity to live in a stable, socially recognized, long-term, loving relationship through a relationship contract.

However, her negative freedom (which must include the freedom to engage with existing social forms) and her self-respect may still be adversely affected. Thus comparative considerations about who else has access to a socially conditioned opportunity continue to be relevant for a person's overall well-being.

That said, the adequacy of all opportunities—whether they are dependent on social forms or not—are contingent on the particular context to some extent. This is because they are sensitive to need. Certain forms of disabilities, for example, may require different or greater opportunities to facilitate the pursuit of a given personal goal. Certain climatic conditions impose greater electricity requirements than others. The adequacy threshold cannot therefore be fixed for all persons or for all times.

At this stage, we need to distinguish between what is the adequate range of opportunities required for our well-being, and what is the adequate range of opportunities that a state is obliged to procure for an individual in order to further her well-being. The feasibility of procuring a particular opportunity, including economic feasibility, is relevant only to the second question. It may be that securing the adequate access to electricity for everyone is simply too expensive, or comes at too high an environmental cost. These pragmatic constraints do not make access to electricity any less valuable for our well-being—but they do require that we may have to settle for less-than-adequate access to some valuable opportunities. Another way of understanding this is to see different opportunities connected through a polycentric web, where our distribution decisions for any one of them impact the distribution of other opportunities.[45] Thus, distribution-related duties for any given opportunity are sensitive to the adequacy requirements of all other opportunities and the costs of procuring them for everyone.

We can now appreciate that the adequacy threshold for some opportunities depends on what others have. Adequacy concerns itself with whether one has enough—thus the standard is essentially sufficientarian rather than egalitarian. Nonetheless, its dependence on what others have (or have had) builds in a comparative dimension to this sufficiency threshold. Furthermore, there is another comparative dimension to this account. Because everyone's well-being counts, distribution schemes must also prioritize the needs of those most in want: if the state cannot immediately secure an adequate range of valuable opportunities to everyone, any programme of distribution must

---

[45] Fuller explains the complexity of polycentric decisions in the context of adjudication: Lon Fuller, 'The Forms and Limits of Adjudication' (1978) 92 Harvard Law Review 353.

ensure that those who have the fewest opportunities have the first claim on the opportunities being distributed.[46]

We can finally turn to the issue of security: what is required is a *secured* access to an adequate range of valuable opportunities. One should not have to fear that the range of the valuable opportunities she has access to will become less than adequate. Nor should she have to live in fear of losing any particular opportunity in which she has invested significantly. And yet, the nature of this basic good is such that its secured enjoyment requires two, countervailing, caveats. On the one hand, because of the interconnectedness of opportunities, some opportunities are unlocked only after certain prior opportunities are accessed. For example, certain employment opportunities are dependent on a person having accessed a particular type of education. A person who has a personal goal of becoming a doctor will only be able to do it after studying medicine at university, which in turn requires her having had a decent school education. Opportunities which constitute the foundation for accessing other important opportunities are therefore critically important.

On the other hand, the concept of security should be understood in light of the fact that accessing any particular opportunity often forecloses the possibility of accessing certain alternative and incompatible opportunities. Pursuing a career as a doctor would normally shut the door to becoming an airline pilot. Effectively excluding the pursuit of some other opportunities is in the nature of opportunities—loss of an opportunity incompatible with one that I have freely pursued is not usually of moral concern.

4.4 Secured Self-Respect

The last basic good we need to consider is secured self-respect. Rousseau famously claimed that 'the first step towards inequality' is taken when 'public esteem acquires a value'.[47] We may agree with Rousseau that the desire for self-respect is the root of much evil, and yet coherently hold, with many contemporary philosophers, that at least in the 'civilized' world we live in, a minimal degree of self-respect is critically important for a person's well-being.[48]

---

[46] Derek Parfit, 'Equality and Priority' (1997) 10 Ratio 202; Roger Crisp, 'Equality, Priority and Compassion' (2003) 113 Ethics 745.

[47] Jean-Jacques Rousseau, *A Discourse upon the Origin and Foundation of the Inequality among Mankind* (R & J Dodsley 1761) 114.

[48] John Rawls, *A Theory of Justice* (Oxford University Press 1999) 440f; Avishai Margalit, *The Decent Society* (Harvard University Press 1996).

Self-respect has two distinct aspects. Status self-respect, corresponding with what Darwall calls 'recognition respect' involves self-respect based simply on our status. Most defensible conceptions of status self-respect draw upon our status as 'persons', since persons are uncontroversially accepted as objects of value (and, somewhat more controversially, objects of ultimate value). 'Evaluative self-respect' corresponds with Darwall's notion of appraisal respect, and denotes our respect for the value and success of our life, character, and personal goals.[49] Evaluative self-respect reflects one's confidence in the value of one's goals and in one's ability to pursue them.[50] Because one's confidence in the value of her goals or means may be misplaced, self-respect serves our well-being only when it is premised on objectively valuable goals and objectively valuable means of pursuing these goals.[51] At the same time, we must always be cautious against over-zealous determination of 'value'.

Self-respect and well-being are symbiotically related—well-being is enhanced by self-respect and self-respect is enhanced by well-being. To put it differently, self-respect counts among the causes as well as the effects of well-being and success in life. Success, we have seen, depends on what is possible for us to achieve in our context. In feudal societies, it was possible for a low-class person to possess self-respect because social mobility was almost impossible—what mattered was whether her life was as successful as it could have been. In our societies built on meritocratic and egalitarian assumptions, success is frequently, but wrongly, assumed to follow hard work and talent and to have little or nothing to do with the lottery of birth. The reference point for everyone has moved up to Steve Jobs. Like the other two basic goods, self-respect has come to acquire a relative dimension. Circumstances and luck are believed to be less responsible for our failures than they used to be. The achievement of others is the parameter by which we have all come to evaluate our lives, and therefore determine how much we respect ourselves.[52]

[49] Stephen Darwall, 'Two Kinds of Respect' (1977) 88 Ethics 36; Joseph Raz, *Value, Respect, and Attachment* (Cambridge University Press 2001); Robin Dillon, 'Respect' Stanford Encyclopaedia of Philosophy <http://plato.stanford.edu/entries/respect> accessed 27 October 2014.

[50] John Rawls, *A Theory of Justice* (Oxford University Press 1999) 440.

[51] Stephen Massey, 'Is Self-Respect a Moral or a Psychological Concept' (1983) 93 Ethics 246. Massey objects to Rawls's claim that self-respect is a *primary* social good, but does not deny my modest proposal that self-respect is *a* social good.

[52] Notice also the tension Bernard Williams identified between equal respect and equality of opportunity at the end of his seminal article on equality: Bernard Williams, 'The Idea of Equality' in Peter Laslett and Walter Runciman (eds), *Philosophy, Politics and Society* (Second Series edn, Blackwell 1962) 130.

Self-respect is a prized good—even persons who claim not to be inter-ested in accessing valuable opportunities tend to desire self-respect. This near-universal craving is an important motivator of our actions. Moreover, the respect that others show to us determines, to some degree, whether and to what extent we respect ourselves. When we enjoy an appropriate level of self-respect, the motivational pull of the desire to have it is modest—we can go about our daily lives content in our comparative worth. Occasional displays of disrespect by others harmlessly bounce off our robust armour of self-belief.

However, when we lack self-respect, the desire to possess it becomes intense, even neurotic. All our actions become geared towards acquiring it. Tormented by the knowledge that we are not worthy of respect, we make efforts to gain the acknowledgment of others and detest slights and trivial occurrences. Respect is a capricious item—the more obviously and consciously we seek it, the less likely we are to get it. As we try harder, demanding what we are due, our esteem in the eyes of others drops further. Thus, a lack of self-respect can easily trigger a vicious cycle, making our lives steadily worse.[53]

We could, of course, also have too much self-respect, when it is more appropriately described as pride or vanity. We should not, therefore, encour-age a culture where no one is ever offended and where trifles become causes of conflict.[54] Like Plato's tamed beast, being always protected from disrespect can make us vain and pathetic.[55] A hyper-sensitive citizenry is inimical to the cherished liberal goal of a tolerant society.[56] Therefore, we need to have an appropriate level of self-respect—neither too much, nor too little.

It was suggested above that respect by others and self-respect are con-nected. But one may ask how this can be if self-respect is a quality internal to a person. It is true that others cannot give it to you if you refuse to have it, and others cannot take it away if you decide resolutely to keep it. Slights do not necessarily injure self-respect, and respect from others does not necessar-ily engender it. Yet, it is hard to deny that one is much more likely to respect oneself if one is treated with respect (or without disrespect) by most persons most of the time. Self-respect is usually enhanced by the secure knowledge

[53] See Rousseau's distinction between *amour-propre* (comparative self-love, one that depends on the opinion of others—translated in the following reference as 'selfishness') and *amour de soi* (the instinc-tive drive towards self-preservation, translated simply as 'self-love'): Jean-Jacques Rousseau, *A Discourse upon the Origin and Foundation of the Inequality among Mankind* (R & J Dodsley 1761) 250, n 15.

[54] Leslie Green, 'Two Worries about Respect for Persons' (2010) 120 Ethics 212; Christopher McCrudden, 'Dignity and the Challenge to Liberty: Reading Andras Sajo's Constitutional Sentiments' in Renata Uitz (ed), *Freedom and its Enemies: The Tragedy of Liberty* (Eleven International 2015).

[55] Plato, *Republic* (Robin Waterfield tr, Oxford University Press 1994) 493a–e.

[56] Pratap Mehta, *The Burden of Democracy* (Penguin 2003) 38f: Mehta diagnoses the pathology of Indian politics as rooted in its overemphasis on the politics of recognition and respect.

that others adopt a considerate attitude towards us, and diminished by the suspicion that we are objects of indifference, disrespect, or condemnation. It is a feature of social beings that our sense of self is sensitive to the judgement of others we live with. In fact, we care not only about how others treat us but also, how they treat us in comparison with their treatment of others—self-respect is doubly relational.

In particular, self-respect is sensitive to three aspects of respect from others. First, disrespect by certain types of persons has a more severe impact on self-respect. These persons include those who matter most to the person concerned personally (her friends, family, and colleagues), and persons who represent her community (officials of the state, religious, and social leaders). Historically, respect from one's religious community was critical. In modern democratic societies, respect or condemnation by the state usually matters more, given its expressive salience in determining who is worthy of respect and who of condemnation.[57] Second, the pervasiveness of disrespect against a person matters to her self-respect. It is easier to shrug off an isolated disrespectful act, but it is much more difficult to do so if one is subjected to disrespect frequently and by a large number of people. Finally, the ostensible ground on which the disrespect of others is based matters. The more strongly one identifies with this ground, the more severe is the impact on one's self-respect. However, if the identification with the ostensible ground of disrespect is felt strongly enough by a critical mass of persons, it could also engender a counter-culture of strong self-respect within the disrespected sub-group. A good example is the emergence of a proud gay sub-culture in certain industrial societies in the late twentieth century.

It is for all of these reasons that it matters what others think of us and why. To promote the basic good of self-respect, therefore, we need to eradicate widespread, systemic, and significantly disrespectful attitudes when they are (morally speaking) misdirected, ie when they are directed against objects that are in fact valuable. A twenty-first-century state has remarkable discourse-influencing expressive powers, and what it says or fails to say matters a great deal. It is essential that this expressive power of the state is never employed to damage our legitimate interests in our self-respect, but only to protect them. That said, there are three important reasons why the expressive power of the state must be deployed with great care. First, given the strong liberal interest in protecting freedom of expression, the extent to which the

---

[57] Tarunabh Khaitan, 'Dignity as an Expressive Norm: Neither Vacuous Nor a Panacea' (2012) 32 Oxford Journal of Legal Studies 1.

state ought to be able to regulate disrespect shown by others is limited. Very often, the best response to bigotry and prejudice by non-state bodies is condemnation (rather than prohibition) of the expression of such bigotry by high-ranking officials of a democratic state. Second, the law of unforeseen consequences applies very strongly to expressive politics. The best of intentions can have very bad consequences. The state must tread very carefully and remain vigilant lest its expressive interventions backfire. Finally, the state must recognize that even its considerable discourse-influencing powers cannot make us respect ourselves. At best it can ensure that societal conditions are such that we are capable of having self-respect. Much caution and humility are required before this treacherous tool is deployed.

4.5 Interconnections between the Three Goods

The three goods are deeply interconnected. A person lacking secured access to any one of them will probably lack access to (or be in danger of losing access to) at least one of the two remaining goods as well. A person who lacks secured negative freedom is likely to be in a relationship of dominance or is unjustifiably interfered with frequently. This compromises one's ability to pursue valuable opportunities, and therefore to lead a successful life. Unjustified interference with one's person or projects is, in addition, usually disrespectful—this can injure a person's self-respect.[58] Being in a relationship of dominance may be compatible with the pursuit of valuable opportunities (if one has a benign master), but it is difficult to possess self-respect while being pervasively controlled by another. When two parties are bound by a relationship of dominance, they are likely to be aware of such a relationship and of the relative position they hold: the dominant party will be conscious of his power, the dominated party will be conscious of his weakness, and both will be conscious of the other's awareness. This will shape the image that the two parties have of themselves and the status that they enjoy in the social setting. A master will not simply enjoy the power of being able to arbitrarily interfere: he will also see himself as superior and will be recognized as such. Conversely, the slave does not only suffer the evil of being vulnerable to the possibility of arbitrary interference: he will also see himself as an inferior and will be perceived as such. Assuming that

---

[58] Jean-Jacques Rousseau, *A Discourse upon the Origin and Foundation of the Inequality among Mankind* (R & J Dodsley 1761) 114–15: 'every voluntary injury became an affront, as besides the mischief, which resulted from it as an injury, the party offended was sure to find in it a contempt for his person more intolerable than the mischief itself'.

enslavement (at least when it is not part of a role-play) is without value, even a proud slave will nonetheless lack self-respect in the objective sense.

Similarly, a person who does not have secured access to an adequate range of valuable opportunities is likely to lead an unsuccessful life, and therefore lack evaluative self-respect. Moreover, if one has very few opportunities, one is likely to be less secure about retaining the few opportunities one does have access to. Finally, if one lacks self-respect, one is unlikely to pursue available valuable opportunities in a way that contributes to a successful life. What emerges then is a complicated web of interrelated basic goods, all of which are necessary in order for a person to lead a flourishing life. It is in every person's paramount interest to have secured and adequate access to each of these basic goods, an interest that justifies our calling them 'basic' goods.

4.6 Comparative but Not Egalitarian

This book supports the growing philosophical opinion that it is freedom rather than equality which provides a better foundation for discrimination law.[59] What these other accounts lack (or, at least, fail to make sufficiently explicit) is the insight that the freedom we are entitled to also depends on the freedom that others enjoy. In other words, our liberty-interest is relative, because the three of the four basic goods that constitute this interest have an essential connection with what others enjoy. Secured negative freedom cannot be enjoyed if there are particularly striking power imbalances between different societal groups. The range of opportunities that is adequate for us to have a flourishing life depends on the range of opportunities it is possible to have, which in turn depends on how much access the better-off people have. Even our self-respect has a relative dimension, inasmuch as it depends on how much respect others show to us, and how successful we believe our lives to be in relation to the success of the lives of others.

Furthermore, the state's duty to secure sufficient liberty to all of us has an inbuilt priority for those who are least free. Thus, this account of freedom is comparative in two significant respects—it aspires to guarantee basic goods which are relative in character, and for those who lack these goods the worst

---

[59] See John Gardner, 'On the Ground of Her Sex(uality)' (1998) 18 Oxford Journal of Legal Studies 167; Hugh Collins, 'Discrimination, Equality and Social Inclusion' (2003) 66 The Modern Law Review 16; Sophia Moreau, 'What is Discrimination?' (2010) 38 Philosophy and Public Affairs 143. Collins combines the fraternal ideal of solidarity with a liberal one (autonomy) to justify discrimination law. Gardner and Moreau use 'personal autonomy' and 'deliberative freedom', respectively.

off have a prior claim to have their access enhanced. Although comparative, this account is decidedly not egalitarian, except perhaps in the weak or general sense that the well-being of *all* persons is morally desirable.[60] The proposed account is non-egalitarian when equality is understood in a strict sense, ie as valuable for its own sake. The theoretical case against the intrinsic value of equality has been ably made by several writers.[61] The liberal-perfectionist theoretical foundation proposed here is more attractive normatively and does a better job of explaining the practice of discrimination law. I will leave the referenced works to defend the claim that strict egalitarianism isn't attractive morally. The second claim that a freedom-based account better explains the practice of discrimination law will be defended in Chapter 5.

If these claims are true, it may seem surprising that lawyers, judges, legislators, and even some theorists continue to use the terms 'equality' and 'anti-discrimination' interchangeably. Constitutional guarantees of equality are often read as guarantees of non-discrimination. Even in common language, one thinks of discrimination *between* A and B more readily than simply discrimination *against* A. Philosophers rooting for a freedom-based account have a tough task at hand.

Besides the obvious suggestion that the validity of a claim has little to do with the numbers who believe in it, several other things may be noted. First, at least at this stage, we are only concerned with the overall purpose of discrimination law and not with how duties of antidiscrimination are distributed. It is perfectly possible to attribute a non-egalitarian purpose to the overall practice, which is pursued through an egalitarian duty in particular cases (say, the duty of equal treatment). This is not the claim that I am going to make, but it is at least coherent.

Second, we have now understood that even a freedom-based account must be comparative in certain respects. It may be that at least some egalitarians are primarily concerned with the relativity of any sufficiency threshold and with the priority of the claims of the worse-off. If that is the case, then they are not the strict egalitarians with whom I am disagreeing, and the debate is just a semantic one.[62]

---

[60] The characterization of this weak claim as 'egalitarian' is controversial. Raz suggests that principles of universal entitlements are egalitarian only in a trivial sense. Joseph Raz, *The Morality of Freedom* (Clarendon Press 1986) 221ff.

[61] Peter Westen, 'The Empty Idea of Equality' (1982) 95 Harvard Law Review 537; Joseph Raz, *The Morality of Freedom* (Clarendon Press 1986) ch 9; Harry Frankfurt, 'Equality as a Moral Ideal' (1987) 98 Ethics 21; Derek Parfit, 'Equality and Priority' (1997) 10 Ratio 202.

[62] For a conception of the right to equality which isn't strictly egalitarian, see Sandra Fredman, 'Substantive Equality Revisited' (forthcoming 2015) International Journal of Constitutional Law.

Third, any measure that successfully pursues the three basic goods this chapter has identified will normally make a society less unequal. The account is non-egalitarian, not necessarily anti-egalitarian. All it discounts is the claim that strict equality is intrinsically desirable. The flip-side of this is that efforts designed to eliminate inequality also often lead to the achievement of non-egalitarian goals, such as the three basic goods we have discussed here. Frankfurt is therefore right in suggesting that even non-egalitarian liberals could (and should) support equality-seeking political projects because of their beneficial side-effects.[63] Just as philosophical anarchism does not necessarily justify political anarchism,[64] philosophical equality-scepticism does not legitimate anti-egalitarian politics.

The language and rhetoric of equality has played an important historical role in facilitating the political acceptance of discrimination law. The basic-goods account presented in this chapter could co-exist with a continued rhetorical role for equality in the political and legal discourse, especially if it is acknowledged that the egalitarian impulse is driven primarily by the need to accommodate the relative nature of freedom.[65] Intellectual hygiene is a pre-occupation of theorists; the primary duty of problem-solving practitioners is to achieve the right outcome, even if they get there by traversing a conceptually meandering route.

4.7 Conclusion

This chapter has explained that in order to live a good life, we need secured access to at least four basic goods: (a) a set of goods which will adequately satisfy one's biological needs; (b) negative freedom, ie freedom from unjustified interference by others in one's person, projects, possessions, relationships, and affairs; (c) an adequate range of valuable opportunities to choose from; and (d) an appropriate level of self-respect. Sufficient and secured access to these goods make a person free and enable her to seek a good life. We have had a deeper look at the last three of these goods, since they are particularly relevant to the discussion in the next chapter. We have learnt that although these goods are freedom-enhancing, how much of each we are entitled to is a relative and contextual judgment rather than an absolute and insular one.

---

[63] Harry Frankfurt, 'Equality and Respect' (1997) 64 Social Research 3, 3.

[64] Robert Wolff, *In Defense of Anarchism* (Harper & Row 1970).

[65] See Frank Michelman, 'Foreword: On Protecting the Poor Through the Fourteenth Amendment' (1969) 83 Harvard Law Review 7.

How much freedom I am morally entitled to depends on how much freedom it is possible to have in my context, which in turn depends on how much freedom the most free enjoy. We have also seen that any efforts to facilitate or improve access to these goods must give priority to the least free. Thus, this account of freedom is comparative, even though it is not egalitarian.

The stage is now set for the next step in our inquiry. In the next chapter, we will see how the general purpose of the practice of discrimination law is to enhance and protect the access of some of the least well-off to these three basic goods. As this freedom-seeking account seeks only to explain the *general purpose* of discrimination law, how the rights and duties in discrimination law come to be distributed in specific cases will be a concern of later chapters.

5

The Point of Discrimination Law

Before we proceed, a recap of where we have reached in our inquiry will be helpful. We started our journey by appreciating that a lot of theoretical confusion regarding discrimination law stems from an inability to distinguish between at least three different theoretical queries: the definitional question which seeks to understand what discrimination law is by identifying its theoretically salient features, the purposive question which tries to understand what discrimination law seeks to do and whether this is justified, and the distributive question which concerns the scope and distribution of the rights and duties under the law. Chapters 2 and 3 dealt with the definitional question. Chapter 4 laid down a general freedom-based framework which will now be relied upon to answer the purposive question. The stage is set for us to inquire into the point of the practice of discrimination law: what is the general justifying aim of this area of law? We will consider what discrimination law seeks to do, and whether what it seeks to do is justified.[1] The subsequent chapters will continue the inquiry by examining the distributive questions. My claim in this chapter is that the point of discrimination law is to secure access to the three basic goods discussed in Chapter 4, when such access is impeded by a person's membership of a relatively disadvantaged group (hereinafter, I will use the term 'basic goods' to exclude a reference to the first basic good concerning biological needs, unless the context implies its inclusion).

5.1 The Goal of Discrimination Law

We will begin with the functional inquiry before embarking on a full-fledged justificatory enterprise in section 5.2. The question at hand is:

---

[1] Notice that the question is framed not as what discrimination law actually *does*, but what it seeks to do. Even the best laid plans go awry. One cannot discover what discrimination law actually does from general conceptual analysis—that would require contextualized empirical investigation.

what is it that discrimination law seeks to do? It is a question that a legislator asks herself before designing any legislation: what is the mischief that the law should seek to correct? It is also a question that a judge, when interpreting or making new law in the course of adjudication, may need to furnish some answer for. But it is, essentially, a legislative rather than an adjudicative question. It does not concern, at least not at any level of detail, the specific rights or obligations of particular persons involved in a given dispute. One may think that simply framing the question as a functional one is question-begging, inasmuch as it might be taken to have assumed that every area of law has some teleological function.[2] This is not so. One could ask this question, at least in a thin sense, for all areas of law. Criminal law punishes persons for certain types of conduct. Contract law enforces certain types of agreement. Tort law compensates for certain types of injuries. It is only in this thin sense that I ask the functional question with respect to discrimination law: what does it do? It should be obvious that our responses turn on the most salient features of a given area of law. These features may relate to the law's subject matter, its mode of operation, or the remedies it provides. Perhaps unlike these other areas of law, it is not immediately obvious what the function of discrimination law is. This difficulty clearly relates to the diversity of tools that this area of law uses, the numerous contexts in which it applies, and the various enforcement mechanisms that are used to effect its implementation. So, in order to discover what it is that discrimination law seeks to do, we need to turn to its essence: the four conditions unearthed in Chapter 2 that all anti-discrimination norms must satisfy. Recall that these were the following:

The Personal Grounds Condition: *The duty-imposing norm in question must require some connection between the act or omission prohibited or mandated by the norm on the one hand and certain attributes or characteristics that persons have, called 'grounds', on the other.*

The Cognate Groups Condition: *A protected ground must be capable of classifying persons into more than one class of persons, loosely called 'groups'.*

The Relative Disadvantage Condition: *Of all groups defined by a given universal order ground, members of at least one group must be significantly more likely to suffer abiding, pervasive, and substantial disadvantage than the members of at least one other cognate group.*

The Eccentric Distribution Condition: *The duty-imposing norm must be designed such that it is likely to distribute the non-remote tangible benefits*

---

[2] See John Gardner, 'What is Tort Law For? Part 1: The Place of Corrective Justice' (2011) 30 Law and Philosophy 1–2.

in question to some, but not all, members of the intended beneficiary group.

These conditions, I argued in Chapter 2, constitute the essence of the practice of discrimination law. They suggest that there are four key concepts that give antidiscrimination norms their character: personal grounds, cognate groups, relative disadvantage, and eccentric distribution of benefits. Discerning the functional objectives of discrimination law from these conditions will be more controversial. But judgments have to be made.

Before we pursue what we can discern from these conditions regarding the functions that discrimination law seeks to perform, we ought also to remind ourselves of the definitions of certain terms I am about to reuse. *Protected grounds* are personal characteristics that satisfy the first three conditions above. They are characteristics with which norms of discrimination law require the acts they regulate to have some connection, and which divide persons into groups such that at least one of those groups is relatively disadvantaged. *Protected groups* are those groups whose members are significantly more likely to suffer abiding, pervasive, and substantial disadvantage than the members of at least one other cognate group. Women, for example, are a protected group. *Cognate groups* are the relatively privileged groups that share a protected ground with protected groups. So, men are cognates of women, because they share the ground 'sex'. It is also worth recalling that when we speak of 'disadvantage' here, we are referring to systemic disadvantage suffered by protected groups, removal of which (I will argue) is the purpose of discrimination law. It does not refer to the injury or harm that may be caused by particular acts or omissions, which we may characterize as 'discriminatory'. To put it differently, past acts of discrimination need not be the reason why a relatively disadvantaged group is protected.

Let us now return to the functional question at hand: what is it that discrimination law does? It should not be controversial that discrimination law is protective in nature—all its duties seek to protect or benefit certain persons under specified circumstances (for brevity, I will use the term 'protection' to include 'benefit'). A superficially attractive, if tautological, claim that can be made is that:

Discrimination law seeks to protect persons from discrimination based on protected grounds. (P1)

P1 not only explains discrimination law in terms of discrimination, it is also too simplistic an account of what discrimination law does to aid understanding. First of all, it fails to account for the salience of groups in discrimination law. This salience is suggested not just by the cognate groups and relative disadvantage conditions, but also by the eccentric distribution condition: this curious non-universal distribution pattern makes sense only if one can see that the intended beneficiaries are groups rather than individuals. This is, of course, entirely compatible with a claim that the primary objects of moral concern are individual persons, not groups: one can be concerned about group disadvantage mainly (even solely) because of the impact it has on individuals.

Second, we also know from Chapter 3 that discrimination law does more than prohibit discrimination *based on* protected grounds. P1 readily captures only the prohibitions on direct discrimination and harassment. Some linguistic juggling is required to show that indirect discrimination is *based on* a protected ground, whereas affirmative action can only be understood as compensating for past acts of discrimination under this formula. We should therefore refine our claim thus:

Discrimination law seeks to benefit some members of protected and cognate groups. (P2)

P2, no doubt controversially, recognizes the centrality of groups in discrimination law (and also, indirectly, of grounds—which are essential to the definition of cognate groups). The clarification that only *some* members benefit accommodates the Eccentric Distribution Condition. It still does not go far enough. We know from Chapter 3 that relative group disadvantage is not simply a qualifying hurdle that a personal ground needs to jump over in order to be protected (as required in the relative disadvantage condition). Even after a ground becomes eligible for protection, we learnt that the protection of discrimination law is largely (or, sometimes, completely) asymmetric—members of the relatively disadvantaged groups tend to receive exclusive or stronger protection (recall that we settled for the somewhat misleading label '*protected* groups' for this reason). In other words, it is not simply the case that 'sex' is a protected ground only because there is a substantial and abiding advantage gap between men and women. It is also the case that discrimination law tends to benefit women more than men. This is not simply because women are more likely to bring a successful case of discrimination in practice, but also because legal doctrine itself tends to permit affirmative action to favour women but not men. If sex was like eye-colour, men would get as much benefit from discrimination law as blue-eyed people: which is none at all. It is hard to escape the conclusion that the ultimate purpose of discrimination law is to make sex as (in)significant as eye-colour. Of the conditions that relate to grounds (ie the first three conditions), only the relative disadvantage condition differentiates sex and eye-colour. For the purposes of discrimination law, sex will become as (in)significant as eye-colour only when women are no longer significantly more likely to suffer abiding, pervasive, and substantial disadvantage than men. Thus:

Discrimination law seeks to reduce (and ultimately remove) any significant advantage gap between a protected group and its cognate groups. (P3)

With the caveat that 'significant' here elliptically refers to 'substantial, abiding, and pervasive' advantage gaps, we now have a reasonably accurate statement of what it is that discrimination law does. This is the big-picture, systemic, concern of discrimination law. There may be considerable opacity between precise rules of antidiscrimination and this overall purpose. But the practice of discrimination law, *on the whole*, is geared towards achieving this goal. We must now turn our attention to whether this goal is morally justified.

5.2 Justification of the Goal

Given that discrimination law seeks to reduce (and ultimately remove) any significant advantage gap between a protected group and its cognate groups, we now need to know whether this is something worth pursuing. Broadly, the question we need to confront is whether reducing substantial, abiding, and pervasive disadvantage suffered by a group in comparison with other cognate groups (hereinafter, 'relative group disadvantage') is of moral concern. As a preliminary objection, one may ask why we ought to be concerned with relative group disadvantage only between groups defined by the same ground. It is possible that groups that are not so defined can also have a significant advantage gap between them. All that is logically required is that the membership of the two groups is (more or less) mutually exclusive (eg whites and Muslims in the United Kingdom—respectively defined by race and religion). If they are not mutually exclusive, we cannot sensibly talk of relative disadvantage between groups. By definition, these groups will (more or less) be mutually exclusive only if most whites in the United Kingdom are not Muslims, and vice versa. Thus, the two groups can be understood to be based on the same ground (whites and Muslim non-whites based on race, or Muslims and white non-Muslims based on religion). Remember that we are using the term 'group' loosely—it is not necessary that the members of the group attach any salience to their affiliation.[3] The fact that there is some overlap between these groups should not bother anyone. People can and do belong to multiple groups— a person with a Jewish mother and a Sikh father may well consider herself

---

[3] However, as we will see shortly, salience of group membership may indeed be relevant to a person's ability to have self-respect. All I am suggesting here is that it is not *necessary*.

Jewish as well as Sikh.[4] All that is required for relative group disadvantage is that the membership of the two groups is *more or less* mutually exclusive. Whenever this is the case, groups are likely to be cognates of each other. The preliminary objection must therefore be rejected. Our focus on relative disadvantage between only protected groups and their cognates is justified.

I will now show that relative group disadvantage is indeed of moral concern. This is because relative group disadvantage disrupts secured access to the basic goods and therefore adversely affects the ability of the members of the disadvantaged group to be free. Members of protected groups do not have secured or adequate access to these goods. This tends to be true of all members of such groups, even those who may seem to be materially well off. Since every person has an interest in her own well-being, members of protected groups have an interest in changing this state of affairs so that they come to have secured access to these basic goods. Moreover, given the fundamental importance of these goods to human flourishing, this interest is particularly weighty. If human freedom is of moral concern, as I will assume it is, protecting the liberty-interest of members of relatively disadvantaged groups is also a legitimate—nay pressing—moral concern.

Let us remind ourselves of the basic goods we are concerned with: secured access to negative freedom, an adequate range of valuable opportunities, and self-respect. Recall the emphasis on *security* of access—it is not enough to have access to the goods here and now. One must also be free from reasonable fear of losing this access. Recall also that we need to have as much negative freedom—ie freedom from unjustified interference—as is possible; but we only need to have optimal (as opposed to maximal or equal) access to a range of valuable opportunities and adequate self-respect in order to lead a good life. With these memory jogs, we can now consider how relative group disadvantage disrupts a person's secured access to each of these goods.

Members of protected groups are, by definition, significantly more likely to suffer abiding, pervasive, and substantial disadvantage compared to members of their cognate groups. Recall that we have understood disadvantage holistically, to include political, socio-cultural, and material disadvantage. Protected groups tend to be disadvantaged in at least two of these three facets. Religious and sexual minorities, for example, tend to be disadvantaged at least politically and socio-culturally. Even if the group as a whole is not materially disadvantaged, its poorer members tend to suffer material disadvantage acutely. Women face greater socio-cultural and material disadvantage

---

[4] On intersectionality generally, see Kimberlé Crenshaw, 'Demarginalising the Intersection of Race and Sex: A Black Feminist Critique of Antidiscrimination Doctrine, Feminist Theory and Antiracist Politics' [1989] The University of Chicago Legal Forum 139.

(and, despite the size of their electorate, even political disadvantage). *Dalits*, Roma, and disabled persons are disadvantaged materially, politically, and socio-culturally.

A multifaceted understanding of disadvantage can relatively easily be restated in terms of a lack of access to basic goods. Socio-cultural and material disadvantage includes being the object of hostility and violence, which results in a breach of negative freedom. All tangible forms of disadvantage can be reframed as a lack of access to valuable opportunities. And socio-cultural disadvantage has crucial links with the ability to have self-respect. These connections between the basic goods and various forms of disadvantage are obvious when we think of disadvantage in an *absolute* and *individual* sense—ie the disadvantage of an individual judged against some non-relative standard of the sort of advantage she ought to have. Our predicament is to see if there are any links between *relative group* disadvantage and the basic goods. To this task I shall now turn my attention.

5.2.1 Negative Freedom

Let us first consider the impact that relative group disadvantage has on one's negative freedom. Power is a function of what you are able to will and achieve; interference is the subjection of the will of another to your own will. Relative group disadvantage makes interference with members of one group by those of another easier—the greater the advantage gap between the groups, the more power the dominant group has over the disadvantaged one. This is because power, in the sense that is relevant to negative freedom, is a relative concept—you have power *over* or *against* someone else. In this sense, it is different from a mere ability to do something. It is easier for the more powerful group to interfere with and even dominate the less powerful. Given how power operates in human societies, it is reasonable to think that a relatively disadvantaged group will remain in danger of being dominated by the more powerful group, in the sense that the will of its members will frequently be subjected to the will of the members of the powerful group. Often, such subjection will be unjustifiable, resulting in the loss of negative freedom. This is particularly likely to be the case when a group suffers socio-cultural disadvantage, in the form of widespread hostility and prejudice. This hostility will often translate into indirect interference (through acts of exclusion or boycott) and sometimes direct interference (crimes, torts). Material and political disadvantage will underline its inability to defend itself against interference and domination. Political indifference could also lead to poor security and policing services in minority neighbourhoods, and therefore to a situation where members of weaker groups are more likely to be victims even of crimes not perpetrated by members of dominant groups.

The supposition that relative group disadvantage is likely to lead to domination of weaker groups, of course, needs corroboration with actual evidence to show that its members are indeed disproportionately more likely to be victims of criminal, tortious, and discriminatory acts. All such acts, when unjustified, result in an unacceptable loss of one's negative freedom. Although my project is theoretical rather than empirical, there appears to be significant evidence from diverse contexts that women, religious minorities, racial minorities, gays and lesbians, transpersons, and disabled persons are indeed disproportionately more likely to have their negative freedom interfered with than members of cognate groups.[5]

It may be that this claim is not always true for all groups in all societies. Even when it is true, not every member of the protected group will necessarily have her negative freedom interfered with. Even so, the power imbalance between groups that necessarily results from relative group disadvantage will make the enjoyment of negative freedom by all members of the weaker groups insecure. The existence of relative group disadvantage generates a pull towards domination. The extent to which a society can resist actual domination while groups continue to have significant advantage gaps between them is fortuitous and inherently unstable. If anything, power is self-sustaining and self-entrenching. For members of disadvantage groups to enjoy secure negative freedom, there is no alternative but to break the nexus between group membership and disadvantage. It is quite right, therefore, for discrimination law to seek to protect relatively disadvantaged groups.

5.2.2 Adequate Range of Valuable Opportunities

Like the absence of secured negative freedom, lacking secured access to an adequate range of valuable opportunities constitutes disadvantage. But we now know that the focus of discrimination law is not to deal with absolute disadvantage faced by individuals. That is a function of welfare law or socio-economic rights. The main purpose of discrimination law is to ameliorate and eradicate any significant relative group disadvantage. How does this impact a person's access to an adequate range of valuable opportunities?

At this stage, we need to recall from Chapter 4 that the adequacy threshold that every individual needs to access in order to live a good life is not fixed, but changes across time and space. In particular, it is pegged to the type of

---

[5] See, for example, Sylvia Walby, Jo Armstrong, and Les Humphreys, *Review of Equality Statistics (UK Equality and Human Rights Commission)* (2008) 65, 84, 88–9; US Census Bureau, *Statistical Abstract of the United States* (2011) 200.

life opportunities it is possible for one to have. This in turn is determined by the life-style of the members of the dominant group and the opportunities they enjoy. This insight had revealed to us that relative disadvantage and absolute disadvantage are not divided by a bright line. Significant relative disadvantage is very likely to translate into absolute disadvantage too. It follows, then, that many members of a protected group are likely to lack access to an adequate range of valuable opportunities.

But the variability of the adequacy threshold only explains why we should care about *relative* disadvantage. It does not, in itself, justify our concern with *group* disadvantage. It probably is the case that many members of relatively disadvantaged groups also suffer absolute disadvantage in the sense of lacking access to an adequate range of valuable options. We still do not know if *most* members lack such access. Again, this is an empirical judgment beyond the scope of this book. But the notion of security once again helps us properly appreciate what it is like to belong to such a group. Recall that one's access to an adequate range of valuable opportunities must be secure. Even when they have adequate access at any given point in time, most, if not all, members of protected groups are unlikely to have confidence in the sustainability and security of such access.

This is the case for several reasons. Although we saw that discrimination law does not insist on proof of any particular cause, human agency is often responsible for relative group disadvantage. Given the serious and high-threshold terms in which we have defined it, it is unlikely to be caused by random factors, although it is possible that some non-human factors may bring it about in exceptional cases. The most obvious of these human factors is the frequent interference with the negative liberty of members of weaker groups. When criminal, tortious, or discriminatory acts against members of a group become endemic, it is not surprising that the access of its members to an adequate range of valuable opportunities is also progressively compromised. We know that the basic goods are interlinked, and denial of any one has implications for access to others. Infrequent violations of one's negative liberty can have devastating effects on one's own life. But when frequent violations are visited upon many members of a group who are relatively powerless to defend themselves, disadvantage acquires a group dimension. When these interferences relate to key opportunities such as one's education, employment, domicile, relationships, and personal safety, they have a ripple effect on all other opportunities one is able to access. Furthermore, if the group suffers relative political disadvantage too, it will find it hard to use the political muscle of the state to provide opportunities to its members. So, even if a rich black man living in the United States enjoys access to an adequate range of valuable opportunities, it may often be the case that he is not secure in his continued access to these opportunities.

Once disadvantage acquires a group dimension, it becomes self-perpetuating and intensifies over time. This is because members of the dominant group acquire an interest in maintaining the status quo which gives them access to greater power and opportunities. This very access also makes them more capable of maintaining this status quo. It is this inertia in favour of relative group disadvantage which makes the institution of discrimination law in most societies such a remarkable political feat—made achievable by a combination of its protection of a multiplicity of grounds which builds a broad coalition of many different vulnerable groups, its incremental and gradual approach to dealing with relative group disadvantage, and the extension of at least some of its protections to dominant groups as well so that everyone has some stake in its success.[6] Without external intervention, the strong connection between existing disadvantage and future disadvantage of a group will result in a vicious cycle of intensifying disadvantage over generations. It is no surprise that members of relatively disadvantaged groups lack secured access to an adequate range of valuable opportunities. For that very reason, discrimination law is justified in treating them as protected groups.

5.2.3 Self-Respect

Finally, relative group disadvantage also inhibits one's ability to have self-respect, if one is a member of a weak and vulnerable group. Of the basic goods we are concerned with, self-respect is the most starkly relative in character. One's ability to have self-respect is a function of the respect shown by others as well as one's standing in relation to others. Relative disadvantage, in particular relative socio-cultural disadvantage, can make it difficult for a person to keep her self-respect. This is so because socio-cultural disadvantage often manifests itself in either the dominant group's indifference towards the need to accommodate the cultural practices of the minority group in the mainstream public sphere, or, what is worse, in hostility, prejudice, and stereotyping of the members of the protected groups. This is especially the case when the group becomes more than a mere collection of individuals—with an understanding of its own existence as a group with a history, a rank, a culture, and a particular relationship with other groups based on the same ground. As Weber explained, 'The power of political structures has a specific internal dynamic. On the basis of this power, the members may pretend to a special "prestige", and their pretensions may influence the external conduct of the power structures.'[7] Relative group disadvantage, which is but a reflection of the enormous power of the dominant group, often results in

---

    [6] See Chapter 6, section 6.5.
    [7] Max Weber, *From Max Weber: Essays in Sociology* (HH Gerth and Wright Mills trs, Routledge & Kegan Paul Ltd 1970) 159.

the coming about of such group consciousness. When group identities get entangled with relative group disadvantage in this way, the socio-cultural disadvantage that the minority group suffers usually becomes acute.[8]

Normally, intense socio-cultural disadvantage makes it difficult for members of the group burdened by it to have self-respect. However, this very same disadvantage may also catalyse a sense of pride in the membership of the group, to counter the prejudicial claims of the dominant group about the worth of its members. The emergence of queer pride and *dalit* politics of recognition in the late twentieth century epitomize this phenomenon.[9] Even so, the continued struggle that many gay people and *dalits* continue to have with internalized homophobia and casteism shows that so long as deep-rooted socio-cultural disadvantages remain, one's ability to be secure in the knowledge that one's life is valuable and worthwhile remains compromised. Gay pride and ubiquitous public statues of Dr Ambedkar (the foremost author of India's Constitution and a *dalit*) may give a person self-respect, but only the eradication of widespread homophobia and casteism can make it secure.

It is true that, under certain circumstances, relative political and material disadvantage is compatible with self-respect. This is especially true in feudal societies, where it is easier to have self-respect and dignity in one's rank-determined low station in life. The near impossibility of social mobility brings with it the solace of the knowledge that one's life could not have been much better than it is. If success in one's life must be measured against what is possible, a person is more likely to retain self-respect if another life is beyond the pale of the possible. Not so in modern industrial democratic states, where the discourse of equality and spectacular, if rare, rags-to-riches narratives serve as constant reminders that any continuing political, socio-cultural, or material disadvantage—even if only relative—must be down to our own choices. The tragedy is that we have come to believe we are free to make of our lives what we will, when in fact our ability to do so remains seriously constrained. Under these circumstances, self-respect becomes a first casualty. The solution must lie in a more realistic assessment of the human condition (without, obviously, turning our back on the idea that all persons deserve recognition and respect simply because they are persons) and the fetters that continue to bind us, alongside attempts to break free of at least some of the most egregious

---

[8] Hellman presents a variation on this theme in terms of 'humiliation' and 'demeaning' treatment suffered by the victims of discrimination: Deborah Hellman, *When is Discrimination Wrong?* (Harvard University Press 2008).

[9] Robin Brontsema, 'A Queer Revolution: Reconceptualizing the Debate over Linguistic Reclamation' (2004) 17 Colorado Research in Linguistics 1; Sonia Sikka, 'Untouchable Cultures: Memory, Power and the Construction of *Dalit* Selfhood' (2012) 19 Identities: Global Studies in Culture and Power 43; Bhimrao Adbedkar, *Annihilation of Caste* (Verso 2014).

constraints. Abiding, pervasive, and substantial relative group disadvantage, which also turns out to be self-perpetuating and ever-intensifying, is one such constraint. In seeking to deal with relative group disadvantage, discrimination law contributes to our ability to have self-respect. In addition, and more directly, discrimination law itself has come to acquire particular expressive salience in our societies. The mere declaration by discrimination law that a relatively disadvantaged group will be treated as a protected group is itself of direct expressive significance for the ability of its members to have self-respect, quite apart from the impact its success may have in breaking the group membership and individual disadvantage nexus.[10] Thus, the need to facilitate our having self-respect also justifies the law's protection of these groups.

5.2.4 Discrimination Law and the Basic Goods

Although relative group disadvantage has an impact on each of the basic goods, given their interrelationship, even an impact on only one of them will affect others. Imagine that a group only faced relative socio-cultural disadvantage and consequently its members struggled to maintain their self-respect. Assume further that they were frequently discriminated against and harassed by the dominant group. As social power translates into economic and political power, it is likely that these vulnerabilities will, over time, impede their access to valuable opportunities. It is the nature of these basic goods that we can securely enjoy any of them only if we have secure access to all of them. In this respect, they are somewhat different from the first basic good—if we do not have secure means to satisfy our basic biological needs, no doubt we will also fail to access the other goods. But the reverse is not true. It is possible for us to have our bodily needs of food, clothing, shelter, and such like fulfilled while the remaining three goods continue to elude. It is no surprise then that different tools (welfare guarantees and socio-economic rights) are needed to provide access to the first basic good.[11]

At any rate, we should now be able to see the connection between relative group disadvantage and certain forms of denial of access to the basic goods. There is one other aspect of this connection which requires some elaboration. Relative group disadvantage affects all members of protected groups, but it does so in varying degrees. Those who are most disadvantaged also tend to

---

[10] Samuel Bagenstos, ' "Rational Discrimination", Accommodation, and the Politics of (Disability) Civil Rights' (2003) 89 Virginia Law Review 825, 844: Discrimination law 'serves an important expressive purpose by offering to previously excluded groups a tangible invitation of admission as full members of society'.

[11] It is true, of course, that not all socio-economic rights relate to the first basic good. The right to education, for example, primarily enhances our access to a range of valuable opportunities.

be most vulnerable to the exercise of social, political, and economic power by the dominant groups. A rich white woman in the United Kingdom, although vulnerable, is likely to be less so than a rich black woman. Both of them are likely to be less vulnerable than a poor black woman, and so on. Given the eccentric distribution condition, discrimination law allocates benefits to members of protected groups without specific reference to their individual level of disadvantage. No obvious prioritarian instinct of benefiting the worst off first can be discerned in the actual distributive pattern of its benefits.

However, at the general level, we can show that discrimination law is compatible with prioritarian impulses. Breaking the group membership and individual disadvantage nexus is likely to benefit the worst off the most (simply because they suffer the most). It so happens that dealing with relative group disadvantage does not easily lend itself to a regime which self-consciously eradicates its effects on those worst affected first. When the nexus is broken, it will be broken for everyone—it simply cannot be broken for some and yet survive for other members of the group. A temporal priority is difficult to build into the overall purpose of discrimination law, although its overall purpose is sensitive to the greater need of the worst off within a protected group.

I do not intend to suggest that nothing more can be done or ought to be done to make discrimination law more prioritarian. Continuing debates on intersectional and multiple-group discrimination or on how affirmative action policies should be framed tell us that there is indeed scope for improvement. However, these reforms are primarily addressed to the distributive worries in discrimination law. We can surmise that discrimination law seeks to reduce and remove relative group disadvantage, which denies to individuals optimal access to the basic goods, and that this denial is the most acute for those who are most disadvantaged.

Since these goods are basic (ie fundamental to human flourishing) reducing and eliminating significant relative group disadvantage is of pressing moral concern. P3 stands vindicated. It should also be clear by now that our concern with relative group disadvantage is based on a concern for individuals. Groups are salient to discrimination law because group membership has a significant impact on the life-chances of a person. On this understanding, it will be a mistake to romanticize groups for their own sake, especially given their capacity to oppress their own members. Group membership is valuable only when, and to the extent that, it adds value to a person's life.[12]

---

[12] We have largely focussed on congruence between the interests of the group as a whole and its individual members. When individual and group interests are in conflict, it may help to remember

5.3 Debate with Egalitarians

We have also seen that our concern for relative group disadvantage springs not from the ideal of equality but from the desirability of a state of affairs where each person is free to pursue a good life. What has been offered is a comparative account of discrimination law, but not an egalitarian one. A liberty-based approach, such as mine, was able to show that the concern with relative group disadvantage is ultimately down to a concern for individual well-being. Indeed, a strictly egalitarian account may struggle to explain discrimination law's obsession with relative group disadvantage. The reason for this should be obvious. Discrimination law is not going to make everyone equal, whatever the currency of equality. It is not even *designed* to make everyone equal. The eccentric distribution condition for antidiscrimination norms *requires* that the substantive benefits of discrimination law are distributed to some—*but not all*—members of protected groups. This condition embodies the focus of discrimination law, which remains firmly on breaking the nexus between individual disadvantage and group membership. It is true that if discrimination law succeeds, the society will become more equal. But that is a side-effect—a more equal society cannot be the general justifying aim of discrimination law. Anyone who sincerely wants to pursue *that* aim must come up with a very different regulatory system.[13]

The elimination of relative group disadvantage will result in a society where relative disadvantage continues to exist between individuals, it is just that it will no longer be tied to the membership of a group. Furthermore, we have been using 'relative group disadvantage' only as a shorthand for substantial, pervasive, and abiding advantage gaps between groups—discrimination law is not concerned about inequality between groups that does not meet this demanding threshold. If one is an egalitarian, it is unclear why one would be concerned only with *significant* relative disadvantage and only between *groups*. Why not remove all forms of relative disadvantage? Liberals and egalitarians (and liberal-egalitarians) can usually agree that some safety nets which secure

---

that groups are valuable for the sake of their members. See generally, Leslie Green, 'Rights of Exit' (1998) 4 Legal Theory 165.

[13] See, for a possible example, Thomas Pikkety, *The Capital in the Twenty-First Century* (Harvard University Press 2014) ch 4. Note that my challenge cannot be met by simply distinguishing between equality of *opportunity* and equality of *results*. We know that opportunities are nested in concatenated heirarchies, such that equal opportunity for a good (say, employment) boils down to little more than a demand for the equality of results in accessing a prior good (education). I, of course, have no substantive quarrel with theorists who call themselves egalitarians but are not, in fact, strict egalitarians.

minimum access to the basic goods are essential. But they diverge over whether the state should do more than that. I have relied on an account of perfectionist freedom to show that relative group disadvantage has implications for well-being in the absolute sense, and therefore should be of moral concern to liberals as well as egalitarians. The same is not true of mere relative individual disadvantage without a group dimension. There is no need for non-egalitarian liberals to be concerned with relative disadvantage between individuals for its own sake, so long as everyone has access to the four basic goods. They can, therefore, explain why it is that discrimination law is concerned with relative group disadvantage but not relative individual disadvantage (at least at the purposive level).

Egalitarians, however, cannot easily make a distinction between group inequality and individual inequality. They will either have to show that a concern with group inequality exhausts one's concern with inequality, or that, as inequalities go, group inequality is of particularly pressing concern. The first option is clearly not available—even after group inequality has been eradicated, individuals will continue to be unequal. The second option may momentarily look attractive. Have I not just argued that relative group disadvantage adversely affects a person's access to three of four basic goods (and, impliedly, that relative disadvantage between individuals, without this group dimension, does not)? Does this not make group inequality particularly pressing, and therefore legitimize a focus solely (or, at least primarily) on addressing this form of inequality? It does, but for liberal rather than egalitarian reasons. An egalitarian will have to establish the priority of group inequality on egalitarian grounds.

In fact, if I believed that equality was valuable for its own sake, then I would see attempts to characterize discrimination law as 'equality law' not just sophistic but also disingenuous.[14] Discrimination law would then be little more than lip-service to the ideal of equality. It would make an insincere promise of equality without the wherewithal or even the ambition of ever achieving—or coming close to achieving—equality. My objection boils down to this: if equality is not a valuable ideal, why pursue it even for groups? If it is a valuable ideal, why stop at inequality between groups, and only when this inequality is particularly grotesque?

A commitment to positive freedom will not be satisfied simply with the successful administration of discrimination law. It will also require that a state have a spate of other legal tools to protect and enhance basic liberty: especially criminal law, tort law, contract law, welfare law, and tax law. Couldn't an egalitarian also claim that discrimination law is only part of the full arsenal of laws required to achieve equality, and that additional laws and policies

---

[14] Alexander Somek, *Engineering Equality: An Essay on European Anti-Discrimination Law* (Oxford University Press 2011) 97–8.

targeting relative individual disadvantage could supplement discrimination law's focus on relative group disadvantage? After all, haven't I admitted that a successful operation of discrimination law will make society less unequal?

The problem with this argument is that it mistakes a side-effect for the primary goal, and ultimately devalues its own commitment to equality. I have shown that the general justifying goal of discrimination law is sufficientarian, and compatible with prioritarianism: it seeks to make sure that we have enough to make us free, and that those who are most unfree deserve special attention. Now, any successful programme whose goals are prioritarian and/or sufficientarian will, given the world we live in, inevitably result in a reduction of inequality. There may well be other laws and policies in a given jurisdiction whose goals are genuinely egalitarian. Discrimination law (and, many other laws whose primary goal is not the pursuit of equality) may well augment and supplement the pursuit of these equality-oriented laws and policies. But this synergy does not transform discrimination law into an egalitarian law. That characterization must turn on the central purpose of the area of law, not a mere side-effect.

The egalitarian support for discrimination law must boil down to the fact that at least its side-effect is supposed to be a reduction in inequality. But what discrimination law achieves for equality is a pittance. Any true egalitarian's support for it should be heavily qualified, and under protest. Other options include diluting one's understanding of what equality requires to such an extent that it leaves little bite to the supposed ideal, or using it merely rhetorically without any real commitment to equality.

Notice the charge I have not laid against the use of equality as the foundational value in discrimination law. The usual reason for worrying about the role of equality in discrimination law is that it has been instrumental in establishing the comparator-analysis in discrimination cases. We know that the role of comparators for establishing direct discrimination is increasingly unnecessary, and quite rightly so.[15] However, this is not a reason to reject equality as the general justifying aim of discrimination law. For, even if achieving a more equal society was indeed the point of discrimination law, it does not automatically follow that judges should use some conception of equality to determine the outcome of cases. This strand of criticism against equality springs from the now-familiar inability to distinguish between the purposive and the distributive questions in discrimination law, and therefore misdirected. The proper ground for rejecting equality is that it fails to explain the central features of the edifice of discrimination law.

There is yet another objection frequently made against equality, to which my comparative-but-not-egalitarian account may also seem

[15] Chapter 3, section 3.3.1.

vulnerable. The objection—called the levelling-down objection—accuses egalitarians of preferring a reduction in the well-being of those already advantaged to an unequal status quo, and (less charitably) of being indifferent between raising the well-being of the disadvantaged and reducing that of the advantaged. Would the same objection not apply to P3, whose main commitment is to reduce and remove any significant gap between a protected group and its cognates?

It would, but in a qualified sense that should not trouble us too much. Since we are not discussing whether any specific person's opportunities should be reduced in any particular case we can focus only on whether it is acceptable to reduce the opportunities available to the dominant group taken as a whole in order to reduce its advantage gap with a protected group. Levelling down at the distributive stage is more evidently unattractive—it can lead to waste, and individuals may have made personal commitments to certain projects based on available advantage which makes their interest in the status quo weightier. At the purposive stage, discrimination law does indeed seek to reduce the advantage gap between groups, but it does not seek to do so through a direct wealth transfer from one group to another. The duty-bearers in discrimination law need not belong to dominant groups. The duty is imposed not by reference to their group membership, but by their control over access to valuable opportunities in a society.[16] Indeed, the group membership of the discriminator is wholly immaterial to a claim of discrimination.[17]

Instead, it opts for an ad hoc allocation of certain tangible benefits to certain members of protected groups and, in the process, seeks to refashion structures and processes which contribute to their disadvantage. Assuming that certain material opportunities are limited in a given society, any allocation of benefits to those who did not have them will inevitably reduce the share of those who used to have them. At this broad societal level, it is an unavoidable price we must pay to optimize the range of opportunities to which members of protected groups have access to. This is, of course, always subject to the caveat that the opportunities of the members of the dominant group should not fall below the adequacy threshold either. This indirect and gradual levelling down achieved at the societal level is an acceptable and necessary price to pay to secure freedom for all.

---

[16] See generally, Chapter 7.
[17] See, for example, UK Equality Act 2010, s 24: for the purposes of establishing direct discrimination 'it does not matter whether [the discriminator] has the protected characteristic'.

5.4 Perfectionism in Discrimination Law

The account of discrimination law presented in this chapter is at variance not only with egalitarian accounts but also with other approaches. In focussing on group-disadvantage rather than ground-irrelevance, my account distances itself from relevance-based accounts. These descriptive relevance-based accounts make the rationalist claim that the purpose of discrimination law is to prohibit discrimination on grounds which are irrelevant to the legitimate objectives of the employer, landlord, or other discriminator. For example, race discrimination is prohibited in employment because race does not usually have any bearing on a person's ability to perform a job.[18] Even assuming that a general legal duty to act rationally can be justified (which will be difficult, if not impossible, alongside a commitment to liberalism), these relevance-based accounts are utterly inadequate to explain the general justifying aim of discrimination law. We know full well that the law prohibits discrimination even in contexts where the ground in question is indeed descriptively relevant to the performance of a job (think pregnancy, certain types of disabilities, and sometimes even race—say, the race of a bartender in a pub whose patrons are largely racist). These relevance-based accounts also show no sensitivity to relative group disadvantage, which we have seen is a key obsession in the legal model.[19] Without this reference to disadvantage, they struggle to explain why the liberty of the victims of discrimination trumps that of the duty-bearers to go about their business without legal interference. As I have shown, the dimension of disadvantage is key to focus our minds on the most egregious denials of liberty in the form of basic goods.

For all their faults, these relevance-based accounts (unlike most egalitarian ones) correctly appreciate that grounds are important to discrimination law. Where they go wrong is in their understanding of the reason why grounds are so important. In this chapter so far, we have understood the significance of grounds only derivatively—as definitional markers for salient groups. But the role of grounds is important in another respect, independent of relative group disadvantage: they are normatively irrelevant. They embody the perfectionist element in discrimination law, and are the reason why anti-perfectionist liberal accounts will also be unsuccessful. Perfectionist liberals are willing to allow the state to make certain (severely constrained) normative

---

[18] Donal Nolan, 'A Right to Meritorius Treatment' in Conor Gearty and Adam Tomkins (eds), *Understanding Human Rights* (Pinter 1996).

[19] Relevance-based accounts do play a limited role in dealing with the distributive questions. See Chapter 6, section 6.6.5.

judgments about what a good life is, whereas anti-perfectionists refuse to do so. Recall from Chapter 4 that a good life is lived in pursuit of value. Recall also that our understanding of value in that chapter was significantly qualified so that it was pluralistic, not too demanding, agent-centred, contextual, and holistic. The account was perfectionist, yet liberal.

I have argued in this chapter that discrimination law facilitates the pursuit of a good life by seeking to reduce and remove significant relative group disadvantage which impede such pursuit by limiting our access to certain basic goods. But only when the membership of a group is valuable (more accurately, not-immoral) will it contribute to a good life. Discrimination law assesses the value of such membership by examining the moral significance of the ground in question. Let us see how.

We learnt in Chapter 3 that a ground's division of persons into more and less advantaged groups is only one of two preconditions that make it eligible for protection. The other condition is that the ground must either be immutable or it must constitute a valuable fundamental choice.[20] We should start by revising P3 to make explicit the qualification inherent in the notion of a 'protected group':

Discrimination law seeks to reduce (and ultimately remove) any significant advantage gap between a protected group (defined by an immutable or valuable ground) and its cognate groups. (P4)

We can rephrase this by saying that discrimination law's central purpose is to ensure that members of groups based on immutable or valuable grounds do not suffer abiding, pervasive, and substantial relative disadvantage. Recall from Chapter 3 that immutability is to be understood expansively to include not just an inability to change the relevant characteristic, but also a lack of control over its acquisition. Furthermore, *effective* immutability will suffice—it is enough to show that changing the characteristic will impose significant personal costs. A mutable ground is also protected so long as it constitutes a valuable fundamental choice. These are but two different ways of determining whether the candidate ground is compatible with the pursuit of a good life.[21] This will always be the case if the ground is immutable.

---

[20] Chapter 3, section 3.1. Notice that a morally thin (anti-perfectionist) account will mainly be able to account for relative disadvantage. It will struggle to explain the additional requirement that the ground must be not-immoral. For the defense of an anti-perfectionist approach to discrimination law, see Deborah Hellman, 'Equality and Unconstitutional Discrimination' in Deborah Hellman and Sophia Moreau (eds), *Philosophical Foundations of Discrimination Law* (Oxford University Press 2013).

[21] Moreau refers to these grounds as 'normatively extraneous': Sophia Moreau, 'What is Discrimination?' (2010) 38 Philosophy and Public Affairs 143, 147.

When it constitutes a fundamental choice, discrimination law cares not just about group disadvantage, but also about whether the group in question is valuable (not-immoral) for its members. It is for this reason that discrimination against terrorist groups is not prohibited by discrimination law, whatever their advantage status—becoming a terrorist is simply not a valuable choice.[22]

Recall from Chapter 2 that the concept of a ground can be said to exist in two orders.[23] It was suggested that in the higher *universal* order, a ground applies to all individuals. In the *particular* order, different instances of a universal ground attach to different people. So, sex is a universal order ground, while maleness is a particular instance of sex. Usually, if one particular instance (say, whiteness) of a given universal order characteristic (race) is compatible with a good (valuable) life, all other particular instances (in this case, blackness, Asian-ness, etc) of that universal order characteristic are also likely to be so. But such results are coincidental, arrived at after considering each particular order characteristic. Let us imagine a hypothetical religious sect, the Stravinskyites, who perform the *Rite of Spring* involving human sacrifice.[24] If performing the *Rite of Spring* is an essential part of being a Stravinskyite, then life as a Stravinskyite is not valuable. Stravinskyism will not qualify as a valuable fundamental choice even though it might be a 'religion'.

This discussion shows that a decision to protect any particular order ground has little to do with how we have assessed *other* particular order grounds that are subsets of the same universal order ground. A person's pregnancy, Christianity, or atheism are all morally valuable characteristics, while her homosexuality, heterosexuality, disability, or blackness are at least morally irrelevant (but potentially morally valuable too, especially if they entail the membership of a nurturing community). What becomes clear is that the fundamental unit of protection qua grounds exists in its particular order (femaleness) rather than in the universal order (sex).

We are now in a position to appreciate the role that (particular order) grounds play in discrimination law. First, they provide the organizational basis for groups. Second, they demand that membership of the group serves perfectionist freedom by being conducive to the pursuit of a flourishing good

---

[22] This is not true of former terrorists, those who have now renounced violence. Our low-threshold judgment of value may not automatically deny them the protections of discrimination law, provided that other conditions are satisfied.

[23] See Chapter 2, paragraph preceding section 2.3.

[24] Igor Stravinsky's ballet *The Rite of Spring*, from which the reference has been borrowed, has human sacrifice as its central theme.

life. Egalitarian accounts tend to ignore the perfectionist role of grounds and focus primarily on disadvantage. Rationalist accounts focus solely on the relevance of the ground in question to the legitimate objectives of a discriminator. Anti-perfectionist accounts cannot distinguish between value-compatible and valueless grounds. All of them miss the point to different degrees. The real relevance that discrimination law seeks is between the particular order ground and a good life. This objective moral assessment of protected grounds is an essential part of discrimination law, as is its relationship to relative group disadvantage.

This insight has important implications for the debate on multiple-ground discrimination. Consider the case of Mackie, a woman of Indian origin who claimed to have been unfairly dismissed.[25] Her womanhood and her Indianness are independently either morally irrelevant or morally valuable traits. In Mackie's case, the respondent company's Indian directors disapproved of Asian women working there, but did not have any problems with men (including Asian men) or non-Asian women. The tribunal found that Mackie 'was not treated less favourably because she was a woman nor simply because she was Indian, but because she was an Indian woman'.[26] In this instance, she belonged to a unique intersectional category, which could not have been captured by her womanhood or her race. Our insight that it is the particular order characteristic of individuals that matters tells us that at least at the normative level, the relevant questions to ask are only these: (i) Is Indian-womanhood a normatively irrelevant or valuable characteristic?; (ii) Does it define a relatively disadvantaged group (Indian women)? If it didn't, we would have asked further if it defined a relatively advantaged group that we have reasons to nonetheless protect.

5.5 Conclusion

In this chapter, I have shown that membership of certain relatively disadvantaged groups has a serious impact on a person's secured access to three primary goods, and therefore to her well-being. We know that protected grounds define the contours of the protectorate of discrimination law, while protected groups add texture to its protection. Although we have somewhat elliptically

[25] *Mackie v G & N Car Sales Ltd t/a Britannia Motor Co* [2004] ET/1806128/03, as summarized in Nicholas Bamforth, Colm O'Cinneide, and Maleiha Malik, *Discrimination Law: Theory and Context* (Sweet & Maxwell 2008) 526.
[26] *Mackie v G & N Car Sales Ltd t/a Britannia Motor Co* [2004] ET/1806128/03.

been referring to protected grounds and groups, the law on discrimination is ultimately about the protection of *persons*. My claim is the general justifying aim of discrimination law is to further the well-being of persons by securing access to the basic goods to those who lack such access because of their affiliation to protected groups. These groups are in turn defined by particular order grounds whose possession is compatible with a good life.

The discussion in this chapter has been at a level of generality, which is all a theoretical work of this nature can afford to do. Some of its implications for particular debates may be obvious, others less so. The criteria we have discussed are no doubt satisfied by other groups which are not (yet) protected by discrimination law in the jurisdictions under discussion. These groups may include the overweight, people without a university education, those with a less-than-average IQ, persons who are not good-looking in the conventional sense, the poor, etc. Many, if not all, of these groups suffer relative and multifaceted disadvantage, and are based on grounds which are either valuable or morally irrelevant (note that our test required *moral* irrelevance of the ground, rather than irrelevance of the characteristic to one's ability to perform a job). Most jurisdictions do not treat these groups as protected groups. In some cases, this is simply an omission that ought to be remedied. In other cases, things are more complicated. It may be that the evidence available does not show that the relative group disadvantage is serious and substantial enough to merit attention. In other cases, it may be that the connection between the characteristic and ability to perform a job makes it too expensive to protect certain groups, at least against discrimination in the employment sector. This reasoning must be used with caution—prohibiting discrimination is always expensive, and there are costs associated with the failure to do so as well. The real question is who should bear the burden, rather than whether the burden should be borne. We will consider this set of concerns in some detail in Chapter 6, section 6.6 and in Chapter 7. Finally, for some of these groups, there may be better tools than discrimination law to address the problem. The poor, for example, are disadvantaged in the relative as well as in the absolute sense. Absolute deprivation, at least of the most egregious kind, is best left to the care of welfare measures and socio-economic rights.

Given the generality of our discussion, we have also glossed over some concerns that arise because of groups which are already protected. The most important of these concerns relate to religious groups. One needs to consider the difference between the principle of non-discrimination on the grounds of religion and the right to freedom of religion. Courts and commentators appear not to have given sufficient attention to the separate scope of these rights in the context of religious minorities. Further examination will be required to see how the material and expressive concerns of some religious groups (owing to their lack of adequate and secured access to the basic goods) is connected with their interest in abiding by the beliefs and practices of their faith.

While these important questions remain unresolved, the general insights of this chapter are still very significant: that discrimination law seeks to reduce (and ultimately remove) any significant advantage gap between a protected group (defined by an immutable or valuable ground) and its cognate groups; and that this objective is morally justified, even laudable.

PART III

DESIGNING THE DUTIES

6

The Antidiscrimination Duty

We now know that the point of discrimination law is to reduce significant, abiding, and pervasive relative group disadvantage. It is time to turn to the implication of this overall purpose for the design of the specific legal duties. Any set of duties imposed by discrimination law must be designed to systemically realize this purpose. Let us recall from Chapter 3, section 3.3.6 that the duties imposed by discrimination law can broadly be classified into two groups. On the one hand, it imposes duties that vest particular persons with reflex rights (we called these duties 'rights-generating'). These duties include the prohibition on direct and indirect discrimination and on ground-based harassment. Remember that the right to reasonable accommodation is a secondary right to which someone becomes entitled upon breach of her primary right not to be discriminated against. As such, it is better understood as a specific type of remedy available for certain types of breaches of the non-discrimination duty. Similarly, affirmative action undertaken to remedy specific acts of historical discrimination by the duty-bearer is also a remedy for the breach of the primary right not to be discriminated against. For this reason, I reserved the term 'affirmative action' only for non-remedial affirmative action measures. Affirmative action duties, whether mandated by law or by contract, are typically non-rights-generating, since they do not usually vest reflex rights in particular persons.

This distinction between rights-generating and non-rights-generating duties maps neatly onto two other ways in which we may classify these duties. The first of these classifications is between action-regarding and non-action-regarding duties.[1] Rights-generating duties—the duty not to discriminate directly or indirectly or not to harass—are action-regarding, inasmuch as they make an essential reference to something done. They are only activated by the duty-bearer doing something. One could see relatively easily why prohibitions on direct discrimination and harassment are action-regarding. Even the prohibition on indirect discrimination is action-regarding, in the sense that it

---

[1] See Elisa Holmes, 'Anti-Discrimination Rights Without Equality' (2005) 68 Modern Law Review 175, 184.

requires a connection between disproportionate impact on a protected group and some policy, rule, or practice. The same is true of a failure to provide reasonable accommodation—it is a failure to make accommodations within the context of a policy, rule, or practice. This is what makes all these duties essentially action-regarding. Affirmative action duties do not necessarily refer to any past action on the part of the duty-bearer upon which the imposition of the duty is conditional. For this reason, these duties are not action-regarding.

What we have then are two sets of duties in discrimination law. On the one hand, we have action-regarding duties which are also rights-generating. On the other hand, we have non-action-regarding and non-rights-generating duties. In this chapter, I am going to show that a third method of classifying these duties also maps onto these two subsets. Breach of the action-regarding and rights-generating duties in discrimination law is always *harmful* (at least when harm is understood capaciously to include expressive injury) to the victim and some element of *wrongfulness* on the part of the duty-bearer. Although the breach of the antidiscrimination duty is always harmful and wrongful, it is only usually (rather than necessarily) *faulty*, as fault (or blame) depends on the state of mind of the wrong-doer. The imposition of non-action-regarding and non-rights-generating duties, on the other hand, does not necessarily entail any prior harm to any victim or wrong (or fault, for that matter) on the part of the duty-bearer. To sum up these classifications, the action-regarding and rights-generating duties that discrimination law imposes are wrong-sensitive; whereas its non-action-regarding and non-rights-generating duties are wrong-insensitive.

This chapter concerns the first set of duties, namely the duty not to discriminate directly or indirectly and the duty to refrain from ground-based harassment. I will show that these three duties are but instances of a single, comprehensive, *antidiscrimination* duty. This duty prohibits certain specific persons from undertaking discriminatory action. In the account that follows, the legal concept of discrimination is presented as a wrongful exacerbation of relative group disadvantage. This effect-based formulation is, admittedly, at variance with a layperson's understanding of the phenomenon. What I have characterized, by way of a rough archetype, as the 'lay' model of discrimination is endorsed by many moral philosophers.[2] This model focusses on the intentional (and therefore blameworthy) reliance by the discriminator on a personal characteristic (a ground, such as sex) of the victim for comparatively adverse treatment. It is concerned with the process of reasoning of the discriminator, rather than the effect of discrimination on the victim. It demands that the personal characteristic ought to have played a *causal* role in the consequent adverse treatment.

---

[2] See Chapter 1, section 1.1.

To show that this endorsement of the lay model is too hasty, this chapter will provide a conceptual restatement of certain aspects of the doctrinal formulation of the antidiscrimination duty clarified in Chapter 3. It will explain the scope and largely asymmetric nature of the protectorate.[3] Towards this goal, it will classify discrimination into its paradigm and collateral forms. Paradigmatic discrimination is discrimination against members of protected (ie relatively disadvantaged) groups. Collateral discrimination takes place against cognate (ie relatively advantaged, or—given our high-threshold understanding of disadvantage—dominant) groups. Furthermore, it will provide a common explanation for all the duties imposed by discrimination law except the duty to undertake affirmative action.[4] The division between paradigmatic and collateral discrimination cuts across, rather than maps onto, the traditional divide between direct and indirect discrimination. The two forms of discrimination are defined in a precise, if somewhat technical, sense below:

Paradigmatic Discrimination:

An action φ by a duty-bearer x is/will be paradigmatically discriminatory if and only if:

(i) φ has/will have a non-remote adverse effect ε on a set of person(s) V (the adverse effect clause); and

(ii) V is/will be constituted entirely or disproportionately by persons who are (or are perceived to be, or are closely associated with) members of a protected group P (the group membership clause); and

(iii) there is a correlation between a person's membership of V and her (actual or perceived, or her associate's) membership of P (the correlation clause); and

(iv) φ-ing lacks adequate justification (the justification clause).

Collateral Discrimination:

An action φ by a duty-bearer x is collaterally discriminatory if and only if:

(i) φ has/will have a non-remote adverse effect ε on a set of person(s) V (the adverse effect clause); and

(ii) V is/will be constituted entirely or disproportionately by persons who are (or are perceived to be or are closely associated with) members of a group C that is a cognate of a protected group P (the group membership clause); and

(iii) there is a correlation between a person's membership of V and her (actual or perceived, or her associate's) membership of C (the correlation clause); and

---

[3] See Chapter 3, section 3.1.   [4] See Chapter 3, section 3.3.

(iv) memberships of groups P and C have expressive salience (the expressive clause); and

(v) φ-ing lacks adequate justification (the justification clause).

The *antidiscrimination duty* on x is to not φ. I will show how the breach of this duty is wrongful. The breach may be more or less wrong. This will depend on many factors, including whether the breach was blameworthy and the extent of blame (especially whether it was committed maliciously, intentionally, recklessly, or negligently). As with most duties, this duty may sometimes be outweighed by x's undefeated right to φ. Most of the following discussion relates to the paradigm case, but should normally apply to the collateral case as well, until we come to discuss its specificity in section 6.5. It is my claim that the paradigm and the collateral cases of discrimination, together, provide the best fit with the broad trends in the progressive development of the anti-discrimination duty, as outlined in Chapter 3. The sections in this chapter are organized on the lines of the different clauses in the definitions.

Barring minor exceptions, my definition is a restatement rather than a revision of the legal doctrine, even as it seeks to clarify the concept of direct discrimination and highlight its conceptual continuity with indirect discrimination and harassment. Even the exceptions only chart a theoretical difference—their practical outcome should still track the legal model outlined in Chapter 3 reasonably closely. What is more, it provides an easier way to explain recent developments with respect to intention, comparators, and intersectionality in the practice of discrimination law—developments that have put pressure on the traditional formulation of the doctrine. That said, I am not necessarily recommending that courts adopt the conceptual definition offered here as a doctrinal test. The definition has been organized the way it is for analytical clarity. There may be practical imperatives that I have the luxury to ignore but courts have to contend with—issues such as determining the appropriate burden of proof—which may merit a different formulation.

6.1 Action-Regarding Duty

The main stems of both definitions contain two implicit elements: *[a]n action φ by a duty-bearer x*. First, only an action can constitute discrimination. Second, the (legal) antidiscrimination duty is not universal, but borne by certain specific duty-bearers alone. Both elements are key to our understanding of this duty.

The first element clarifies that the antidiscrimination duty is action-regarding. The action φ could of course be an omission, so long as it is an omission made in the course of doing an act. If I 'omit' to step on the brakes while driving a car, I have nonetheless 'acted'.[5] Discrimination law considers such 'omissions' to be acts, as is evident from its prohibition of indirect discrimination and provision for reasonable accommodation.[6] In the same vein, an act includes a set of interrelated acts. Often, the adverse effect follows not from a single rule or practice, but through a combination of two or more rules or practices of an employer. For example, the quasi-automatic channelling of a disproportionate number of Roma children to special schools designed for mentally disabled students in the Czech Republic was a result not of a single policy or practice. It was, instead, the combined outcome of a whole host of practices:

> [T]he assessment of Roma children in the Ostrava region did not take into account the language and culture of the children, or their prior learning experiences, or their unfamiliarity with the demands of the testing situation. Single rather than multiple sources of evidence were used. Testing was done in a single administration, not over time. Evidence was not obtained in realistic or authentic settings where children could demonstrate their skills. Undue emphasis was placed on individually administered, standardised tests normed on other populations.[7]

It will defeat the purpose of discrimination law if the discriminator is allowed to avoid liability by simply breaking down the offending rule or practice into several distinct components. It is important, therefore, that a combination of acts of the same duty-bearer should also be liable to challenge as discriminatory. Expansive though our understanding of what an 'act' is, there cannot be discrimination without a discriminatory act. It is this action-regarding nature of the antidiscrimination duty which distinguishes it from the genuinely non-action-regarding duty to undertake non-remedial affirmative action.

The second element is also crucial. The antidiscrimination duty is not imposed indiscriminately. Instead, as we will see in Chapter 7, it is imposed on a carefully selected group of duty-bearers, who have a weaker claim to negative freedom owing to their public character and who exercise significant control over our access to basic goods. Contrast this with the tort law duty not to act negligently, which is indeed imposed universally. Or, for that

---

[5] See generally, Herbert Hart and Tony Honoré, *Causation in the Law* (2nd edn, Clarendon Press 1985) 138–40.

[6] See generally, Samuel Bagenstos, '"Rational Discrimination", Accommodation, and the Politics of (Disability) Civil Rights' (2003) 89 Virginia Law Review 825.

[7] *DH v Czech Republic* (2008) 47 EHRR 3 [44].

matter, the criminal law duty not to kill or rape. These duties are universal in the sense that they apply to everyone. Perhaps the antidiscrimination duty in the moral sense is also universal. It is morally wrong of us to refuse to seek the friendship of persons belonging to certain racial groups, or rule out the possibility of dating someone from another caste. The legal prohibition on discrimination, however, is not universal. A limited application of this duty is key to its legitimacy, as will become clear in Chapter 7.

6.2 The Adverse Effect Clause

The adverse effect clause, which isolates the element of *harm* in discriminatory acts, is common to the two definitions: φ *has/will have a non-remote adverse effect* ε *on a set of person(s)* V. Let us examine the different elements of this clause. First, the clause requires that the adverse effect ε is a proximate (ie non-remote) consequence of the action of the duty-bearer. This underlines not only the action-regarding nature of the duty, but also introduces a requirement of a causal link between the prohibited act φ and a key ingredient of discrimination: its adverse effect ε. There can be no discrimination unless this causal link between a particular act and an adverse effect has been established.[8] Tort lawyers are familiar with the concept of remoteness, although it plays a somewhat different role in the tort of negligence than it does in this definition.[9] This is not the place to visit tort law debates. Suffice it to note that there must be some such remoteness qualification to exclude, well, remote consequences of x's actions. To give one example, x's donation to a political party with a conservative economic agenda is too remote a cause of the consequent adverse effects of its government's policies on racial minorities and women to qualify as discriminatory.[10]

Second, this clause only entails the requirement that φ causes/will cause ε. This causation requirement must not be carried over to the next, group membership, clause of the definition. An example may bring the difference out clearly. Imagine that a medical council administers a test to determine the candidates' suitability for a general practice licence. As long as there is *somebody* who has been found ineligible under the test (or that V is not an empty set), the adverse effect clause is satisfied. Suppose that, for whatever

---

[8] *Wards Cove Packing Co v Atonio* 490 US 642 (1989) 657.

[9] See, for example, John Cartwright, 'Remoteness of Damage in Contract and Tort: A Reconsideration' (1996) 55 Cambridge Law Review 488.

[10] I am grateful to John Gardner for this example. Note that this donation may not count as 'discrimination' for a variety of other reasons too—it may be justifiable; or political donors, qua political donations, may not bear the antidiscrimination duty's burden. Even if it did constitute discrimination, x may yet have had an undefeated right to make the donation anyway.

reason, white candidates were disproportionately more likely to pass this test than candidates belonging to other racial groups. The adverse effect clause does *not* require that there be a causal link between φ and this disproportionate adverse impact *on racial minorities*.[11] There is no need, for example, to point to any particular feature of the test to explain *why* racial minorities performed disproportionately badly. To put this more generally, the adverse effect clause should not be read to require that φ is responsible for an adverse effect on members of a protected (or cognate) group. The correlation clause will make it clear that for that relationship, a mere correlation will suffice. The current clause only requires that the adverse effect on the persons in the set V be caused by an act of the duty-bearer.

6.2.1 Tangible and Expressive Effects

Third, the adverse effect ε of φ-ing is to be understood broadly. Recall from Chapter 3 that we recognized a group's disadvantage in political, socio-cultural, and material dimensions. If a polling station only allows access to the voting booths via steps, its 'omission' to provide a step-free access has an adverse *political* effect on wheelchair users (since they are denied the exercise of their franchise). When a same-sex couple is barred from participating in a couples' dance event, they suffer socio-cultural adverse effect. Indian income tax law, by recognizing the separate legal personality of the Hindu family and allowing it to claim tax deductions in addition to each individual member, has an adverse *material* effect on non-Hindus (whose families are not similarly recognized as distinct legal persons). Relative group disadvantage at the systemic level has to cross the threshold of substantiality, abidingness, and pervasiveness to merit consideration. There is no such threshold requirement at the particular level—any amount of adverse effect will qualify.

In fact, the adverse effect may be tangible or it may be solely expressive or symbolic. Often, tangible effects are accompanied by expressive effects. Each of the three examples used above involve a tangible adverse effect on a wheelchair user, a same-sex couple, and a Muslim citizen. Simultaneously, they also express unwholesome attitudes towards these people. But there are some acts whose non-remote adverse effects for the victim are entirely symbolic. Consider a national census which does not allow an atheist to self-identify as such under the religion column; or a state which provides all the material benefits of marriage to same-sex couples but describes their relationship as a 'civil partnership'; or a dance club that charges men but allows women to

---

[11] See generally, *R (BAPIO Action Ltd) v Royal College of General Practitioners* [2014] EWHC 1416.

enter without a fee. In these cases, there are adverse expressive effects for atheists, gay people, and women, respectively. In the last example, women actually benefit materially from not having to pay an entry fee—they nonetheless suffer an expressive injury because the arrangement objectifies them to lure in male clientele.[12] Discrimination law recognizes these expressive acts simply because they can also exacerbate relative group disadvantage. They may worsen existing socio-cultural disadvantages suffered by the protected group because they may endorse existing prejudices and harmful stereotypes. Furthermore, symbolic acts can also have very tangible, if somewhat remote, effects in the long term.

Acknowledging the importance of expressive effects clarifies some issues pertaining to the role of subjective malice and intention in discrimination law. In section 6.2.2, I am going to defend the fact that the law no longer insists on proof of subjective malice or intention to discriminate. It is the effect on the victim that matters, not the reasons of the discriminator. At this stage, note that if malice or discriminatory intent is discovered, there is invariably going to be an expressive adverse effect on the targets of the malice or mal-intent. These subjective states of mind may not be necessary to prove discrimination, but their existence would often be sufficient. This explanation should also help us deal with mixed-motive cases.[13] Suppose that a decision is taken for some legitimate reasons and some discriminatory reasons, and that it would have been taken even if the discriminatory reasons were not present. Even so, the mere fact that discriminatory reasons were relied upon should be sufficient cause for adverse expressive effects on those at the receiving end.

Expressive harm is the most important, and often the only, non-remote adverse effect of ground-sensitive harassment.[14] This type of harassment has come to be seen as an integral part of discrimination law. As the US Supreme Court recognized, the law's reach 'is not limited to "economic" or "tangible" discrimination'.[15] Any understanding of discrimination that fails to acknowledge this reality will, for that reason, be impoverished. I will show shortly that one of the attractions of my definition is that it provides a common conceptual foundation for direct and

[12] Tamas Szigeti, 'Stereotyping as Direct Discrimination?' Oxford Human Rights Law Blog <http://ohrh.law.ox.ac.uk/?p=3803> accessed 22 September 2014. This example also demonstrates that the same act can simultaneously amount to paradigmatic discrimination against a protected group (women) and collateral discrimination against a cognate group (men).

[13] *Price Waterhouse v Hopkins* 490 US 228 (1989).

[14] I use the qualifier 'ground-sensitive' only to distinguish say sexual/racial harassment (which is a concern of discrimination law) from harassment unconnected with a ground such as sex or race (which isn't).

[15] *Meritor Savings Bank v Vinson* 477 US 57 (1986) 64.

indirect discrimination (while maintaining their distinctiveness). For now, notice that the prohibition of harassment is also entailed in this definition.

The recognition of adverse expressive effect is by no means unproblematic. Apart from concerns about the institutional competence of courts to evaluate this effect, its unguarded recognition could expand the reach of discrimination law in significant and problematic ways.[16] It is all the more important, therefore, that the adverse effect clause excludes remote effects from its ambit. Drawing a line between remote and non-remote instances of adverse expressive effects is likely to be more difficult than for material effects. Is the expressive injury suffered by a single gay man due to the non-availability of same-sex marriage in his society too remote? What about that of his mother (who suffers at least some expressive injury in her own right, as a gay man's mother)? Relative judgments are easier to make: it should be clear in our example that the adverse expressive effect on a gay couple is the least remote, whereas that on the mother is the most remote. Drawing a bright line to separate cases that are too remote is an admittedly difficult problem, but not one that lawyers are unfamiliar with. In fact, some scholars and judges have (wrongly) come to regard expressive injustice as the primary, even the sole, concern of discrimination law.[17] These scholars are wrong only in their insistence on the primacy or exclusivity of the expressive concern—its importance is difficult to deny.

6.2.2 Comparative and Non-Comparative Effects

All the examples used in the two preceding paragraphs involve acts that have an adverse effect in a comparative sense. If no one had the vote, we would have a problem, but it would not be a problem that would concern discrimination law. In general, discrimination law will not be engaged in other examples either: so long as there was no dance competition; if every family (or no family) was recognized as a separate person able to claim tax deductions; if the census did not ask the religion question, or there was no census at all; if all couples or no couples were allowed to 'marry'; or if dance clubs charged everyone or no one or there were no dance clubs. These are primarily acts of discrimination only because the adverse effect is *comparative*—it falls on members of a protected group but not its cognates.

---

[16] Tarunabh Khaitan, 'Dignity as an Expressive Norm: Neither Vacuous Nor a Panacea' (2012) 32 Oxford Journal of Legal Studies 1, 15ff.

[17] Deborah Hellman, *When is Discrimination Wrong?* (Harvard University Press 2008); Cary Franklin, 'The Anti-Stereotyping Principle In Constitutional Sex Discrimination Law' (2010) 20 New York University Law Review 101. In *R v Kapp* [2008] 2 SCR 483, the Canadian Supreme Court sought to abolish the pre-eminence of expressive concerns in its early jurisprudence, without denying its role altogether.

But at the level of particular acts, *non-comparative* adverse effects will also suffice. We know from our discussion in Chapter 3 that courts no longer insist on proof of comparative adverse effect in cases where there is no appropriate comparator (such as those involving pregnancy discrimination); where a comparator analysis ends up frustrating claims that seem legitimate otherwise (for example, intersectional discrimination against, say, *dalit* women, who may suffer no clear adversity when compared separately to non-*dalits* or to men); or where it draws attention away from the parochialism of dominant norms (by, for example, demanding that a disabled complainant establish they are 'like' a non-disabled comparator in all other respects).

These examples capture an important truth about contemporary discrimination law—when it comes to the characterization of *particular* acts as discriminatory, it cares for non-comparative adverse effects as much as it does for comparative ones. A complainant is usually allowed to show *either* that there has been discrimination *between* her and an appropriate comparator, *or* that there has been discrimination *against* her.[18] Contrast this with the sole *systemic* concern of discrimination law: reducing and eliminating *relative* group disadvantage.[19] One could say that discrimination law is necessarily comparative at its systemic level concern with groups, but not necessarily so at its particular level engagement with individual cases.

In fact, some scholars have suggested that even in the particular cases where a comparator analysis is performed, this is done heuristically—only to discern the reasons behind the act in question.[20] Although I have some sympathy with this account of the use of comparators, if taken too far, we would be back to the lay approach that focusses on the reasons of the discriminator rather than the effects on the victim. We need a better, victim-oriented, explanation of the heuristically useful rather than conceptually essential role that comparators perform in discrimination law. This explanation is found in the recognition of expressive adverse effects: almost every instance of comparative adversity will entail a symbolic injury. Each of our examples of tangible comparative harm—the denial of the vote to disabled persons, competing opportunity to the same-sex dancing partners, and differential taxes on Muslims—also amount to expressive harm to the victims involved in the absolute sense. The

---

[18] Leslie Green, 'Sex-Neutral Marriage' [2011] Current Legal Problems 1, 13–14.

[19] There is, of course, an overlap between the intended beneficiaries of welfare law and of discrimination law. The overlap, however, is coincidental rather than conceptual.

[20] Elisa Holmes, 'Anti-Discrimination Rights Without Equality' (2005) 68 Modern Law Review 175, 186; Denise Réaume, 'Dignity, Equality and Comparison' in Deborah Hellman and Sophia Moreau (eds), *Philosophical Foundations of Discrimination Law* (Oxford University Press 2013).

law's cognizance of their expressive injury does not require proof that this injury is comparative. Indeed, it is not even clear whether it is possible to sensibly distinguish comparative and non-comparative expressive injuries. It is true that this expressive adversity is, at least in part, constituted by the bad reasons of the discriminator. Like many other differences between them, the distinction between the lay and the legal models here lies in what they choose to emphasize (reasons of the discriminator or the effect on the victim)—we don't need to insist that the two are unrelated. This concession does not reintroduce the establishment of the mental state of the discriminator as a requirement—it is only an acknowledgement that subjective *mens rea* remains relevant to various inquiries in discrimination law. Whether there was expressive adversity is one such inquiry, whether the discrimination was justified is another. So long as our conception of adverse effects is capacious enough to include expressive effects, comparative adversity can be seen as merely evidencing absolute adversity in the expressive sense. That persistently elusive and troublesome character—the appropriate comparator—can safely be pushed further along the margins of doctrinal irrelevance without any damage.

6.2.3 The Levelling-Down Objection

Understanding comparative tangible discrimination as expressive discrimination has another attraction. It reveals precisely what is wrong with 'levelling down', which occurs when a discriminator who provides a benefit to some takes it away rather than extending it to those discriminated against. Some of the examples I have used above may appear to tolerate levelling down. This is not true: levelling down may sometimes be justified, but discrimination law is, by default, hostile to it. To understand why, we need to distinguish between the *absence* of a benefit to anyone in the first place (where no one may have a claim of discrimination) and a comprehensive *rollback* of a benefit in response to demands for its extension to a previously discriminated group (when there may still be a claim of discrimination). A levelling-down strategy adopted mainly to avoid extending the benefit in question to a protected group is likely to have an expressive adverse effect on this group. To understand this claim better, let us look at the same-sex marriage example in some detail.

In our example, a state provides exactly the same rights and duties for different-sex and same-sex couples, but characterizes their relationships as 'marriage' and 'civil partnership', respectively. Given certain background conditions, including the social salience of 'marriage' and significant opposition to same-sex marriages from some (primarily religious) groups, I have assumed that this arrangement has adverse expressive effects on same-sex couples: it signifies the state's endorsement of the sentiment that same-sex relationships do not deserve the label. This will be the case even without any material or political injury.[21]

If our example was slightly different and there was no social institution of marriage in that society, same-sex couples would have no claim of discrimination against the legal characterization of all romantic/sexual adult relationship agreements as 'civil partnerships'. In our example, expressive injury is caused because a socially salient institution called 'marriage' already exists, and the label is permitted to different-sex couples but denied to same-sex couples. Now, assume that the state responds to complaints of discrimination by resorting to 'levelling down' by withdrawing its availability to different-sex couples rather than extending it to same-sex couples. Now, the law recognizes civil partnerships for everyone and marriage for none. There may be good reasons for this regime,[22] but when the motivation is to deny the label to same-sex couples, there is clear expressive harm to them.[23] An appreciation of adverse expressive effects shows why levelling down is not, generally, an acceptable response to comparative discrimination.

Finally, the adverse effect clause speaks of a set of adversely affected person(s) V. It should be obvious that the set could contain just one individual or several persons. These are only persons proximately (non-remotely) affected by φ. The next clause further explores the constitution of this set. For now, it is worth noticing that the set of proximately affected persons V is distinct from 'protected groups'. An employer who refuses to grant paid leave to his part-time workers, who are disproportionately women, adversely affects part-time workers, whether male or female, who work for him. This is the set of people who constitute V, which is evidently distinct from the relevant protected group in this case, which is women.

6.3 The Group Membership Clause

The group membership clause is substantively common to the two forms of discrimination. The only difference is that the relevant group for paradigmatic discrimination is a protected group, whereas discrimination involving

---

[21] Suzanne Goldberg, 'Marriage as Monopoly: History, Tradition, Incrementalism, and the Marriage/Civil Union Distinction' (2009) 41 Connecticut Law Review 1397.

[22] Cass Sunstein and Richard Thaler, *Nudge: Improving Decisions about Health, Wealth and Happiness* (Yale University Press 2008) ch 13.

[23] Expressive harm can, of course, also be inflicted without any motive to do so. What matters is the social salience of the expressive act—motives behind it are only sometimes relevant to this salience.

members of a cognate group is collateral. Recall that protected groups are those groups, defined by protected grounds, whose members are significantly more likely to suffer abiding, substantial, and pervasive disadvantage compared with members of its cognate groups (ie other relatively advantaged groups defined by the same ground). Women, for example, constitute a protected group in most societies, whereas men are their cognates. The distinction between paradigmatic discrimination and collateral discrimination brings home the point that an additional clause needs to be satisfied before men are protected from discrimination. I have labelled this the 'expressive clause' and we will examine it in due course. Before that, let us grasp the import of the group membership clause. For paradigmatic discrimination, this clause requires that *V is/will be constituted entirely or disproportionately by persons who are (or are perceived to be or are closely associated with) members of a protected group P*. For collateral discrimination, the condition is that *V [be] constituted entirely or disproportionately by persons who are (or are perceived to be or are closely associated with) members of a group C that is a cognate of a protected group P*. This clause establishes the scope of the protectorate of discrimination law: members of protected groups or (sometimes) their cognates.

6.3.1 Systemic Wrongfulness

The group membership clause embodies the key rationale behind prohibiting discriminatory conduct: to prevent the exacerbation of relative group disadvantage. It assumes that when members of a protected group are adversely affected, the advantage gap with their cognates is widened. The clause does not demand that a link between the adverse effect caused and the worsening relative group disadvantage be established in each and every case. The assumption works at the systemic level: individual acts of discrimination against protected groups, taken as a whole, plausibly worsen relative group disadvantage. Especially when such acts are widespread, as is often the case with respect to members of protected groups, their collective impact on relative group disadvantage can be significant. This is the wrongfulness of discrimination *at a systemic level*. The wrongfulness of discrimination at the level of *particular* acts will be revealed when we discuss the correlation clause. Given this claim, the prohibition of collateral discrimination may not immediately make sense. We will come to that issue later. For now, although I will explain the clause with reference only to protected groups, everything said here should also apply to their cognate groups.

Basically, the group membership clause interrogates the composition of the set V that is adversely affected by φ in relation to protected groups. The definition includes those who may not actually be members of P, but are perceived to be so by others, or associated closely with such members. These non-members also deserve to be protected because the discrimination they suffer is linked inextricably to their perceived group membership or to the membership of their associates. A camp straight boy who has homophobic insults hurled at him by a school bully, a Sikh man whose attacker thinks he is Muslim, or a carer who is fired for taking time off to look after her disabled son all suffer from discrimination. They suffer because gay people, Muslims, and disabled people are relatively disadvantaged. Their predicament shows us that it is not just members of protected groups who suffer due to relative group disadvantage. This is why the protection of associates and mistaken victims is justified.[24] References to members of a protected group will hereinafter include these allied beneficiaries.

6.3.2 Direct and Indirect Discrimination

Cases where V is constituted *entirely* by members of P are relatively easy to distinguish. The requirement here is simply that everyone adversely affected by ϕ belongs to the same protected group (they could, for example, all be women, or blacks, or *dalits*). Note that the converse is not necessary: not all women need to be adversely affected by ϕ; the fact that everyone affected is a woman will suffice. This will usually be the case when ϕ, on its face, singles out women for adverse treatment. For example, an employer who administers a policy of paying his female employees 10 per cent less than his male workers clearly satisfies the group membership clause: everyone he adversely affects is a woman. There may be other occasions when V is entirely constituted by members of P. Suppose an employer has a policy of firing any employee who becomes pregnant.[25] Even though the policy, on the face of it, says nothing about sex, it is obvious that (given biological realities) everyone directly adversely affected by this policy will be a woman. In the much-criticized case of *James*, the House of Lords simply acknowledged that it is not just underlying biological realities which can result in an exact correspondence between the adverse effects of a facially neutral action and the membership of a protected group.[26] In *James*, only members of a cognate group (men) were adversely affected by a

---

[24] Whether the expressive clause would justify a similar extension with respect to collateral discrimination could be controversial. Given that the actual cases where such extensions of collateral discrimination will be practically relevant are likely to be negligible anyway, I err towards their inclusion.

[25] See *Air India v Nargesh Meerza* (1981) 4 SCC 335; C-177/88 *Dekker v Stichting (VJV-Centrum) Plus* [1991] IRLR 27.

[26] For criticism, see John Finnis, 'Directly Discriminatory Decisions: A Missed Opportunity' (2010) 126 Law Quarterly Review 491.

benefit linked to pensionable age—not because they were biologically men, but because of a legally unimpeachable background rule which laid down different ages when men and women become pensionable.[27] All these cases have been treated as cases of *direct* discrimination by courts. We can therefore say that discrimination is direct when the adversely affected set V is constituted *entirely* by members of a protected (or cognate) group.[28]

Indirect discrimination occurs when members of P constitute V *disproportionately*. Determining this is less straightforward. Two problems are involved. First, one needs to know the relevant pool in relation to which a judgment of disproportionality needs to be made.[29] In this regard, Lord Justice Mustill suggested that the relevant pool against which disproportionality is to be judged should include everyone who satisfies all the other conditions of selection, except the one(s) that is/are being challenged.[30] This is easier to do in some cases than others. Consider an easy example first. Let us say that a company x decides to give a one-off bonus pay to every employee who has worked for it for more than 15 continuous years. There are two criteria for eligibility for the bonus:

(i)   the person must be an employee of x; and

(ii) he or she should have worked for x for a continuous period of more than 15 years.

The rule that is under challenge as potentially indirectly discriminatory is (ii). Under the Mustill formula, the relevant pool consists of everyone who satisfies (i), ie all the employees of x. Say the total number of employees who work for x are 150, and the total number of women in this group are 40. It is this pool against which those adversely affected need to be compared. Let us assume further that the adversely affected set V, ie employees who have not worked for 15 continuous years with this employer, contains 100 employees, of whom 35 are women. It turns out that the ratio of the number of women adversely affected to the number of women in the relevant pool is 35:40. Compare this to the ratio of men adversely affected to the total number of

---

[27] *James v Eastleigh Borough Council* [1990] 2 AC 751.

[28] C-73/08 *Bressol v Gouvernement de la Communauté Française* [2010] 3 CMLR 559 [56]: 'I take there to be direct discrimination when the category of those receiving a certain advantage and the category of those suffering a correlative disadvantage coincide exactly with the respective categories of persons distinguished only by applying a prohibited classification.' This suggestion by Advocate General Sharpston is broader than my proposal: it requires not only that V is entirely a sub-set of some protected group (as I do), but also that no beneficiary belongs to this group (which I don't) in order to establish (paradigmatic) direct discrimination. See also, *Bull v Hall* [2013] UKSC 73 [29]; *Brooks v Canada Safeway Ltd* [1989] 1 SCR 1219 [41], [47].

[29] See generally, *Wards Cove Packing Co v Atonio* 490 US 642 (1989) 650–1.

[30] *Jones v Chief Adjudication Officer* [1990] IRLR 533 [36].

men in the relevant pool, which is 45:110. It turns out that 87.5 per cent of all women who could have been adversely affected were so affected, whereas the same number for men was 49.1 per cent. Even a rule of thumb analysis will suffice to conclude that women disproportionately constitute the adversely affected group V in this example.

Cases are harder when the relevant pool is more difficult to determine. Consider an employer who wants to hire 50 workers for a low-skilled factory job. In order to be eligible, say, every aspirant must

(i)   be between the age of 18 and 55 on the date of appointment;

(ii) be living within, or willing to move to live within, a 30 mile radius from the factory; and

(iii) have an undergraduate university degree.

The group of 50 workers he eventually hires includes 4 black people, 35 white people, and the remaining 11 from other racial groups. An unsuccessful black aspirant challenges requirement (iii) as indirectly discriminatory against blacks.[31] In order to determine whether the group membership clause has been satisfied in this case, we need to know—under the Mustill formula—what the relevant pool of people who satisfied all conditions other than (iii) is, and what the racial composition of this pool is. The trouble is that in most cases it is almost impossible to determine this pool with any degree of certainty. Does one consider the entire population of the local area between the ages of 18 and 55 as the relevant pool? Even if one thinks this is appropriate, what counts as 'local' area, given that some people living elsewhere may be willing to move. Does one look only for those who might be considering a low-skilled factory job? Or, does the relevant pool only contain those who in fact want this particular job? These questions should clarify that the main difficulty is epistemic rather than conceptual—even so, it is hardly a trivial matter for a court trying to solve a real-world problem. Ultimately, the law must settle this issue by relying on its ability to deem certain facts as legally acceptable (as it does, for example, with a bright line age of majority). In doing so, it should consider what data is readily available, the relative position of the party which bears the evidentiary burden, and the broader objective that discrimination law seeks to achieve. In many cases, this will result in treating the entire population in the relevant age group living in the normal catchment area of that factory as the relevant pool for determining disproportionality. This rough determination will usually be more acceptable than rejecting the claim because of the epistemic difficulties involved.

---

[31] I will ignore additional concerns with respect to age discrimination—the concern is legitimate, but beside the point I hope to make.

The second, related, problem in determining whether the group membership clause is satisfied is the type of evidence required to judge disproportionality. My example concerning the bonus pay assumed that the relevant statistical data was available, at least when the relevant pool was clearly defined. This will not always be the case. Again, if the epistemic constraint imposed by the absence of such data results in the wholesale rejection of indirect discrimination claims, the very purpose of discrimination law could be compromised. Therefore, courts increasingly, and rightly, make judgments of disproportionality on a rule-of-thumb basis rather than strict statistical analysis.[32]

6.3.3 A Common Definition

This explanation shows how the different tools that discrimination law employs share conceptual and normative continuity. It accommodates the prohibition on indirect discrimination and harassment quite readily. Indirect discrimination is explicitly understood in terms of disproportionate adverse effect and the definition I have offered tracks this understanding. Even the prohibition on discriminatory harassment requires some sort of adverse effect—usually an expressive effect in the form of intimidation, humiliation, or offence.[33] In fact, an effect-based understanding of harassment is preferable to one that focusses on the harasser's conduct because it sits more comfortably with the recent doctrinal dilution (even abandonment) of the requirement of intention to harass in discrimination law.[34] The only (somewhat) adventurous aspect of this focus on effects is the recognition, with Doyle, that even 'direct discriminations on a proscribed ground ... produce disparate impacts that correlate with that proscribed ground'.[35] I will shortly argue that the current doctrinal approach to direct discrimination is better reflected by focussing on effects of the discriminatory act rather than the reasoning of the discriminator.

Although I have proposed a conceptually common foundation for direct and indirect discrimination and harassment, one should not conclude that there are no differences between these concepts. All jurisdictions, with the possible exception of Canada,[36] make a distinction between these forms of discrimination.

---

[32] This move was bolstered by a change in EU law from statistical evidence to proof of 'particular disadvantage'. See Framework Directive 2000/78/EC, art 2(2)(b); *Homer v Chief Constable of West Yorkshire Police* [2012] UKSC 15.

[33] See, for example, UK Equality Act 2010, s 26. See also, Elizabeth Anderson, 'Recent Thinking about Sexual Harassment: A Review Essay' (2006) 34 Philosophy and Public Affairs 284.

[34] See Chapter 3, section 3.3.4.

[35] Oran Doyle, 'Direct Discrimination, Indirect Discrimination and Autonomy' (2007) 27 Oxford Journal of Legal Studies 537, 542.

[36] *British Columbia (Public Service Employee Relations Commission) v BCGEU* [1999] 3 SCR 3.

The distinction between direct and indirect discrimination in particular is most relevant when it comes to the issue of justification. The definition offered here does not erase these differences, as we will realize while discussing justification. Under the definition I am defending here, discrimination is direct when V is constituted *entirely* by members of P and indirect when members of P *disproportionately* constitute V. Although a difference of degree rather than kind, it is not insignificant for that reason.

In one respect, this is at variance with the manner in which the distinction is drawn in practice. If there is evidence that an act was motivated by racial prejudice, in practice it would be classified as an act of *direct* discrimination even if the set of affected persons is disproportionately (rather than entirely) black. This is a doctrinal hangover from a malice-based understanding of direct discrimination in the early years. It nonetheless performs a useful function in denying to the malicious discriminator the possibility of satisfying the normally easier justification standard for indirect discrimination. Classifying this as indirect discrimination in my conceptual scheme makes little difference because it is doubtful that malicious acts could ever be justified (more on justification later). Practice often needs to draw bright lines to avoid unnecessary procedural burdens on the complainant and the court—sometimes this comes at the cost of conceptual clarity and theorists just need to live with practically useful messiness.

6.3.4 Lay and Legal Models

An entirely effects-based understanding of direct discrimination, as reflected in the group membership clause, is likely to be controversial. It stands in stark contrast to the lay appreciation of the problem of direct discrimination rooted in the *reasoning* of the discriminator. The lay model ascribes some causal role to a protected *ground* as a basis for φ-ing. Under this approach, the wrongness of discrimination lies in the reliance by the discriminator on a personal characteristic which is descriptively irrelevant to the distribution at hand. Under my victim-oriented definition, the central concern is with the impact of discrimination on *groups*, whereas the lay perpetrator-oriented understanding focusses on the discriminator's reasons. The lay model inspired the manner in which judges initially framed the doctrinal inquiry to determine whether direct discrimination had taken place (legislatures have typically been taciturn when it comes to defining discrimination, leaving the task to judges). Seeking to examine the discriminator's reasons, the judges asked whether the act was 'based on', 'because of', or 'on the grounds of' a protected characteristic. There is little doubt that, at least outside of the United States, judges have shifted the emphasis from grounds to groups, although some of the work performed by the original requirement of ground-based causation is now done by what I have characterized as the correlation clause.[37] Substantively the doctrine is undeniably effects-oriented. Even so, the lay model continues to be remarkably popular with moral philosophers, in part because it captures the lay understanding. For instance, Gardner suggested that 'the wrongfulness of discrimination is fundamentally linked to the fact that an improper ground of discrimination figures in the *operative* premises of the discriminator's thinking'; this led him to the controversial conclusion that direct discrimination was the 'paradigm case' of wrongful discrimination, and that the legal prohibition on indirect discrimination constituted a 'secondary paradigm'.[38]

Theorists who continue to insist on a causal role for protected grounds are largely drawing upon and seeking to preserve the lay understanding of the concept. In law, however, the term 'discrimination' has acquired a special, technical, meaning which overlaps with, but is not concurrent with, its ordinary meaning. At best, some courts have retained the lay *form* in which the inquiry is framed. It is easy to see why they would do so—after all, a legal approach to discrimination that is compatible with the lay model is more likely to claim legitimacy successfully. This is no trivial concern for a perpetually controversial area of law. The more daring of courts have been most upfront about this shift from the lay motive-based understanding of discrimination to the new effects-based approach. The Canadian Supreme Court, for example, has openly acknowledged that in discrimination law, 'the principal concern is the *effect* of the impugned law'.[39] Although it hasn't endorsed this position as explicitly, the South African Constitutional Court tends to spend very little time determining whether an allegedly discriminatory act was 'based on' a prohibited ground.[40] It has also made it clear that this requirement does not necessitate proof of subjective discriminatory intent.[41] The Court appears to assume this whenever protected groups are adversely affected. As two scholars put it: 'Falling within a listed ground

[37] Note that even in the group membership clause, grounds continue to play an implicit role, inasmuch as they *define* protected and cognate groups.

[38] John Gardner, 'On the Ground of Her Sex(uality)' (1998) 18 Oxford Journal of Legal Studies 167, 182. Emphasis in the original. Note that Gardner uses the term 'paradigm' differently from me. He characterizes an effects-based approach as the 'radical critique', at 187.

[39] *British Columbia (Public Service Employee Relations Commission) v BCGEU* [1999] 3 SCR 3 [47]. Emphasis in the original. See also, *Quebec v A* 2013 SCC 5 [196].

[40] Catherine Albertyn and Beth Goldblatt, 'Equality' in Stuart Woolman, Theunis Roux, and Michael Bishop (eds), *Constitutional Law of South Africa* (2nd edn, Juta 2009) 35–46: 'In the Constitutional Court's jurisprudence to date, there has been little dispute over ... [whether] discrimination is based on a prohibited ground.'

[41] *Pretoria City Council v Walker* 1998 (2) SA 363 [39].

enables a group to get through step one without anything further.'[42] Most of the analysis focusses instead on the nature of the adverse effect and its justification (what the Court terms its 'unfairness' analysis), whether the discrimination alleged is direct or indirect.

But even other courts which appear to keep the *form* of the inquiry close to the lay model are substantively asking the effects question. The United Kingdom's highest court is one example, whose decision in *James* has already been cited. There was no doubt in that case that the sex of affected persons played no role in the reasoning behind the action of the city council. It was genuinely only concerned with whether a person was of 'pensionable age'. Even so, the House of Lords held that the council had discriminated directly, because but for the sex of the affected person, he would not have suffered the adverse effect of the action concerned.[43] Implicit in the ruling is the additional proposition that it is unnecessary to prove any discriminatory intent in order to prove direct discrimination—yet another nail in the coffin of any approach that prioritizes the actual reasoning of the discriminator. As the dissenting judge complained, the ruling 'reduces to insignificance the words "on the ground of"'.[44] Traditionalists have no option but to deny the correctness of the decision.[45] The problem, however, is that the emphasis on adverse effects is now too entrenched in the jurisprudence of courts around the common law world to be dismissed as a mistake. The lay understanding of discrimination no longer reflects the legal doctrine on direct discrimination.

6.3.5 Doctrinal Difficulties with the Lay Model

The lay approach leads to several doctrinal problems—problems that an effects-based understanding of direct discrimination is best placed to resolve. The first of these problems is with the recognition of intersectional discrimination. Consider an employer who refuses to hire Asian women—he has no problem hiring non-Asian women, nor does he mind employing any men. He just believes that *Asian* women should not work outside their home.[46] The lay approach will struggle to identify the precise ground that has played a role in the reasoning of the employer—it is neither her race nor her sex which motivated

---

[42] Catherine Albertyn and Beth Goldblatt, 'Equality' in Stuart Woolman, Theunis Roux, and Michael Bishop (eds), *Constitutional Law of South Africa* (2nd edn, Juta 2009) 35–45.

[43] *James v Eastleigh Borough Council* [1990] 2 AC 751, 774. See also, Sandra Fredman, *Discrimination Law* (2nd edn, Oxford University Press 2011) 205.

[44] *James v Eastleigh Borough Council* [1990] 2 AC 751, 780.

[45] John Gardner, 'On the Ground of Her Sex(uality)' (1998) 18 Oxford Journal of Legal Studies 167, 182–3.

[46] *Mackie v G & N Car Sales Ltd t/a Britannia Motor Co* [2004] ET/1806128/03.

his refusal. It is a unique intersection of these characteristics. A discriminator-centric explanation is indeed possible, but will require much contortion in the form of imaginary, hybrid, grounds. By contrast, a victim-centred, effects-based, approach has no trouble recognizing intersectional discrimination. Since Asians as well as women are both protected groups, the Asian women who have been refused employment will be able to satisfy this clause twice over. Instead of demanding that the claimant must choose between her racial and her sexual identity before bringing the claim, or claim under a made-up hybrid 'ground', the law can sincerely acknowledge the especially pernicious nature of intersectional discrimination inasmuch as it puts a weight on her membership of two different protected groups (Asians and women).

The second problem with the lay understanding is that some of its academic proponents are forced, like Gardner, to give normative priority to direct discrimination and therefore characterize it as the central case of discrimination. This entails the shunting of indirect discrimination to the 'moral margins' of the phenomenon of discrimination, prohibited mainly due to 'institutional considerations'.[47] Doyle is right in calling this characterization into question as inadequately capturing the fact that in many cases—he cites sexual orientation discrimination—the incidence of indirect discrimination is temporally prior to direct discrimination and often has more pernicious implications for the victims. Because of its relatively hidden nature, indirect discrimination may even be more difficult to notice and challenge.[48]

Theorists who adopt the lay process-based approach to direct discrimination but want to avoid distinguishing it too sharply from indirect discrimination often suggest that the prohibition on indirect discrimination merely 'expand[s]' the relevant range of grounds. A ground which would not otherwise be a forbidden ground of discrimination (say, physical strength) becomes a forbidden ground of discrimination because it bears a certain relationship to the prohibited ground of distinction (sex).[49] Fishkin makes the same point by telling us that 'the majority of the future job applicants who benefited from the removal of the high school diploma requirement [which the *Griggs* court found to be indirectly discriminatory against blacks] were white'.[50] In some ways, these theorists are also suggesting a common conceptual foundation

[47] John Gardner, 'On the Ground of Her Sex(uality)' (1998) 18 Oxford Journal of Legal Studies 167, 183.

[48] Oran Doyle, 'Direct Discrimination, Indirect Discrimination and Autonomy' (2007) 27 Oxford Journal of Legal Studies 537, 549ff.

[49] Elisa Holmes, 'Anti-Discrimination Rights Without Equality' (2005) 68 Modern Law Review 175, 184.

[50] Joseph Fishkin, *Bottlenecks: A New Theory of Equal Opportunity* (Oxford University Press 2014) 247.

for direct and indirect discrimination—only from a direction opposite to my own. Instead of casting direct discrimination in the image of indirect discrimination (as I have done), they seek to do the opposite by suggesting that indirect discrimination is direct discrimination, just on different grounds. At any rate, Fishkin's approach maintains the conceptual (and possibly normative) priority of direct discrimination.

This analysis is problematic. Any theory of discrimination law needs to give an account of why certain characteristics (race, sex) are protected.[51] If all that indirect discrimination does is create new grounds of protection from direct discrimination, these new grounds (physical strength, educational qualification) need to jump through the same normative hoops that race and sex have crossed in order to be able to claim conceptual continuity. It should be obvious that discrimination law regimes do not treat these two categories of 'grounds' in the same way. The prohibition on race or sex discrimination is *comprehensive*. The prohibition on discrimination based on physical strength is *contingent*: only when such discrimination has an adverse effect on protected groups such as black people does it qualify for protection. White people who benefit from the voiding of a rule that indirectly discriminated against black people decidedly piggyback on the happy (or unhappy, depending on your point of view) coincidence that their lot has been cast with black people *in the particular context of this case*.[52] I do not deny that highlighting its trans-racial benefits may make indirect discrimination more palatable politically. We will learn shortly that this is a very important concern that often underpins the protection of cognate groups. But this fact does not detract from the primary purpose behind the prohibition of indirect discrimination, which is to seek to reduce and eliminate substantial, abiding, and pervasive relative group disadvantage in our societies. Pretending that discrimination law can deal with other types of disadvantages too, such as those based on educational qualifications, exaggerates its capabilities and distorts our understanding of its key functions. In sum, it is almost impossible to recognize the importance of indirect discrimination and still be faithful to a reasons-based lay model of what discrimination entails.

The final problem with the lay model is that it encourages hostility to affirmative action. If direct discrimination entails the discriminator's reliance on a protected ground in his reasoning, affirmative action automatically becomes suspect. The lay model makes affirmative action presumptively unacceptable because it treats it as directly discriminatory. One only needs to look

---

[51] I have given this account in Chapter 5, section 5.4.
[52] See generally, *Griggs v Duke Power Co* 401 US 424 (1971).

at reactionary rollback of protection in the US jurisprudence to realize the importance of acknowledging the conceptual and normative continuity not only between the prohibition on direct and indirect discrimination but also between this prohibition on the one hand and the provision for affirmative action on the other.[53] Law-makers outside the United States tend to see affirmative action as part of discrimination law and furthering the same goals, rather than as inimical to the prohibition on discrimination. Of course, we have to be careful when designing affirmative action measures. But the effects-oriented, group-based, legal model correctly recognizes their presumptive validity.

If we think that recognizing intersectional discrimination is important, that indirect discrimination is more than a mere adjunct to direct discrimination, and that affirmative action measures are sometimes necessary, we have reasons to prefer the legal model. There may be other benefits for the further development of the doctrine in a progressive direction: for example, an effect-based approach is likely to take cases involving implicit bias much more seriously than the motive-based lay approach.[54] We have these normative reasons in addition to the descriptive one: that the lay model simply fails to describe the contemporary shape of discrimination law in the first place. The arguments in this section boil down to this: law's understanding of discrimination (as explained in Chapter 3) is different from, and better than, how a layperson usually understands the phenomenon. If the two understandings ought to converge, this is an instance where society could do well to follow law's lead.

6.4 The Correlation Clause

After the adverse effect and the group membership clauses have been satisfied, our definition requires the satisfaction of the correlation clause. For paradigmatic discrimination, it requires that *there is a correlation between a person's membership of V and her (actual or perceived, or her associate's) membership of P*. Put simply, this clause requires that there is a correlation between the claimant suffering adverse effect and her membership of the protected group. This clause basically connects the adverse effect clause and the group

---

[53] *Ricci v DeStefano* 557 US 557 (2009); *Gratz v Bollinger* 539 US 244 (2003).

[54] Samuel Bagenstos, 'Implicit Bias, "Science," and Antidiscrimination Law' (2007) 1 Harvard Law and Policy Review 477. See also, Patrick Shin, 'Liability for Unconscious Discrimination? A Thought Experiment in the Theory of Employment Discrimination Law' (2010) 62 Hastings Law Journal 67, 100: 'the argument in favor of liability for unconscious discrimination truly is an argument for moving our conception of discrimination away from the paradigm of individual human action and more toward a conception that defines it as something like the expression of our persistent structures of social inequality'.

membership clause with a correlation requirement. In the case of collateral discrimination, the relevant correlation required is between *membership of V and her (actual or perceived, or her associate's) membership of C*. Except where the context suggests otherwise, all that is said for P here applies to C as well.

6.4.1 Causation to Correlation

In section 6.3 I rejected the requirement that discrimination is 'based on', 'because of', or 'on the ground of' a protected ground as no longer reflecting the practical reality of discrimination law.[55] That said, simply satisfying the adverse effect clause will not be sufficient either. Although courts no longer insist that sex discrimination is 'on the ground of' sex, they do still require (at least) a correlation between the adverse effect of the challenged act and the victim's membership of a protected group. As Shin points out, the law recognizes a wide range of forms this correlation could take: from a clear case of malice where there is prejudice against a group, to cases where the action is based on mistaken stereotypical assumptions about the abilities of the members of a group, to those where there is 'rational' statistical connection between group membership and a person's abilities.[56] In indirect discrimination cases, it is clearly not necessary that the discriminatory act *caused* the disproportionate adverse effect on members of a protected group.[57] To continue with our example concerning bonus pay in the previous section, it may be that the disproportionate impact on female employees was *caused* by the employer having begun to hire women in significant numbers only recently, or by the fact that the attrition rates for women employees was much higher than men (maybe because they tend to shoulder child-care responsibilities more frequently than men). Some such explanation as to why the bonus rule affects women disproportionately establishes causation. No such causal explanation is, however, demanded by law. All that is necessary is that there is a *correlation* between the adverse effect suffered and group membership.[58] Shin believes that the multiple manifestations of the correlation requirement expose a 'messy plurality' of underlying moral concerns in

[55] Contrast, incidentally, between discrimination on the *ground* of sex and sex as a protected *ground*—the first implies causation, which courts no longer insist on. The second uses ground interchangeably with personal characteristic.
[56] Patrick Shin, 'Is There a Unitary Concept of Discrimination?' in Deborah Hellman and Sophia Moreau (eds), *Philosophical Foundations of Discrimination Law* (Oxford University Press 2013) 172–3.
[57] Sandra Fredman, 'Addressing Disparate Impact: Indirect Discrimination and the Public Sector Equality Duty' (2014) 43 Industrial Law Journal 349.
[58] For reasons that will become clear later in this section, a finding of disproportionate adverse effect in indirect discrimination cases will normally *entail* a satisfaction of the correlation clause.

discrimination law.[59] In fact, however, these diverse means of establishing the requisite correlation are all animated by the same impulse: that the existence of such correlation identifies a second wrong, common to all *particular* acts of discrimination.

6.4.2 Wrongfulness of Particular Acts

We saw in Chapter 5 that the systemic goal of discrimination law is to reduce and eliminate relative group disadvantage. Now, we know that the group membership clause connects the prohibition of discrimination with the pursuit of that goal. The systemic goal would have been better pursued with a definition of discrimination that did not include the correlation clause. If the goal is to reduce relative group disadvantage, should an adverse effect on disadvantaged groups not suffice as a basis for prohibition? If the law wants to close the advantage gap between men and women, why not prohibit all acts which adversely affect women? Surely that would be a quicker way to get to the goal? What justifies the *additional* demand that the adverse effect suffered by women was *correlated* to the fact that they were women?

The reason is that although an approach without the correlation clause might be more efficient in seeking the overall systemic goal of discrimination law, and may even be justifiable when imposed on the state, regulation of private conduct by a liberal state needs to rest on surer footings. If a person opens a corner shop close to an existing one run by a woman and drives her out of business, the adverse effect clause and the group membership clause would have been satisfied. But, without more, there would be no correlation between adverse effect and group membership. In demanding a correlation over and above mere adversity, the correlation clause relies on our foundational assumption that the membership of these groups is either immutable or fundamentally valuable.[60] Since this is the case, we ought not to suffer adverse consequences *because of* our membership of these groups. But this is precisely what happens when the correlation clause is satisfied. We suffer adverse effects which have some correlation with our group membership—whether it is prejudice against our group, or stereotypical assumptions about our abilities, or statistically accurate, but nonetheless essentializing, features of our group, or even correlations where the chain of causation between the act and the effect is not obvious. Where there is such correlation, we suffer

---

[59] Patrick Shin, 'Is There a Unitary Concept of Discrimination?' in Deborah Hellman and Sophia Moreau (eds), *Philosophical Foundations of Discrimination Law* (Oxford University Press 2013) 172.

[60] See Chapter 5, section 5.4.

because of our group membership (or our perceived membership, or close association with members). When a graduation requirement disproportionately excludes blacks, a black victim suffers because she belongs to a group with low university enrollment. No such statement can be made with regard to the sex of the out-competed businesswoman in the preceding example.

This is what makes particular acts of discrimination wrongful—they impose costs on membership of groups whose membership is morally irrelevant or even valuable.[61] It is significant that the correlation clause examines the issue from the victim's point of view. It establishes that she suffered because of her group membership. This wrongfulness of *particular* acts of discrimination, in combination with the fact that their *systemic* impact is to exacerbate freedom-denying relative group disadvantage, makes them especially pernicious. Discriminatory acts are therefore doubly wrongful. On their own, neither wrong may justify the imposition of the antidiscrimination duty. Taken together, they have sufficient weight to do so, at least with respect to a select group of duty-bearers.

At this stage, one may raise a plausible objection: is this not a reintroduction of the 'because of' formula embedded in the lay model of discrimination? It may seem so, but is not in fact the case. The correlation clause is quite distinct from the 'because-of-her-sex' requirement in the lay model we are rejecting. This model asks whether *the discriminator acted* as he did because of the victim's protected characteristic: the legal model, on the other hand, demands to know whether *the victim suffered* on account of her membership of a protected group. This reinforces the victim-focussed group-orientation of the definition I have been defending.

Careful readers of this book may insist that one problem continues to linger. They will recall the first of the four conditions, noted far back in Chapter 2, which together give norms of discrimination law their identity as norms of *discrimination* law. Recall that this first (personal grounds) condition was that *[t]he duty-imposing norm in question must require some connection between the act or omission prohibited or mandated by the norm on the one hand and certain attributes or characteristics that persons have, called 'grounds', on the other.*

Does the correlation clause now call for an abandonment of the personal grounds condition? The two seem to be in tension. First, we are now focussed not on 'some connection' but on a 'correlation'. Second, the correlation we seek is between a person's membership of a protected *group* and her being adversely affected by φ, rather than its connection with a protected *ground*.

---

[61] See generally, Sophia Moreau, 'What is Discrimination?' (2010) 38 Philosophy and Public Affairs 143. Note that I speak of *moral* irrelevance rather than *descriptive* irrelevance. Membership of a group may be *morally* irrelevant even when the ground in question is rationally related to the distribution at hand.

In fact, doesn't this second tension show that the personal grounds condition is simply an expression of the lay, ground-focussed, model of discrimination that I have been arguing against?

The simple answer is that they are not incompatible. The tension between the correlation clause and the personal grounds condition is only apparent, the former is in fact little more than a refinement of the latter. The first tension is easier to explain away. The move away from 'some connection' is required because it is too broad. Every time the group membership clause is satisfied, one could say that *some* connection has been established. It may, for example, be said to be satisfied in the case of the out-competed businesswoman. Any connection, however tenuous, could amount to 'some connection'—it sets the threshold too low. A demand of causation, on the other hand, sets it too high—in many indirect discrimination cases, the adverse effect is not *caused* by one's membership of the protected group. Correlation lies somewhere in between these two extremes— of course, every causal relationship will satisfy the correlation requirement. But many non-causal relationships will also qualify, although some tenuous relationships may not. In setting this intermediate threshold, the correlation clause imposes an *additional* requirement, over and above the requirement imposed by the group membership clause. Merely requiring 'some connection' could make whole swathes of human activity potentially discriminatory, and require the final justification clause to do most of the work. The correlation clause performs a gatekeeping function, and is essential for establishing the wrongfulness of discrimination. The move from 'some connection' to 'correlation' simply preserves these functions.

An example should clarify the difference. Suppose a jury finds a woman guilty of shop-lifting and the judge sentences her in accordance with the law. The adverse effect and the group membership clauses are clearly satisfied— there is an adverse effect on a person who is a member of a protected group. No doubt, assuming the trial was fair, the sentence will be justifiable under the final clause of the definition. But the correlation clause will intervene to ensure that the inquiry does not even get to that stage. Since (in our example) there is no correlation between her sentence (the adverse effect) and her membership of a protected group (women), the correlation clause is not satisfied. There is no discrimination. Consider what would happen if the facts were slightly different. If the jury had convicted her on the assumption that of all the potential suspects, a woman was more likely to have shop-lifted a make-up kit, there would have been a causal link between her group membership and the adverse effect. The correlation clause would have been satisfied. Of course, much less than a causal link could also satisfy the clause. Suppose there is no causal evidence that the jury assumed that shop-lifters are women. Even then, if we know that juries disproportionately (or worse, exclusively) find women defendants guilty of shop-lifting, in relation to men, the correlation clause will be satisfied.

This scenario introduces an important caveat to the claim that the correlation clause is an *additional* requirement, over and above the group membership clause. The caveat is this: if the set of victims V is large enough, the satisfaction of the group membership clause will normally *entail* a satisfaction of the correlation clause. If only a handful of persons are adversely affected by an act, the fact they are all (or disproportionately) women could be due to random factors. However, the larger the set of those adversely affected, the less likely it is that the satisfaction of the group membership clause is down to randomness. If there are only two professors of philosophy at a university, the fact that they both happen to be men satisfies the group membership condition but not, without more, the correlation condition. However, if over 50 years, the university appoints 70 philosophy professors, only 2 of whom are women, we can more or less safely assume a correlation between the adverse affect (non-hire) and group membership (women). This will be a safe assumption even if we cannot *explain* by pointing to any particular feature of the hiring policy or its administration why this is the case (we would, of course, still need to show that *an act* had this adverse effect, in order to satisfy the adverse effect clause). Now, indirect discrimination claims typically involve a large set of adversely affected persons. This is not surprising, because it is very difficult to establish disproportionality with a very small set. It is not surprising, then, that there is no separate requirement to establish that the correlation clause has been satisfied in indirect discrimination cases. In practice—and this is the important point—the proof of disproportionality is, in itself, sufficient proof of non-random correlation. The vestigial 'because of' or 'on the ground of' requirement now performs the limited role of demanding a correlation between the adverse effect and group membership in direct discrimination cases involving a relatively small number of victims. Whether entailed in the group membership clause or established separately, conceptually the correlation clause is an important independent requirement.

The second tension between the correlation clause and the personal grounds condition may seem more significant. This tension is manifested in the move from demanding a relationship between an act and the *ground* in the latter formula to a relationship with *group* membership in the former one. It is this tension which makes my rejection of the ground-based lay model of discrimination look suspicious. But appearances are deceptive here. There is a difference between 'grounds' as personal characteristics (such as sex) which the personal grounds condition refers to and 'on the grounds of' (or, 'based on', 'because of', etc) as a causation requirement which the lay model demands. While *grounds* as personal characteristics (since they define protected groups, such as women) are implicit in the group-based approach, there is no requirement in this formula that discrimination should be *on the grounds of* sex, race, etc. Grounds, as used in the personal grounds condition, continue to be implicit in the correlation clause.

I hope readers are now reassured that this clause is no more than a refinement of the original condition we learnt in Chapter 2. It is, nonetheless, a necessary refinement. We have already seen that direct reliance on grounds by the lay model, even in the personal characteristics sense, have led to difficulties with comparators and intersectionality. Equally importantly, demanding a correlation between the adverse effect suffered and the victim's membership of the group (say, women) *contextualizes* the relationship in a manner that a correlation with the relevant personal ground (her sex) may not. We know that a person suffers discrimination not because she possesses a sex, but because that sex happens to be female. We are more likely to acknowledge the (negative or positive, true or false) stereotypes that exist about women, or the role that their educational disadvantage plays in limiting their access to opportunities, if we focus on women as a group rather than sex as a ground. Furthermore, this contextualization also helps us appreciate that the same conduct may amount to harassment when directed at certain persons—because of the specific history of their group—but may not be so when directed at others. Consider, for example, an employee who leaves a banana skin on a white colleague's table. Assuming that there are no black employees around and barring any other special considerations, the act may be a prank, possibly a nuisance, but is unlikely to be viewed as racial harassment by the target or by spectators. Even in rare cases—say if the skin is left inside his shoes, or the act is repeated frequently—when it may qualify as *harassment*, it will still not be *racial* harassment (and, therefore, not a concern of discrimination law). If, however, the victim was black, the pernicious racist history of comparisons between black people and apes is very likely to characterize this as an act of racial harassment. Our understanding directs attention to the contextual history of black people, rather than considering the phenomenon of race in the abstract.

The point is not that some of these issues cannot be resolved under a grounds-oriented formulation. It is rather that defining the correlation requirement in terms of groups is less distracting and more straightforward.

6.5 The Expressive Clause

I have labelled discrimination faced by members of cognate groups 'collateral'. For collateral discrimination to be established, an additional—expressive—clause needs to be satisfied. This clause requires that *Memberships of groups P and C have expressive salience.* Recall that P denotes relatively disadvantaged protected groups whereas C denotes their cognate dominant groups. The clause simply states that in order for members of the cognate groups to be protected, memberships of the cognate group and the protected group both need to have expressive salience. The rationale for this clause, I will explain later in this section, is that when it is satisfied asymmetric protection from discrimination can result in damaging societal consequences (for the protected group itself, as well as for society at large). We will learn that symmetric protection from paradigmatic as well as collateral discrimination is sometimes necessary to prevent the exacerbation of relative group disadvantage.

Membership of a group has expressive salience in a society when such membership is a source of important (and usually valued) personal identity to a critical mass of its members, and when this importance is recognized by a critical mass of the rest of the population of that society. When this is the case, group membership becomes imbued with significant social and cultural meaning. Members tend to take pride in their membership and celebrate it. They are likely to be sensitive to actions which are seen as insulting this pride.[62] Solidarity with other members of the group is often a feature of groups whose membership is characterized by expressive salience. These groups care deeply about the absolute and relative disadvantage that their members face. Groups with expressive salience are organic social entities: they are more than a mere collection of their individual members, often with a sense of their history (or mythology) and a distinct sub-culture.

On the face of it, it may be puzzling why a group's expressive salience should matter in determining whether its member has faced discrimination. Let me explain. One of the enduring debates in discrimination law is the question of symmetry of protection. If the point of discrimination law is to remedy relative group disadvantage, as I have argued it is, why is it that members of cognate groups are also protected from discrimination? We learnt in Chapter 3 that most jurisdictions offer *largely* asymmetric protection, inasmuch as they permit affirmative action measures to benefit protected groups, while typically prohibiting discrimination symmetrically for grounds such as race and sex and asymmetrically for disability and pregnancy. But why prohibit discrimination against men, straight people, and white people in the first place? Why not against the able-bodied and the not-pregnant? Is this all down to doctrinal confusion? The expressive clause shows that there may well be a method underlying this apparent madness.

---

[62] Tarunabh Khaitan, 'Dignity as an Expressive Norm: Neither Vacuous Nor a Panacea' (2012) 32 Oxford Journal of Legal Studies 1.

Let it be clear that for theorists who fundamentally accept that the point of discrimination law is to protect disadvantaged groups, certain explanations for protecting members of (some but not all) dominant groups will simply not do. Some theorists explain this symmetric protection on the ground of administrative convenience. Hellman, for example, says this is the case because 'Laws must generalize'.[63] The problem with this *administrative* explanation is that discrimination law is very happy to make the distinction between protected and cognate groups in several other contexts, including its asymmetric protection of disability or provisions for affirmative action. It is not clear what the special administrative burden is in refusing the protection from discrimination to cognate groups. Whether a person belongs to a particular group is usually not a controversial question (except, in the context of disability, where much judicial time is spent figuring out who is disabled and who isn't). A completely asymmetric approach would often reduce rather than increase the administrative burden. Alternatively, Hellman may have a principled rather than a pragmatic point in mind—laws must generalize because of the operation of some background principle which requires general (equal?) treatment. This, however, is also suspect, again because discrimination law is quite comfortable with non-general norms in certain contexts. There must be another explanation. One promising explanation puts the occasional symmetry in the antidiscrimination duty down to *political* expediency. It is easier for discrimination law to claim legitimacy if it carries the dominant groups along, which is what limited symmetry could facilitate. Where such legitimacy is not a worry—in the case of the able-bodied—the protection offered is asymmetric. This is a promising explanation, and may even be historically accurate. In the rest of the section, I am going to tease out a principled justification lurking behind this political expedient.

To do so, we need to first analyse different categories of groups and examine which are more likely to have expressive salience. Men, heterosexuals, cisgendered persons, middle-aged persons, and able-bodied persons constitute cognate groups in most societies. On the other hand, *different* religious, racial, and caste groups may be cognate groups in different societies, depending on their political, material, and social power in that society. Only the latter set of religious, racial, and caste groups seek to constitute the nation in their own image. In other words, potentially national groups (ie groups that have the potential to exclusively constitute a nation) such as those based on religion, race, language, tribe, or (possibly) caste tend to seek insular, endogamous,

---

[63] Deborah Hellman, *When is Discrimination Wrong?* (Harvard University Press 2008) 37.

homogenous familial, and national arrangements.[64] This means that there is usually an inter-generational identity between its members (ie different generations of its members are likely to be linked by blood and marital ties, and effects of direct discrimination on one generation are usually carried over to the next).[65] They are *potentially* national because these identity groups tend to want to, and have the potential to, constitute a nation (sometimes even a nation-state).[66] This potential has often been realized in the past few centuries. Given their political ambitions, these groups have often been involved in significant political violence (as perpetrators or victims, often both). Non-national identities based on sex, sexual orientation, gender, age, and disability, on the other hand, are usually not so insular and tend to cut across the family and the nation.[67] Members of the same family will usually include men as well as women, and often include disabled people as well as able-bodied people, or heterosexuals as well as (possibly closeted) homosexuals. Even when the dominant non-national groups try to purge their families and nations of their protected counterparts (usually homosexuals, disabled people, the transgendered, or the old), very rarely do these group identities come to fundamentally define nationhood. Many of the non-national protected groups, with the obvious exception of women, are permanent numerical minorities in most societies. Sometimes, they constitute a 'group' only in the loose sense of the term signifying a collection of individuals.[68]

The point of the rule-of-thumb distinction between potentially national and non-national groups is this. Potentially national groups almost invariably have expressive salience. It also follows that if a ground defines potentially national groups, the protected groups defined by it as well as their cognates are both likely to have expressive salience. Expressive salience of potentially national groups is, in other words, likely to be symmetric. For instance, all racial groups in a given society, whether protected or cognate, are likely to have expressive salience. The one exception to this is non-believers, who do constitute a group with a common religious status, but tend not to be potentially

---

[64] See generally, Benedict Anderson, *Imagined Communities: Reflections on the Origin and the Spread of Nationalism* (revised edn, Verso 2006).

[65] Oran Doyle, 'Direct Discrimination, Indirect Discrimination and Autonomy' (2007) 27 Oxford Journal of Legal Studies 537, 548–9.

[66] I include groups that have in fact acquired national characteristics within the scope of 'potentially' national.

[67] Activists have talked of the feminist nation and the queer nation. These claims of nationhood, however, have never been considered with adequate degree of seriousness by most members of the relevant groups. Inasmuch as a nation is an imagined community that resides principally in the minds of its nationals, this failure is sufficient to justify my calling these identities non-national.

[68] These are admittedly rough generalizations, and one may be able to point to exceptional cases.

national. Although normally symmetric, it is not necessary that the intensity with which such salience is felt by the members of rival potentially national groups is equal. Often, members of disadvantaged protected groups feel this salience with greater intensity than those of the dominant cognate groups.[69]

Non-national groups, on the other hand, may or may not have expressive salience. And they may have it asymmetrically, in the sense that it is possible for a protected group to have expressive salience but for its cognate to not have it. For example, those who are not-pregnant do not invest any expressive salience in this status as a group (even though, for particular individuals, not being/having been pregnant may be quite significant). Similarly, of the groups defined on the grounds of disability-status, the group consisting of able-bodied people does not have any expressive salience in most societies. Even among the protected disabled groups, it is probably only the deaf community which can currently be said to have significant expressive salience.[70] On the other hand, gays and lesbians have strenuously built a politics around their sexual identity in the past five decades or so. This has also led to the emergence of a weak, but noticeable, straight identity among heterosexuals. By contrast, both men and women have had expressive salience for a long time.

These are empirical claims, based on little more than armchair sociology—one may not accept them without further nuance or qualifications. I will take them to be, *broadly speaking*, true. What matters more, however, is the conceptual claim—that members of cognate groups are protected from discrimination only if the expressive clause is satisfied.[71] The starting point of this defence is the recognition of the complex relationship between expressive salience of group membership and relative group disadvantage, and of the impact of discrimination law on the expressive salience of a group.

Relative group disadvantage and expressive salience of the membership of a group often have a symbiotic relationship. Members of a group which suffers substantial, abiding, and pervasive relative disadvantage, especially in the socio-cultural dimension, have historically internalized these disadvantages. *Dalits*, women, homosexuals, and many other groups that have suffered unspeakable socio-cultural (expressive) disadvantage have, for centuries, believed that they deserve this disadvantage. One could say that their

---

[69] Beverly Tatum, '*Why are All the Black Kids Sitting Together in the Cafeteria?' And Other Conversations about Race* (Basic Books 1997) 93.

[70] Irene Leigh, Alan Marcus, Patricia Dobosh, and Thomas Allen, 'Deaf/Hearing Cultural Identity Paradigms: Modifications of the Deaf Identity Development Scale' (1998) 3 Journal of Deaf Studies and Deaf Education 329.

[71] In practice, determining whether the expressive clause is satisfied for a given group in a particular society may be difficult, especially for groups defined by grounds such as age. See *Gosselin v Quebec* [2002] 4 SCR 429.

identities have had negative expressive salience. These negative self-beliefs are likely to be challenged sooner or later, especially under democratic conditions.[72] The surest way to challenge socio-cultural disadvantage attached to one's group membership is to change the expressive connotations associated with such membership—a process that first happens internally within the group, but sooner or later leaks out to outsiders. The group starts taking pride in its identity and rejects the demeaning cultural meanings associated with it. Because this nascent pride in the membership is likely to be fragile, the group is likely to be vigilant against any expressive attacks and condemn demeaning behaviour or attitudes of others.

So long as the disadvantaged group's membership had negative expressive salience, the dominant group's members were able to enjoy their privileges unconsciously or sub-consciously. It is not really necessary for the members of the dominant group to consciously take pride in their membership. But when the disadvantaged group starts to assert its pride, one of the ways in which the dominant group may seek to retain its privileges is by investing its own membership with expressive salience. Mehta puts it pithily: 'The dispossessed may engage in [the politics of self-respect] because their structural position warrants it; the privileged may be susceptible because of gnawing anxiety and uncertainty about their status in a rapidly changing world.'[73] To sum up the discussion so far, under conditions of substantial, abiding, and pervasive relative group disadvantage (especially when this disadvantage is socio-cultural), it is quite likely that the membership of the protected group will come to have expressive salience. Whether the dominant (cognate) group's membership also acquires expressive salience is a question of sociological fact, although it is likely that potentially national groups will acquire this more readily than non-national groups.

But when this does happen, it can lead to a pernicious and competitive politics of expression—relevant groups come to treat it as a zero-sum game where an insult to one group generates pride in another. Again, drawing upon his insights into the politics of expression in India, Mehta puts it best: 'the struggles to affirm one's moral worth do not necessarily take the form of a demand for justice. Rather that struggle can express itself as much through a competitive debasement of others as it can in a demand for reciprocity and mutual recognition.'[74] Given the unbalanced scales, the protected group, only beginning to emerge from a history of socio-cultural disadvantage, is

---

[72] Democracy (with universal suffrage) entails a fundamental recognition of everyone's moral worth. Once this first step towards self-respect has been taken, the rest is bound to follow.

[73] Pratap Mehta, *The Burden of Democracy* (Penguin 2003) 51.

[74] Pratap Mehta, *The Burden of Democracy* (Penguin 2003) 45.

likely to be faced with concerted attempts to put it back to its erstwhile social and cultural place. What is worse, this debasing politics also essentializes the supposed 'cultures' of both the dominant and disadvantaged groups, making them resistant to any internal dissenting or reforming voices. There are no victors in this type of culture war—only losers.

Under these circumstances, any expressive intervention by the state must take care to ensure that it does not end up adding fuel to this politics of competitive debasement between rival groups. The state and its law are particularly powerful players in expressive politics. Look no further than the continuing expressive impact of the recognition of caste and religion as administrative categories by the colonial government in British India, to be wary of the role the state can play.[75] We were cautioned in Chapter 4 that the expressive power of the state is a treacherous tool that should be deployed with great caution. This is because expressive politics frequently has unforeseen consequences, because an individual's right to freedom of expression is an important liberal value, and because the state can at best facilitate the conditions under which persons feel able to have self-respect—it cannot force anyone to possess this good.[76] Now we have another reason why the state ought to be wary—even with the best will in the world, it could easily end up encouraging an expressive politics of competitive misrecognition rather than a politics of mutual recognition and reciprocity. It could accentuate the dominant group's perceived (even if false) sense of victimhood, catalysing its efforts to consolidate the salience of its membership. In turn, this could undermine efforts to reduce the socio-cultural disadvantage of the protected group. Relative group disadvantage cannot be reduced without de-intensifying this politics of competitive expressivism. In the context of symmetric expressive salience between protected and cognate groups, seemingly partisan state expression in favour of the disadvantaged unfortunately has the potential to accentuate rather than ameliorate the expressive disadvantage that a protected group faces.

The state's problem is that once it commits to having some sort of discrimination law, it no longer has the option of non-expression (although it is doubtful whether it ever has this option, with or without discrimination law). The very enactment and shape of discrimination law has considerable expressive currency in most societies. Even within discrimination law, its general approach to the question of symmetry appears to have the greatest expressive import

---

[75] The issue is a complex one. See generally, Nicholas Dirks, *Castes of Mind: Colonialism and the Making of Modern India* (Princeton University Press 2001); Michael Anderson, *Islamic Law and the Colonial Encounter in British India* (Grabels 1996).

[76] See Chapter 4, section 4.4.

(alongside its approach to cases where a discrimination claim clashes with the freedom of religion).[77] For a legal tool designed to end relative group disadvantage, this may seem ironic. But we live in the world we do. In this world, an asymmetric antidiscrimination duty that did not, at least formally, protect dominant groups that have expressive salience will be (often wrongly) seen as implying that their interests do not count. This is likely to catalyse retaliation (including expressive retaliation), often targeted at the protected group. Given the impossibility of non-expression, the next best alternative is a default preference for expressive even-handedness between salient groups, unless there are robust reasons for apparent partisanship which outweigh this preference.

The upshot of the discussion is this: sometimes the best way to eliminate disadvantage faced by black people is to ban discrimination against black people as well as white. This is the case when both blackness and whiteness have come to acquire expressive salience in a particular society. It should be clear that the protection of dominant groups from discrimination piggybacks on the disadvantage of protected groups. The main reason white people are protected from discrimination in law is that the absence of such protection may exacerbate the relative group disadvantage suffered by black people. Without their mutual expressive salience, discrimination against white people will be the same as discrimination against the able-bodied or those who are not-pregnant: it may be irrational, even immoral, but not, without more, debilitating enough to merit legal intervention. This does not, of course, imbue discrimination law with any entrenched partisanship. If social facts change, and white people become a relatively disadvantaged group in any society, they must constitute protected groups.

Expressive symmetry has another implication. In many cases of collateral discrimination, although the particular adverse effect is suffered by members of dominant groups, they are not the only victims. Members of protected groups may also suffer expressive adversity because of collateral discrimination—so a collaterally discriminatory act often harms both white and black people, men and women, Christians and Muslims, at the same time. Sometimes this particular adverse effect can be quite severe.[78] Consider a regime of conscription for men alone.[79] This amounts to collateral

---

[77] On the latter, see *Eweida v United Kingdom* [2013] ECHR 37; *Bull v Hall* [2013] UKSC 73.

[78] Sex discrimination against men who do not conform to the mainstream norms of 'masculinity' is one example. However, a better way to understand this may be to view non-conforming men as a relatively disadvantaged group who suffer paradigmatic discrimination, rather than a dominant group which face collateral discrimination. See John Kang, 'The Burdens of Manliness' (2010) 33 Harvard Journal of Law and Gender 477.

[79] This, by the way, is one instance where a levelling-down solution may be the best outcome—ending conscription rather than extending it to women.

discrimination because men lose significant liberty, but it also causes expressive injury to women, who are judged as too weak to be conscripted. The systemic adverse effect is, of course, to expand the advantage gap between men and women by furthering the socio-cultural disadvantage suffered by women (and, possibly, material disadvantage too, if conscription is not too demanding and handsomely compensated). What follows is that when the expressive clause is satisfied, collateral discrimination against men could sometimes also amount to paradigmatic discrimination against women. The difference may simply boil down to who is able to bring a claim.

Furthermore, we all carry multiple characteristics, and discrimination law will protect white women, disabled white people, and white gays and lesbians in any case. Its apparent partisanship is in fact recognition of the priority deserved by the more pressing interests of *disadvantaged* groups, howsoever constituted. It will be a relatively small, and exceptionally privileged, section of any population which does not belong to any disadvantaged group protected by discrimination law. For this reason, discrimination law, properly understood, could encourage a fellowship of the disadvantaged, where coalitions are built across different facets of disadvantage.[80] Instead of being divisive, it could encourage social solidarity and cohesion. Sometimes this may require concessions in the form of symmetric protection because the state's apparent (even if misunderstood) partisanship in the face of symmetric expressive salience could lead to social 'balkanization'. As Siegel perceptively puts it, 'Race-conscious resentments among the racially privileged matter because, if ignored, they may inhibit the amelioration of racial stratification and because these resentments may reflect displaced expressions of other forms of inequality.'[81]

To sum up, when neither group has sufficient expressive salience, or when only the protected group has it, there is no need for symmetric protection. However, when the protected group *and* its cognate group(s) have expressive salience, symmetric protection under the antidiscrimination duty may become desirable. This preserves some semblance of expressive even-handedness by the state, and is therefore more conducive to a politics of reciprocal recognition rather than one of competitive debasement. Of course, there are contexts (such as affirmative action) in which asymmetry is necessary, even required.[82] But

[80] Tarunabh Khaitan, 'Reading *Swaraj* into Article 15: A New Deal for all Minorities' (2009) 2 NUJS Law Review 419.

[81] Reva Siegel, 'From Colorblindness to Antibalkanization: An Emerging Ground of Decision in Race Equality Cases' (2011) 120 The Yale Law Journal 1278, 1300. See also, Hugh Collins, 'Social Inclusion: A Better Approach to Equality Issues?' (2004-2005) 14 Transnational Law and Contemporary Problems 897.

[82] In Chapter 8, section 8.2.4, I will explain that the asymmetry in discrimination is better understood as 'priority' rather than 'partisanship'.

a default acceptance of symmetric protection for all groups with expressive salience allows the state to dodge an expressive minefield at relatively little cost. This is because, given relative group disadvantage, cases of direct discrimination against members of dominant groups will be few (assuming the law does not characterize affirmative action as discrimination). When there are genuine cases of discrimination, the material advantage at stake is likely to be small. Since norms of dominant groups underlie most of our social institutions, instances where a dominant group is being discriminated against indirectly will be even rarer. In practice, therefore, a formal symmetric protection for dominant as well as vulnerable groups is likely to make little difference to the objective of eliminating relative group disadvantage. What is more, it might even aid that pursuit. This defence of occasional symmetry has some resonance with the pragmatic concern that giving the dominant group a stake in the regime is more likely to ensure its stability. The principled exploration of this pragmatic concern in terms of expressive salience brings out nuances that will become very important when we come to consider the legitimacy of affirmative action.

6.6 The Justification Clause

The final clause, common to both paradigmatic and collateral discrimination, is the justification clause: φ-*ing lacks adequate justification*. Whether a conduct should be called 'discriminatory' only if it is unjustified is a fraught question. One view might be that characterizing a conduct that satisfies all clauses of the definition except the justification clause as 'discriminatory' captures the sense that it is being permitted with some regret and that in an ideal world it should not have happened in the first place. This view seeks to capture the wrongfulness of conduct that perpetuates relative group disadvantage, even when it is permitted by law. There is something to this view. It is based on the correct factual premise that 'discrimination' has come to acquire a powerful normative currency in our societies, and the label conveys moral condemnation of the act. We have already seen that the legal model of discrimination is out of sync with the lay model. However, the legitimacy of the embattled legal model is likely to be less threatened if unneccesary divergence from the lay model is avoided. For this reason, it will be unwise to call at least some types of justified conduct discriminatory.

6.6.1 Justification and Proportionality

Some justifications are based on the 'proportionality' of the duty-bearer's conduct. Proportionality is a technical term, and interpreted in many different ways. I understand an act to be proportionate if it seeks to achieve a legitimate (and, sometimes, sufficiently important) objective, is suitable and necessary for achieving that objective, and is proportionate in the narrow sense (ie the benefit that is likely to accrue is not outweighed by the harm done by the discriminatory act).[83] The legitimacy of an objective will depend on the nature of the enterprise—objectives that are legitimate for a business to pursue may not be legitimate for the state, for example. The *raison d'être* of the enterprise is an important consideration. Apart from legitimacy, discrimination law also tends to demand that the objective is sufficiently important to its *raison d'être*, rather than merely incidental to it. Suitability and necessity inquiries are primarily factual, whereas the narrow proportionality inquiry is normative as well as factual. Most stages of the inquiry demand particular regard to the competing interests of the discriminator and the victim—we will examine some of these interests later in the section. Proportionality is a means-ends inquiry. Note also that 'proportionality', used in the context of justification, is different from the 'disproportionality' required to establish indirect discrimination.

6.6.2 Permitted and Justified Discrimination

There is, however, another way of 'justifying' discriminatory conduct. I may decide not to have any disabled friends. Such a decision would be morally reprehensible, but I ought to be permitted to make it anyway given the strong autonomy interest I have in freely determining who I should be friends with. This conduct does indeed merit being labelled discriminatory (and the lay model would agree), even if it is 'justified' in a manner of speaking.[84] I do not treat this type of defence of discriminatory conduct as a *justification* under the final clause. The correct way to understand this is as (wrongful) discriminatory conduct that I have a right to engage in anyway—before this right, my antidiscrimination duty gives way. We might call it *permitted* discrimination, to contrast it with *justified* discrimination. Justified discrimination is only *prima*

---

[83] For Alexy, rights that admit limitations are 'principles' or 'optimization requirements' which require the realization of something to the greatest extent possible, given countervailing concerns: see generally, Robert Alexy, *A Theory of Constitutional Rights* (Julian Rivers tr, Oxford University Press 2002) 58.

[84] On intimate discrimination generally, see Elizabeth Emens, 'Intimate Discrimination: The State's Role in the Accidents of Sex and Love' (2009) 122 Harvard Law Review 1307.

facie wrongful, whereas permitted discrimination may even be wrong *all-things-considered*. In this section we are concerned mainly with justified, rather than permitted, discrimination.

Before we consider what might amount to 'justification' in this sense, a caveat on language: despite what I have just said, it is cumbersome to refer to conduct that has satisfied the other clauses of the definition but not (yet) the justification clause as 'prima facie discriminatory'. I will therefore loosely refer to such conduct as 'discriminatory' before considering whether it can be justified. Readers, I hope, will forgive this imprecision for the sake of readability.

6.6.3 Legislative and Judicial Determination

We know from Chapter 3 that most jurisdictions allow the justification of indirect discrimination, some allow it for direct discrimination, and none allow it for harassment (although an employer could justify certain breaches of her positive duty to protect her employees from harassment by co-workers).[85] Jurisdictions (such as the United Kingdom) whose statutory provisions do not allow the adjudicative justification of direct discrimination tend to have numerous statutory exceptions to the prohibition on discrimination. These jurisdictions also tend to permit justification of direct discrimination in their constitutional provisions.[86] While a failure to provide reasonable accommodation cannot be justified, most of the justification-related considerations are looked into while determining the 'reasonableness' of the accommodation sought. Where no justification plea is allowed in law, what we essentially have is a general *legislative* determination that the possibility of a justification defence succeeding is small enough to merit blanket exclusion. In these cases, the legislature simply removes a requirement which it thinks could lead to a waste of judicial resources in most cases, although its absence may result in a few genuinely justifiable cases falling through the cracks. It is not surprising that there is a significant body of opinion in the United Kingdom that holds that the resulting unfairness is not outweighed by the regulatory convenience of the blanket rule.[87] That said, even when its justification is possible, justifying direct discrimination is likely to be more difficult than justifying indirect

---

[85] *Faragher v Boca Raton* 524 US 775 (1998).

[86] In the UK, direct discrimination cannot normally be justified only under the Equality Act. However, under its constitutional provision—Article 14 of the European Convention of Human Rights, made enforceable by the Human Rights Act of 1998—direct discrimination is justifiable. Even under the Equality Act, direct discrimination is acceptable if it is a proportionate pursuit of a 'genuine occupational requirement': schedule 9, para 1.

[87] *R (on the application of E) v Governing Body of JFS* [2009] UKSC 15 [9].

discrimination. The rationale for this will become clear once we examine the factors to which a justification analysis is sensitive.

Before we examine what these factors are, note that just as legislatures sometimes deem certain categories of discrimination to be unjustifiable for regulatory reasons, they also do the opposite. Frequently, they deem certain types of discriminatory conduct to be justified—this is usually expressed through exceptions carved out from the general prohibitions on discrimination, especially with respect to grounds such as age, relgion, or disability.[88] As Lady Hale acknowledged in the British context: 'The distinction between direct discrimination … and indirect discrimination … is crucial: not because direct discrimination can never be justified, … but because the justifications are expressed in the legislation.'[89] We will appreciate at least some of the numerous and apparently messy legislative exceptions and inconsistencies in antidiscrimination legislation better if we allow for the possibility that it is sometimes wise to make judgments over *justified* and *permitted* discrimination generally, rather than leaving the determination in particular cases to judges. Criticism is due only when these general legislative judgments are wrong, or when the regulatory benefits of a clear rule are outweighed by the unfairness that results from the denial of individual adjudicative assessment of each case based on all relevant factors.[90]

6.6.4 Wrongfulness and Standard of Review

A proportionality analysis can employ a varying standard of review. A low-intensity review is deferential to the assertions and judgments of the discriminator. A high-standard review is more sceptical. In a constitutional context, standards of review are determined on the basis of institutional considerations.[91] The US Supreme Court famously employs different standards of review depending on what ground of discrimination is implicated.[92] The institutional considerations are no doubt relevant, especially when the proportionality analysis is being conducted by judges. However, the standard of review that is employed in discrimination law can also be understood to be sensitive to the degree of

---

[88] Most jurisdictions, for example, have some notion of an age of majority for young children, below which their rights are significantly limited.

[89] *Bull v Hall* [2013] UKSC 73 [16].

[90] Duncan Kennedy, 'Form and Substance in Private Law Adjudication' (1976) 89 Harvard Law Review 1658.

[91] Tarunabh Khaitan, 'Beyond Reasonableness: A Rigorous Standard of Review for Article 15 Infringement' (2008) 50 Journal of the Indian Law Institute 177.

[92] See Suzanne Goldberg, 'Equality Without Tiers' (2004) 77 Southern California Law Review 481.

wrongness of the discriminator's act. This connection is not evident in the doctrine, but there are strong reasons to accept that it exists.

So far we have learnt that discrimination is wrongful because it exacerbates substantial, pervasive, and abiding relative group disadvantage, and because it makes the victim suffer because of her normatively irrelevant or valuable group membership. These two features are common to all acts of discrimination and legitimate their regulation by the state. But not all discriminatory acts are wrong to the same extent—certain states of the discriminator's mind attract more blame than others.

None of the clauses in the definition of discrimination stipulate any particular state of mind that the discriminator must possess. In this sense, the liability in discrimination law is strict. This is, by and large, an accurate reflection of the practice of discrimination law outside the United States. That is not to deny that discrimination is often malicious, intentional, reckless, or negligent.[93] The presence of these mental states respectively organizes discriminatory acts on a sliding scale of decreasing blameworthiness (with the absence of relevant mens rea defining one end of the spectrum—at this point, the action is simply wrongful but not blameworthy).[94] In general, we can say that the higher the degree of blame, the more difficult it is in law to justify discriminatory conduct. This is in keeping with the usual approach to civil liability, which does not necessarily depend on proof of subjective mens rea, but its existence can expand liability or result in higher damages.

It is doubtful that malicious or intentional discrimination is ever justified. Harassment usually entails malice or intention and is, for that reason, not justifiable. This is as good as the law demanding an extremely high standard of review to determine justifiability of malicious or intentional discrimination.

Given the exact correspondence between those affected by direct discrimination and membership of a protected (or expressively salient cognate) group, it is likely that direct discrimination will usually entail at least a reckless disregard for the risk that the victim could suffer because of her group membership. Even in *James*, the city council can be said to have been reckless to the possibility that men will be adversely affected because of their being men when it gave concessions to those of pensionable age (in a context where women reached the

---

[93] Denise Réaume, 'Harm and Fault in Discrimination Law' (2001) 2 Theoretical Inquiries in Law 349.

[94] *R (on the application of E) v Governing Body of JFS* [2009] UKSC 15 [9]: 'Nothing that I say in this judgment should be read as giving rise to criticism on moral grounds of the admissions policy of JFS in particular or the policies of Jewish faith schools in general, let alone as suggesting that these policies are "racist" as that word is generally understood.'

pensionable age sooner than men).[95] Had they not been so reckless, they could still have achieved their objective of being generous to those on low income by providing concessions to persons actually living on pensions, rather than relying on the proxy of pensionable age which was so closely connected with sex. As the dissenting judge Lord Griffiths recognized, this would not have been unlawful.[96] What is usually referred to as subconscious bias in the American literature is probably better explained as a possibly reckless (or, at least, negligent) reliance on deep-seated, if unacknowledged, prejudice or stereotypical assumption.[97] Frequently the mens rea in direct discrimination cases will be stronger than mere recklessness or negligence. Most jurisdictions recognize this by making justification in direct discrimination cases harder, if not impossible. Difficulties arise in those rare cases where there is no blame whatsoever—because these cases exist, at least some of them may be able to satisfy even high-threshold justification requirements. It is for this reason that, subject to regulatory concerns, it may be wise for the law to allow some possibility of justifying direct discrimination.

The typical case of indirect discrimination is somewhat different. At least after the disproportionate adverse effect on a protected group has been pointed out to the duty-bearer, continuing indirect discrimination will at least entail negligence. Under the conceptual distinction I have drawn, it is possible for a discriminator to discriminate indirectly with malice, intention, or recklessness. But when these elements are absent, the action is wrongful without being blameworthy (or involves a lower degree of blame). Hence, the relatively easier justifiability of indirect discrimination—or, which is the same thing, a more deferential standard of review for this type of discrimination.

As with other areas of civil liability such as torts and contract, the mental state of the discriminator is also relevant to the question of remedies. Jurisdictions frequently do not allow the award of damages if discrimination is not intentional, or make it easier to award damages, sometimes including special damages, when it is so.[98]

---

[95] Ignore, for this discussion, the fact that *James* was in fact a case of collateral rather than paradigmatic discrimination.

[96] *James v Eastleigh Borough Council* [1990] 2 AC 751, 768.

[97] Samuel Bagenstos, 'Implicit Bias, "Science," and Antidiscrimination Law' (2007) 1 Harvard Law and Policy Review 477, 483f. On moral responsibility for unconscious bias, see Patrick Shin, 'Liability for Unconscious Discrimination? A Thought Experiment in the Theory of Employment Discrimination Law' (2010) 62 Hastings Law Journal 67, 93ff. See also, Charles Lawrence, 'The Id, the Ego, and Equal Protection: Reckoning with Unconscious Racism' (1987) 39 Stanford Law Review 317.

[98] UK Equality Act 2010, s 124(4) and (5); 42 USC § 1981a; Canadian Human Rights Act 1985, s 53(3).

Thus, the existence and level of blame in the duty-bearer's conduct is an important factor under the justification clause—it determines the intensity with which the conduct in question will be judged. In the absence of blame higher than mere negligence (ie in most indirect discrimination cases), the proportionality-based justification requirements will be easier to satisfy. Where there is greater blame, on the other hand, justification may be very difficult, or even impossible. The distinction between direct and indirect discrimination, normally, tracks the level of blame (or fault) that attaches to the discriminatory act. This discussion should clarify why jurisdictions treat as directly discriminatory conduct that under my definition would count as indirect discrimination, if there is evidence of mens rea higher than mere negligence. The practical effect is simply to apply a very demanding standard of review, but this is achieved through the conceptually messy path of conflating the nature of adverse effect with mens rea-based blameworthiness. The two are related but distinct. Practical difficulties in adducing proof of subjective mental states explain why the law tracks fault elliptically through the direct-indirect distinction. It follows that the mental state of the discriminator is not irrelevant to discrimination law—only that it is relevant at a different stage and for a different purpose than is supposed by the lay model.

6.6.5 Interests of the Duty-Bearer

The costs of antidiscrimination are often borne solely by the duty-bearer in private contexts, but one that could sometimes be distributed more broadly (through, say, insurance). Prohibiting discrimination can be expensive (so can failing to prohibit it, incidentally: the main question is *who* should bear these costs). This is not because, as some wrongly suppose, discrimination law seeks to undercut merit. The antidiscrimination duty does not require any employer, for example, to hire someone who is under-qualified.[99] Certainly, the duty requires an interrogation of what is understood as 'merit', and often exposes majoritarian biases that masquerade as requirements of merit. But this exposure only makes a workplace more meritocratic, not less. There are non-financial costs associated with discrimination too, but we will focus on the financial alone, since they tend to be more controversial. The pecuniary costs of antidiscrimination are usually of three types: transitional, informational, and accommodative.

Before we examine these costs, note that the question of whether financial costs can be considered for justifying discrimination is contentious. The European Court of Justice appears not to accept 'purely financial

---

[99] *Equal Employment Opportunity Commission v Wyoming* 460 US 226 (1983) 239.

considerations' as a justification at all,[100] although Canadian courts have recognized that they cannot always be ignored.[101] Since we understand the concept of justification in an institutionally neutral sense, it is clear that even in EU law, financial considerations do justify discrimination. The difference is that this judgment is made by the legislature rather than judges. How else could we explain EU law's permission for age discrimination in jobs where the employer invests in training the staff?[102] Similarly, the UK Equality Act makes exceptions for landlords with 'small premises',[103] while Title VII of the US Civil Rights Act only applies to persons who employ 15 or more workers.[104]

The question is not whether financial costs are relevant (they clearly are), but how and when they are relevant. Minimizing financial costs is surely a *legitimate* interest of any enterprise. The main question is whether it is sufficiently weighty to override competing claims of discrimination. In most cases, it will not be a sufficiently weighty objective.

That the prohibition of discrimination imposes costs is no secret. If this mere fact can be relied upon to justify all forms of discriminatory conduct, there would be little point to the antidiscrimination duty. In fact, its costliness is already accounted for in the law's cautious and conservative imposition of the antidiscrimination duty on a select group of persons.[105] Furthermore, with respect to enterprises whose main objective is to make profit, the duty is typically imposed on their competitors too, at least those within national borders. Competitive disadvantage will not, usually, be a valid plea. The cost of the duty must have a certain exceptional quality for it to be of significance. In effect, the cost has to be so substantial that it threatens the very existence of the enterprise. The background assumption is that the enterprise itself is legitimate, and should not be forced to shut down operations because of discrimination law. There may be exceptions, for example an association whose only goal is to promote racism: it has no legitimate *raison d'être*.[106] In fact, this limited accommodation of means-end 'rationality' of certain types of discrimination shows us that relevance-based concerns are not entirely alien to discrimination law. We have rightly rejected accounts explaining the wrongness of discrimination based on the notion that discriminatory

---

[100] C-236/09 *Association belge des Consommateurs Test-Achats v Conseil des ministres* [2012] 1WLR [68].

[101] *Newfoundland and Labrador Association of Public and Private Employees v Treasury Board* 2004 SCC 66; see also, Hester Lessard, ' "Dollars Versus [Equality] Rights": Money and the Limits on Distributive Justice' (2012) 58 Supreme Court Law Review (2d) 299.

[102] Framework Directive, Art 6(1)(c).   [103] Schedule 5, paras 3–4.

[104] 42 USC § 2000e(b).   [105] See Chapter 7.

[106] cf *Boy Scouts of America v Dale* 530 US 640 (2000).

conduct is irrelevant to any legitimate objective—this, we know well, is not always the case. Descriptive relevance, instead of being an explanatory foundation, acts as a limiting principle, urging us to tolerate discrimination when the discriminatory conduct is unavoidably necessary to pursue a very important objective. With this qualification in place, let us look at the three types of costs that a duty-bearer may be called upon to incur.

Transitional costs are essentially compliance costs, incurred during the process of changing the discriminatory rules, practices, or conduct. These may also include legal costs, especially if the legal requirements are difficult to understand. These costs are common to all laws seeking to regulate behaviour and ought not to be part of the justification analysis. That said, there is merit in the law seeking to minimize transitional costs, especially by providing clear, uncomplicated guidelines as far as this is possible. Courts must always remember that the success of the law in achieving its objective will depend largely on voluntary compliance without need for adjudication. Voluntary compliance, in turn, will happen readily only when the antidiscrimination norms are internalized by the duty-bearers. If the availability of justification is uncertain, the scope of the antidiscrimination duty becomes unpredictable, thereby making norm internalization difficult. It is not surprising that legislatures are often tempted to draw clear, if rigid, justification rules to avoid some of the costs incurred in sending confused messages to the duty-bearers, even at the cost of injustice in some cases.

The second type of cost imposed by the antidiscrimination duty is *informational*. A prohibition on direct discrimination may impose information costs, inasmuch as it prohibits reliance on a person's membership of certain groups as a proxy for relevant considerations. If the proxy is spurious, ie if it bears no real correlation to the ostensible qualification, there is no information cost (in fact, some misinformation is avoided). It is only when group membership is a non-spurious proxy—it does indeed serve as a rule-of-thumb criterion for judging a candidate—that outlawing direct discrimination incurs information costs because the duty-bearer has to gather relevant information from other sources. This may often require individualized assessment of criteria which were previously judged through proxies. Not all non-spurious proxies are the same. Some proxies correlate to group membership because of existing socio-cultural norms (women are more likely to care for children than men) or because of the reaction of other persons (a black cop may be less effective in a racist all-white neighbourhood).[107] These proxies do predict

---

[107] Larry Alexander, 'What Makes Wrongful Discrimination Wrong? Biases, Preferences, Stereotypes and Proxies' (1992) 141 University of Pennsylvania Law Review 149, 168–71.

with statistical accuracy, but their accuracy is a result of existing relative group disadvantage. Allowing justifications based on these proxies will frustrate the main objective of discrimination law. At any rate, these proxies are only contingently non-spurious because an effective antidiscrimination regime should change these socio-cultural norms and the reaction of others, rendering their proxy-role spurious over time.[108]

The main difficulty with respect to information costs arises when the use of stable, non-spurious, proxies is prohibited. These proxies are usually true because of biological factors—for example, that women tend to live longer than men, or that white people are more susceptible to certain diseases than non-white people, or that completely blind persons cannot see. They are not dependent on social or cultural contingencies. For such proxies, the better they are in their role as proxies for genuinely relevant qualifications, the more wasteful the information cost of individualized assessment will be. At one extreme are cases where the proxy is always accurate. For example, complete blindness is a good proxy in all jobs that essentially require an ability to see, such as an airline pilot or a bus driver. In these cases, it is clearly a waste of time, effort, and money to insist on individualized assessment. Difficulty arises in cases where the proxy is a good one, but not always accurate— for example, advanced age as a proxy for visual acuity. Many, but not all, over-65-year-olds have eye-sight so poor that they cannot work effectively as airline pilots. Prohibiting age discrimination in these cases will impose a significant information cost on the airline, and it ought to be a relevant consideration in determining whether the discrimination is justified. The more accurate a proxy one's membership of a group is for some other judgment, the higher is the opportunity cost for the duty-bearer being required to collect information individually. Given that age and certain types of disabilities are often good, non-spurious, proxies for certain relevant qualifications, it is no surprise that the antidiscrimination duty is often less demanding with respect to groups defined by these grounds.

Even highly accurate, stable, non-spurious proxies can sometimes be legitimately prohibited by discrimination law. The sex of a young woman is a good proxy for her likelihood of becoming pregnant. If pregnancy affects one's performance of certain jobs, the prohibition of sex discrimination may impose significant costs on the employer. Even so, the cost on young women of permitting this discrimination is particularly high, which tips the scales decisively in favour of prohibition. Notice that the cost incurred in the

---

[108] Frederick Schauer, *Profiles, Probabilities and Stereotypes* (Harvard University Press 2003) 140–1.

prohibition of pregnancy discrimination is not informational, but accommodative (we will see in a moment what that is). It is not informational because even an individualized assessment to determine which female candidates are likely to become pregnant is prohibited by discrimination law. The law does not merely bar the use of sex as a proxy for pregnancy, it rules out the use of pregnancy as a relevant criterion entirely.

The third type of cost that the antidiscrimination duty imposes is *accommodative*. This is the cost incurred by a duty-bearer to facilitate a person's access to a relevant opportunity. This often requires the extension or withdrawal of existing benefits and burdens (allowing women to become members of an exclusively male club), the grant of special benefits (pregnancy leave), the revision of or the provision for exceptions from dominant norms (weekly holidays on Fridays for practising Muslims or a weekly holiday on the day of your choice or different physical fitness requirements for male and female candidates for a fire-fighting job), or the installation of special structural features (non-step access for wheelchair users). Discrimination law requires the individual duty-bearer to incur the accommodative costs related to her enterprise. It may seem unfair to some that an employer who happens to have a disabled employee has to bear accommodative costs but one who does not manages to avoid it. This 'unfairness' is no different from that often entailed in tort liabilities. Like the risk of incurring tort liability, there is no obvious reason why the risk of incurring accommodative costs cannot be distributed across duty-bearers more generally through an insurance arrangement.[109] In the long run, the incidence of accommodative costs is likely to fall on all employers in any case.

It is not the imposition of these three costs—transitional, informational, and accommodative—in general that is the problem. We will see in Chapter 7 why the imposition of the antidiscrimination duty, including the costs it entails, is normally legitimate. The justification clause caters for those exceptional cases where these costs are impossibly high, in relation to the benefits that antidiscrimination is likely to bring about. This has to be considered in light of the means of the duty-bearer in question.[110] Often, public duty-bearers have deeper pockets than private ones and may be able to absorb greater costs. A large multi-national corporation with thousands of employees is also

---

[109] Issacharoff and Nelson cite a German regime requiring employers who do not have disabled employees to contribute to a fund to pass on the accommodative costs to all employers: Samuel Issacharoff and Justin Nelson, 'Discrimination with a Difference: Can Employment Discrimination Law Accommodate the Americans with Disability Act?' (2000–1) 79 North Carolina Law Review 308, 355–6.

[110] Americans with Disabilities Act, 42 USC 12111(10).

in a very different position compared to a small firm with five. Determined thus in light of affordability, when the law insists on antidiscrimination in the face of excessive costs, sometimes the only option before the duty-bearer will be to abandon an objective critical to the enterprise (eventually, the enterprise itself). In those rare circumstances, the need to mitigate the financial cost of less blameworthy discrimination may justify it.

6.6.6 Interests of the Victims

Any justification analysis must also consider the cost incurred if the discriminatory act is allowed to take place. Particularly relevant are the nature and scale of the specific adverse effect ε that φ has on its immediate victims, as well as of the systemic impact of φ on relative group disadvantage. This impact may be particularly severe in a case involving state action, especially if it has a general legislative character. The more grievous the impact that the act has on relative group disadvantage and on its specific victims, the more difficult its justification ought to be. There are other costs attendant to discrimination, which may be accounted for as well. It is often the case that the only difference between discrimination and non-discrimination is who bears the cost: the victim bears it when the conduct is not prohibited, the duty-bearer pays when it is not.

Finally, the expressive costs of discrimination, although difficult to measure, are too important to be ignored in any proportionality analysis: a court must consider the message that the law will send to the duty-bearers and to others by allowing (or refusing to allow) certain justifications. The expressive costs of allowing the justification of malicious, intentional, or reckless discriminatory conduct are usually too high.

6.6.7 Interests of Third Parties

Discrimination sometimes imposes costs on persons and groups other than members of protected groups. A racial indirectly discriminatory rule will often have numerically more white victims than black. Emens has pointed out that antidiscrimination measures benefit not just members of protected groups but also third parties.[111] For example, a ramp installed for disabled persons is also helpful for parents using a pushchair. Insofar as the antidiscrimination duty weeds out certain irrelevant considerations from any selection criteria, even the duty-bearer benefits from its operation. Further still,

---

[111] Elizabeth Emens, 'Integrating Accommodation' (2007–2008) 156 University of Pennsylvania Law Review 839.

there are moral benefits that flow from (at least voluntary) compliance with the antidiscrimination rule: it prevents one from doing something wrongful. These benefits will also be lost if the discriminatory conduct is allowed. The question is whether these third-party benefits should enter the justification analysis. I think not. These attendant benefits are incidental to the primary purpose of discrimination law, which is to reduce the relative group disadvantage faced by members of protected groups. It is a good thing that others also benefit from the prohibition of discrimination. But securing these third-party benefits is not its goal. When it comes to assessing the costs of allowing discrimination, only those connected with the purpose of discrimination law ought to be relevant to a justification analysis. If the operation of the anti-discrimination norm imposes incidental costs on third parties rather than conferring benefits to them, a justification analysis will be right in normally ignoring these costs too.

This familiar proportionality inquiry requires a contextual, and typically adjudicative, judgment, taking relevant factors into account. If, after such evaluation, it is found that φ-ing lacks adequate justification, it would amount to discrimination.

6.7 Conclusion

The antidiscrimination duty protects the interest of victims of certain acts in not being made to suffer for their membership of protected groups, and the interest of members of protected groups in not having their group suffer substantial, abiding, and pervasive relative disadvantage. The dual purpose of this duty helps us make sense of the eccentric distribution condition for antidiscrimination norms that we discerned in Chapter 2: *the duty-imposing norm must be designed such that it is likely to distribute the non-remote tangible benefits in question to some, but not all, members of the intended beneficiary group.* The duty delivers *non-remote and tangible* benefits only to claimants who bring an action (although remote and expressive benefits are usually shared with non-claimants; in addition, constitutional remedies against the state may tangibly benefit non-claimants as well). These claimant-beneficiaries are not selected by any need-based criterion. Instead, they are those who happened to get caught by some discriminatory conduct and had the resources to bring an action. It is only the cumulative effect of a critical mass of such actions, including the deterrent effect of the threat of these actions and the internalization of the antidiscrimination norm, which systemically connects the antidiscrimination duty with its broader purpose of ameliorating relative group disadvantage.

This duty manifests itself into a *right* to bring a claim when its breach leads to/will lead to an adverse effect ε' on actual persons. This inquiry is not about whether an action was discriminatory, but to determine who can challenge it. Thus, adverse effect (ε') on a particular member p of group P (or on a particular member c of group C in case of the collateral duty) results in the crystallization of the antidiscrimination duty into a right in p (or c) to ask x to undo or amend φ and (sometimes) compensate for ε'. ε' must fall within the set of the non-remote adverse effects ε. Although φ-ing itself constitutes a breach of x's duty, typically it is not until ε' comes about that p (or c) becomes invested with a right against x. This is hardly exceptionable. In the tort of negligence, a person who has spilled a slippery substance on the pavement outside her home but does not bother cleaning it up has already breached her duty of care. However, her neighbour does not acquire the right to make a claim until he actually slips and suffers injury because of her breach. This should not be taken to mean that the incidence of ε' is a *conceptual* requirement for φ to be challenged. Who should have the right to bring a claim is a regulatory decision based on a variety of concerns, including case management, the injury suffered, and other such concerns. Nothing prevents the law from allowing a regulator or a third person to bring an action in the absence of any person who has suffered ε'.[112]

The definition of discrimination we began with stands vindicated. Let us recap: discrimination is either paradigmatic or collateral. An action φ by a duty-bearer x is/will be paradigmatically discriminatory if and only if,

(i) φ has/will have a non-remote adverse effect ε on a set of person(s) V (the adverse effect clause); and

(ii) V is/will be constituted entirely or disproportionately by persons who are (or are perceived to be or are closely associated with) members of a protected group P (the group membership clause); and

(iii) there is a correlation between a person's membership of V and her (actual or perceived, or her associate's) membership of P (the correlation clause); and

(iv) φ-ing lacks adequate justification (the justification clause).

---

[112] Case C-54/07 *Centrum voor gelijkheid van kansen en voor racismebestrijding v Firma Feryn NY* [2008] ECR I-5187.

On the other hand, an action φ by a duty-bearer x is collaterally discriminatory if and only if,

(i) φ has/will have a non-remote adverse effect ε on a set of person(s) V (the adverse effect clause); and

(ii) V is/will be constituted entirely or disproportionately by persons who are (or are perceived to be or are closely associated with) members of a group C that is a cognate of a protected group P (the group membership clause); and

(iii) there is a correlation between a person's membership of V and her (actual or perceived, or her associate's) membership of C (the correlation clause); and

(iv) memberships of groups P and C have expressive salience (the expressive clause); and

(v) φ-ing lacks adequate justification (the justification clause).

The *antidiscrimination duty* on x is to not φ. The primary wrongfulness of discriminatory conduct lies in the fact that it makes a person suffer because of her morally irrelevant or even valuable membership of a group. This wrongfulness may amount to fault, depending on the state of mind of the discriminator. The antidiscrimination duty protects two interests: it protects a *particular* interest of individuals to avoid the adverse effects of φ. It also furthers the interest of members of protected groups against their group suffering relative group disadvantage. These definitions provide a common conceptual and normative foundation for all action-regarding, rights-generating, wrong-based duties in discrimination law. The classification separates the paradigmatic cases of discrimination, which hurt members of protected groups, from collateral discrimination, where members of dominant cognate groups are the victims. The possibility of justification ensures that the duty is not too demanding. We will now turn to an allied concern: on whom can a liberal state legitimately impose this antidiscrimination duty?

7

The Duty-Bearers

We will now turn to consider the legitimacy of the imposition of the anti-discrimination duty on relevant duty-bearers. I have assumed, with the liberal consensus, that a state has the duty to facilitate human flourishing for all its citizens,[1] and that it can legitimately call upon non-state actors (within reason) to assist it in the performance of this duty.[2] I have further assumed that state coercion is easier to justify when it is a response to wrongful conduct; and that coercion should normally be proportionate to the level of wrong, interests, and ability of the duty-bearer, so that the duty is not too demanding. The proportionality requirement implies that normally (a limited) interference with property is easier to justify than interference with life or liberty, and that the nature and extent of the benefits that the coercive measure will bring about must be sufficient in order to justify it. I take these propositions to be relatively uncontroversial, and vindicated by the normative commitments of most states that call themselves 'liberal'. I understand that my reliance on current practice does not prove any of these normative claims—it only shows that they are widely shared. A proper defence of these liberal assumptions lies far beyond the scope of this book.

The antidiscrimination duty is normally enforced coercively under statute, although it may sometimes be enforced contractually. The legitimacy of the duty is in doubt only in the case of coercive enforcement—the legitimacy of consent-based contractual enforcement will be assumed for the purposes of this chapter. When enforced coercively, the duty may appear to be very

---

[1] Joseph Raz, *The Morality of Freedom* (Clarendon Press 1986) 415: 'Governments are subject to autonomy-based duties to provide the conditions of autonomy for people who lack them.'

[2] See, for example, Martha Nussbaum, *Frontiers of Justice: Disability, Nationality, Species Membership* (Harvard University Press 2006) 280: 'humanity is under a collective obligation to find ways of living and cooperating together so that all human beings have decent lives'. See also, Joseph Raz, *The Morality of Freedom* (Clarendon Press 1986) 408: the principle of autonomy 'yields duties which go far beyond the negative duties of non-interference' and includes mandatory duties; he accepts that these duties may be 'counteracted by conflicting reasons'.

demanding. Compliance with the antidiscrimination duty can be expensive. We learnt in Chapter 6 that the antidiscrimination duty imposes transitional, informational, and accommodative costs. Contrary to what many tend to believe, these costs are incurred not only when the remedy of reasonable accommodation is ordered, but even when other remedies follow a finding of direct or indirect discrimination. Furthermore, the duty regulates not only contractual relations (where it may be viewed as an implied term of the contract) but also pre-contractual relations—for example, it prohibits an employer from discriminating while making hiring decisions, even though there is clearly no contract between the employer and the applicant. This feature of the duty may appear particularly intrusive in relation to the duty-bearer's negative freedom.

As such, the coercive imposition of the duty calls for justification. Before we look at why its imposition on specific persons is justified, consider that the duty seeks a compelling objective. We know from Chapter 5 that the point of discrimination law is to facilitate access to three basic goods to those who lack such access by ameliorating and eliminating pervasive, abiding, and substantial relative group disadvantage. This objective manifests in the antidiscrimination duty through the operation of the group membership clause. Given the necessity of basic goods for a flourishing life, this is a compelling objective, one which a liberal state can legitimately pursue through proportionate means. In this chapter, therefore, we are concerned with the legitimacy of the *extent* of the burden imposed, rather than *whether* it can be imposed at all.

The duty is legitimate only because it is imposed discriminately. But even for the specific bearers of its burdens, there are several features that dilute its seeming demandingness. The first of these features is the fact that discrimination law uses civil rather than criminal tools to coerce, and that it interferes with a duty-bearer's property rather than his or her person.[3] The use of criminal sanctions, especially imprisonment, typically imposes a heavier justificatory burden because their impact on one's negative freedom is so pervasive. The expressive stigma attached to a criminal sanction tends to be greater than a civil one, even in relation to the highly expressive civil wrong

---

[3] cf Indian Protection of Civil Rights Act 1955, ss 5–7, and Indian Equal Remuneration Act 1976, ss 5 and 10, which criminalize certain forms of direct discrimination based on caste and sex, respectively. These provisions are exceptional—in fact, India's reliance on criminal law to deal with discrimination may be a reason why judges have (rightly) shied away from interpreting the phenomenon of discrimination expansively. Following legal practice, I have kept hate crime legislation—which typically increases the penalty for a crime when motivated by a discriminatory animus—outside my understanding of 'discrimination law'.

of discrimination. The move to civil enforcement therefore makes the duty less demanding.

Second, we know from Chapter 6 that the antidiscrimination duty is doubly wrong-sensitive. Discriminatory conduct is wrongful at the systemic level because it exacerbates the existing advantage gap between groups. We know from Chapter 5 that this advantage gap has significant adverse consequences for the liberty interests of the members of the protected groups. At the particular level, every instance of discrimination makes a person suffer some adverse effect owing merely to her membership of a normatively irrelevant or even valuable group. Thus, discrimination is doubly wrongful. If the duty did not entail the correlation clause,[4] mere adverse effect on members of a protected group would suffice to constitute discrimination. So, a judgment finding a woman guilty of an offence would have been potentially discriminatory, subject to the justification clause. On the other hand, if all that was required was that my actions did not make anyone suffer on the basis of their belonging to certain groups whose membership is morally irrelevant or valuable, there would be no requirement of direct or indirect adverse effect on a protected group. On this understanding, an employer who refuses to hire a blue-eyed person or someone whose name began with the letter 'W' would have discriminated. We know that neither of these categories of conduct actually amount to discrimination,[5] because the level of wrongfulness involved is not sufficient. The requirement that the two types of wrongs must be present *together* to constitute discrimination is key to the legitimacy of its prohibition. The wrongfulness of discrimination implies that every act of discrimination incurs certain costs—the question that law has to settle is who should shoulder these costs.[6] Imposing these costs on the select group of duty-bearers makes the antidiscrimination duty less demanding than any wrong-insensitive coercive distributive regime, such as the duty to pay one's taxes. It also makes the duty less demanding than one where only one of the two wrongs might be present.

Finally, the possibility of justification, when it exists, further ameliorates much of its demandingness. A consideration of the legitimate interests of the duty-bearer as well as of the level of her fault is typically built into the duty. It is true that it is not necessary to establish fault in order to prove discrimination. However, the justification clause does consider whether there is fault

---

[4] See Chapter 6, section 6.4.   [5] They may still be illegal for other reasons.

[6] I am assuming, with John Gardner, that wrongs are often sufficient justification for the imposition of civil liability—the existence of some fault on the part of the duty-bearer is not essential. See generally, John Gardner, 'Obligations and Outcomes in the Law of Torts' in Peter Cane (ed), *Relating to Responsibility: Essays for Tony Honoré on his Eightieth Birthday* (Hart 2001).

and how much—justification is easier the less blameworthy the duty-bearer is. Even when justification is not possible, the duty may be defeated if one has a *right* to discriminate. These features make the duty even more likely to be legitimate.

Any remaining legitimacy concerns are mitigated by three features that relate to the character of those who bear the antidiscrimination duty. First, the antidiscrimination duty is *not imposed universally*. Compare it to the duty to take reasonable care in the law of torts—everyone has an obligation to take due care to ensure that another is not harmed by her negligence. No prior gatekeeping role is performed by the designation of a specific class of persons as duty-bearers. Discrimination law is different. We all may have a moral duty to refrain from certain types of discrimination. But only some of us, acting in certain specified capacities, have the legal obligation to refrain from discrimination.

Second, even though its chief role is to tackle relative group disadvantage, discrimination law does not make members of the dominant group bear the burdens of antidiscrimination. In contrast to a progressive taxation regime, a duty-bearer in discrimination law 'is under this duty not on account of his own relative advantages, but on account of his status', as a (prospective) employer, landlord, etc.[7] Whether a duty-bearer belongs to the same group as the complainant or a different group is typically irrelevant to the determination of whether discrimination has taken place.[8] This second feature may look strange, but sound reasons buttress this approach.

One needs to imagine how a duty to reduce relative group disadvantage could be imposed on members of dominant groups. It could take the shape of a wrong-insensitive (when it is not conditional on some prior wrong), non-action-regarding (when it is not conditional on some prior act) duty on all members of dominant groups to pay an advantage tax or undertake affirmative action. Alternatively (or additionally), the duty could be wrong-sensitive and action-regarding, like the antidiscrimination duty. If the latter, the duty could be imposed in the same manner as it is imposed on the state. In other words, it could govern every action that any member of the dominant group would undertake. Or, it could be imposed less indiscriminately, to govern only certain types of actions of these members (such as actions they undertake in the capacity of an employer, landlord, or seller of goods or services).

---

[7] John Gardner, 'Liberals and Unlawful Discrimination' (1989) 9 Oxford Journal of Legal Studies 1, 10.

[8] UK Equality Act 2010, s 24.

All but the last of these duties will be too demanding. We know that wrong-insensitive duties have a heavier proportionality burden to discharge than wrong-sensitive ones: so do duties that govern all actions of a person rather than a few (relatively) public ones. The final duty will be similar to the current regime, except that it will only impose the antidiscrimination duty on those employers (say) who also belong to dominant groups. Since most of us belong to some protected group or the other, the pool of persons who only belong to dominant groups is likely to be very small—comprising middle-aged, white, male, heterosexual, able-bodied persons with the domin-ant religion, and language. Alternatively, a rule forbidding members of a dominant group from discriminating only against members of their correla-tive protected group will expand the pool of duty-bearers, but is likely to be administratively cumbersome.

Even if it is possible to design an efficient and proportionate duty which applies only to members of dominant groups, there is a simple reason why it would still be a bad idea. Any such duty is likely to have extremely high expressive costs.[9] The expressive costs of a duty which is conscious of the victim's group membership but not the duty-bearer's is high enough. Infusing both dimensions with group-consciousness is likely to generate a great deal of animosity among the members of dominant groups, not only against the state but also against persons belonging to protected groups. Any such approach to reducing relative group disadvantage is very likely to be self-defeating. All in all, to impose the antidiscrimination duty (or, for that matter, the affirmative action duty) on members of dominant groups qua such membership would be a distinctly unsound policy.

Third, the antidiscrimination duty is imposed *selectively* and *unidirec-tionally*. Recall from Chapter 3 that, generally, the antidiscrimination duty applies to the state, employers, landlords, and providers of goods and services to the public. It tends to govern all actions of the state, but for other duty-bearers the scope of the duty is not similarly comprehensive. So, the law prohibits an employer from discriminating only when she is acting in her capacity as an employer (say when she is hiring employees, allowing leave, managing the workplace, allocating duties); not when she is a commuter, a shopper, or a parent. It is quite possible that a duty-bearer in one context (say, an employer) could be the victim of discrimination in another (as a consumer). What is more, the duty is imposed unidirectionally—it applies to an employer in dealing with her employees but not to the employee when

---

[9] Chapter 6, section 6.5.

interacting with the employer.[10] Similarly, it applies to the landlord but not the tenant, to the retailer but not the consumer and so on. These are a strange set of arrangements. The rationale behind them is not immediately obvious. It is surprising, then, that most discrimination law theorists ignore this ostensibly bizarre set-up. At best, some scholars have commented upon the legitimacy of the application of the antidiscrimination duty on private employers.[11] These explanations, although important, worked until the time when the antidiscrimination duty was restricted to the state and the employer. Today, however, the duty has extended to other private persons, although the extension has typically been unidirectional. These developments call for an updated explanation.

These three features further dilute the demandingness of the duty. In the rest of this chapter, I will argue that there are two broad parameters by which the law determines who the bearers of the antidiscrimination duty ought to be. The first of these parameters is the severity of the impact that the duty has on the bearer's negative freedom. If a person has a more 'public' character, her interest in negative liberty is weaker, and the imposition of the duty more likely to be legitimate. The second parameter is the optimality of the choice of a particular duty-bearer in achieving the goal (of eliminating relative group disadvantage). This will depend on its ability to affect another person's access to the basic goods. It is against these parameters, taken together, that the choice of certain persons as bearers of the antidiscrimination duty can be justified. I will show that the duty is only imposed when persons are acting in a capacity that entitles them to a relatively weaker negative liberty claim, and only if it is necessary to impose it for the achievement of the main purpose of discrimination law. Together, these considerations reflect a move in law towards an approach that seeks to *balance* the competing interests of the duty-bearer and the victims, rather than to recognize 'a completely insulated private sphere' of freedom.[12] These considerations satisfy any remaining demandingness or proportionality concerns with respect to the imposition of the antidiscrimination duty.

---

[10] An employee can have antidiscrimination duties, but only to other employees. These horizontal duties are either a manifestation of the employer's duty not only to refrain from discrimination but also to protect from it, or of the possibility of attributing acts of an employee (including discriminatory acts) to the employer.

[11] John Gardner, 'Liberals and Unlawful Discrimination' (1989) 9 Oxford Journal of Legal Studies 1.

[12] Hugh Collins, 'The Vanishing Freedom to Choose a Contractual Partner' (2013) 76 Law and Contemporary Problems 71, 88.

7.1 Public Character

My claim in this section is that the antidiscrimination duty is only imposed on those persons who have a sufficiently public character. This is another way of saying that the duty is borne mainly by those who, for a variety of reasons, have a relatively weak claim to an interest in being allowed to discriminate. This is also a reason why the duty is not usually imposed universally. We know that the antidiscrimination duty is an action-regarding duty. All non-state persons have some claim to negative liberty. In most cases, a person's interest in negative liberty is strong enough to trump the duty not to discriminate. This is why the duty is not imposed indiscriminately.[13] Instead, a select group of duty-bearers, whose interest in negative liberty is weak, alone bear its burden.

In this regard, it should be uncontroversial that the state is special. Given its unique position in contemporary societies, in particular its ability to exercise enormous coercive power and its claims to represent the collective will and pursue the general good, state action requires special justification.[14] Even those who reject the liberal precept that any restrictions on natural persons need to be defensible are likely to accept that the state may not do anything without good justification. The state, qua state, has no claim to negative freedom in the manner that natural (and some legal) persons do. Since discrimination is wrongful, and (by definition) unjustified, the state must not discriminate. This is not, however the only reason why the state ought not to discriminate. There are strong additional reasons why a democratic state should not only refrain from discrimination, but must reflect its

---

[13] There may be exceptional circumstances, such as post-apartheid South Africa, where the enormity of the problem could potentially justify a broader application of the duty. The strength of the interest on the other side of the scale—in this case the enormity of the problem of relative group disadvantage—has to be quite substantial to justify a near-universal application. Even then, it is unlikely that its application in all contexts can be defended.

[14] Nicholas Bamforth, 'The Public Law—Private Law Distinction: A Comparative and Philosophical Approach' in Peter Leyland and Terry Woods (eds), *Administrative Law Facing the Future: Old Constraints and New Horizons* (Blackstone 1997) 136, 138. The demand for a special normative justification for state action is in turn reflected in the requirement of legal justification for state action. Thus, 'a public body ... enjoys no such thing as an unfettered discretion ... For private persons, the rule is that you may do anything you choose which the law does not prohibit. It means that the freedoms of the private citizen are not conditional upon some distinct and affirmative justification for which he must burrow in the law books. Such a notion would be anathema to our English legal traditions. But for public bodies the rule is opposite, and so of another character altogether. It is that any action to be taken must be justified by positive law.' *R v Somerset County Council, ex parte Fewings* [1995] 1 All ER 513, 524.

social diversity in its institutions. Suk correctly explains that 'The absence of women or other socially undervalued groups in the institutions that exercise power within a democracy compromises the legitimacy of those institutions, raising questions about whether they can justly govern everyone they purport to represent.'[15] In combination, these reasons not only lead to a very strong presumption against discrimination by the state, they also impose allied duties on the state. The state plays an important facilitative role in helping us organize our affairs. It enforces our contracts and wills, recognizes the legal personality of our corporations, protects us from torts and crimes, and organizes the sharing of property on divorce. The antidiscrimination rationale prohibits the state from being a party to discrimination by other persons, for example by allowing its institutions to enforce discriminatory contracts.[16] It also bears the primary burden of affirmative action, an issue that we will explore in Chapter 8.

In most jurisdictions, the state is governed by constitutional as well as the statutory antidiscrimination regimes. Although there is usually a significant overlap, there may be material differences in procedure, forum, and substantive rules. In general, the paradigmatic public-ness of the state is reflected in its regulation by constitutional provisions. This often means that the state shoulders a heavier burden of antidiscrimination and affirmative action duties than private persons. In some cases, however, its very public character might also allow the state access to certain justificatory grounds that may not be available to private persons (especially when they concern national security). Furthermore, statutory regimes regulate the state only when it acts in the capacity of an employer, landlord, or provider of goods and services. Constitutional provisions are the ones that apply to all state action.

There will, of course, be difficult cases concerning discrimination by state officials when they are wearing two different hats—an agent of the state on the one hand and a private person on the other. A recent case where a marriage registrar refused to conduct same-sex partnership ceremonies because of her religious beliefs is a good example.[17] These are no doubt hard cases which call for a balancing of the weight of the state's interest in not discriminating and the strength of the individual's personal right to do so. Assuming that the person in question has not been compelled to work as a state official,

---

[15] Julie Suk, 'Quotas and Consequences: A Transnational Re-Evaluation' in Deborah Hellman and Sophia Moreau (eds), *Philosophical Foundations of Discrimination Law* (Oxford University Press 2013) 245.

[16] *Shelley v Kramer* 334 US 1 (1948).

[17] *Ladele v London Borough of Islington* [2009] EWCA Civ 1357.

one can generally say that (unlike in a purely non-state context) the private right involved in these hybrid cases has to be exceptionally compelling to outweigh the state's fundamental duty to secure access to the basic goods for all its citizens.

Unlike the state, non-state persons have an interest in their negative liberty. The strength of our interest in our negative liberty depends on a number of factors, including the 'public-ness' of the capacity in which we propose to act. Implicit in the claim is the notion that the traditional approach to the public-private divide as embodying two discrete sets is a mistake. Most of us wear different hats, and act in varyingly public and private capacities. Instead of a sharp line dividing public and private bodies, it is better to appreciate that most persons lie somewhere on a spectrum, depending on the specific *function* they are performing at the relevant time: the state, perhaps when acting as a legislator, sits at the extreme end of public-ness, while an adult all by herself lost in her thoughts lies at the extreme private end of this spectrum. The more private the capacity in which we propose to act, the stronger is our liberty interest in doing that act. This notion of privacy takes on board feminist criticisms of the traditional understanding of the concept, which draws a sharp line between the public and the private sphere and understands them only in spatial terms (inside one's home or outside it). My understanding, on the other hand, sees the divide in terms of degree, and primarily in functional terms. My understanding also preserves the liberal intuition 'that in a just society there will be an area of liberty in which private people are permitted to express their preferences'.[18]

The two extremes of the legislating state and the private thinker encompass between them a range of different persons characterized by varying degrees of public-ness. Altruistic bodies, such as charities, are more state-like than those that seek profit. When their stated altruistic goals are combined with tax benefits, the public character of charities becomes even more pronounced. This may, however, be counterbalanced by a right to the freedom of religion for religious charities. Further along the spectrum, bodies whose relationships are overwhelmingly monetized are more public than those whose relationships are not so monetized. Businesses, for this reason, are more public than families, friendships, or (possibly) clubs.[19] Generally, the more intimate and the less monetized the interaction between two persons, the more private is the relationship. It may seem contradictory to claim that both altruism and

[18] Larry Alexander, 'What Makes Wrongful Discrimination Wrong? Biases, Preferences, Stereotypes and Proxies' (1992) 141 University of Pennsylvania Law Review 149, 154–5.

[19] See Hugh Collins, 'The Vanishing Freedom to Choose a Contractual Partner' (2013) 76 Law and Contemporary Problems 71, 83f.

monetization give a relationship a public character. But there is no contradiction if we appreciate that only certain types of altruistic relationships are of a public character—altruism typical of the state and of charities, where the benevolence is motivated not by personal likes and dislikes but by the very character of the charitable institution. This sort of altruism depersonalizes relationships just as monetization does.

These general comments aside, let us focus on the particular bearers of the antidiscrimination duty, and the duty's unidirectional character. Non-state employers, landlords, and providers of goods and services almost invariably either have monetized relationships or are a charity. This already imbues them with a modicum of public-ness. The rest of this section will show that employers, landlords, and providers of goods and services are more 'public' than employees, tenants, and consumers, respectively. The reasons why employers are quasi-public are different from those that characterize the public-ness of other duty-bearers. An employer's public character is based on the institutional power she enjoys in contemporary industrial societies; landlords, retailers, service-providers, and certain types of associations, on the other hand, have *assumed* a degree of public-ness by offering to serve the public generally.

In our societies, the position of employers is unique amongst non-state actors. Relationships that are characterized by a significant power dynamic are a matter of public concern. This is because power has the capacity to dominate, to abuse, and to corrupt. The liberal suspicion of the state is based predominantly on the sheer extent of its coercive power. But the power to subject the will of another to one's own will, as a social phenomenon, is the same whether the source of power is the state or a private employer.[20] Behind the feminist slogan—'the personal is the political'—lies the recognition that the power that men have over women in the 'privacy' of their homes gives the relationship between them a political, and therefore public, character; thereby justifying its legal regulation. The employer has a quasi-public character for the same reason:

[T]he relation between an employer and an isolated employee or worker is typically a relation between a bearer of power and one who is not a bearer of power. In its inception it is an act of submission, in its operation it is a condition of subordination, however much the submission and the subordination may be concealed by that indispensable figment of the legal mind known as the 'contract of employment.' The main object of labour law has always been, and we venture to say will always be, to be a

---

[20] Otto Kahn-Freund, *Kahn-Freund's Labour and the Law* (Paul Davies and Mark Freedland eds, 3rd edn, Stevens 1983) 14.

countervailing force to counteract the inequality of bargaining power which is inherent and must be inherent in the employment relationship.[21]

This social power of the employer precedes a contract of employment, and extends over job-seekers too. Because she wields such enormous power, an employer is a state-like body, albeit in a limited domain. It is this public-ness of her character that has justified regulations requiring provisions for health and safety at work, payment of minimum wage, prohibition of unfair dismissal, and provision for retirement pensions. Because of her power, the employer has a relatively weaker claim to negative freedom. This is what justifies the imposition of the antidiscrimination duty on the employer.

Other duty-bearers may also be powerful, but usually not to the same degree as an employer. Their public character is drawn from a different source: it is voluntarily assumed. As an English judge acknowledged three centuries ago, a common caller 'has made profession of a trade which is for the public good, and has thereby exposed and vested an interest of himself in all the King's subjects that will employ him in the way of his trade'.[22] In this case, Chief Justice Holt recognized the incidence of a general duty to serve the public on at least three common callers: the inn-keeper, the blacksmith, and the common carrier. Simpson challenges the suggestion that this duty was applicable to all common callers, although he acknowledges it did apply to quite a few others.[23] There were other, more specific, duties which also attached to particular common callers. For example, the common jailer had the duty to provide prisoners with food and act as a surety if any prisoner escaped.[24] Most relevant for our purpose is Simpson's explanation of who could be considered a *common* caller. This was not a legal term of art, but a question of fact: 'The adjective "common" as applied to such persons as hangmen, prostitutes, informers, Serjeants, labourers, attorneys, innkeepers, carriers, originally means no more than available to or for the public, or generally available.'[25] The factual question is whether the person has set up an enterprise to serve the public generally—cooks tended not to be common callers because 'medieval cooks were found retained in private employment, and

[21] Otto Kahn-Freund, *Kahn-Freund's Labour and the Law* (Paul Davies and Mark Freedland eds, 3rd edn, Stevens 1983) 18. See also, John Gardner, 'Liberals and Unlawful Discrimination' (1989) 9 Oxford Journal of Legal Studies 1, 11: 'the formation and preservation of the employment relation involves a peculiarly large amount of control for one of the parties (the employer)'.

[22] *Lane v Cotton* [1558–1774] All ER Rep 109 KB, 114. See also, *Indian Medical Association v Union of India* AIR 2011 SC 2365 [113], where the Indian Supreme Court endorsed a similar argument.

[23] Brian Simpson, *A History of the Common Law of Contract: The Rise of the Action of Assumpsit* (2nd edn, Clarendon Press 1987) 229–34.

[24] Brian Simpson, *A History of the Common Law of Contract: The Rise of the Action of Assumpsit* (2nd edn, Clarendon Press 1987) 232.

[25] Brian Simpson, *A History of the Common Law of Contract: The Rise of the Action of Assumpsit* (2nd edn, Clarendon Press 1987) 230.

do not cook for all and sundry'.[26] It was not necessary for a common caller to be a skilled professional—there existed a category of the common labourer, who 'could be retained in service by any member of the public who cared to hire him'.[27]

Landlords and providers of goods and services will typically fall within the scope of this understanding of common callers. These duty-bearers do normally set up an enterprise to serve the public generally. In fact, legal provisions applying to this group sometimes explicitly require that their 'goods, services, facilities or accommodation [are] customarily available to the general public',[28] or that they are 'concerned with the provision of a service to the public or a section of the public'.[29] In this sense, they have voluntarily assumed a degree of public-ness, which dilutes any privacy-based claim to negative liberty. Of course, the claim may yet survive this assumption of a public role. We no longer consider it just to coerce a labourer or a prostitute to serve anyone willing to pay, even if they held themselves out as a *common* labourer or a *common* prostitute. Given the deeply personal nature of the 'service' they provide, the cost of such coercion to their negative liberty will be too large. At any rate, for most of the other common callers, their voluntary assumption of a public character will normally defeat claims that their negative liberty entitles them to discriminate.

Thus, in general, the typical employer, landlord, retailer, or service-provider has a public character when she acts in these capacities.[30] There will of course be hard cases at the borderline. A small employer with a single employee will be less public than a large factory employing thousands of workers. Where the landlord shares a house with the tenant, the negative liberty interest is stronger. Determining whether clubs and associations—a unique category of service-providers—have the requisite degree of public-ness to legitimate the imposition of the antidiscrimination duty upon them is notoriously difficult.[31] Apart from those we have already seen, other factors will be relevant too. These include the consideration of whether the putative duty-bearer is a natural or a legal person (for legal personality is usually recognized in aid of some public function); its size, powers, and functions;

[26] Brian Simpson, *A History of the Common Law of Contract: The Rise of the Action of Assumpsit* (2nd edn, Clarendon Press 1987) 231.

[27] Brian Simpson, *A History of the Common Law of Contract: The Rise of the Action of Assumpsit* (2nd edn, Clarendon Press 1987) 231.

[28] Canadian Human Rights Act 1985, s 5.   [29] UK Equality Act 2010, s 29.

[30] For a less generous understanding of what amounts to public-ness, see Alfred Avins, 'What is a Place of "Public" Accommodation?' (1968) 52 Marquette Law Review 1.

[31] Stuart White, 'Freedom of Association and the Right to Exclude' (1997) 5 The Journal of Political Philosophy 373.

any aid, licence, subsidy, or grant it receives from the state; its turnover and profits; and the nature of the normal activities of the enterprise.

The possibility of justification, inherent in the definition of discrimination, will allow for the consideration of any legitimate interests that a person may have in discriminating, including their interest in negative liberty. Even when the conduct is not justifiable (say, because the interest in discriminating is not legitimate), it may be permitted: the proposed framework preserves the possibility that the antidiscrimination duty may be defeated by a countervailing right. This is because persons sometimes have a right to do wrong.[32] Hurtful speech is often unjustified, yet one may have the right to speak it. Investing my savings in a doomed enterprise is irrational, but I normally have a right to make the investment anyway. In discrimination law, the most common instance is when the right to freedom of religion is invoked to seek an exemption from the antidiscrimination duty.[33] This right to do wrong will be weak for the relatively public persons upon whom the antidiscrimination duty is imposed. Even so, the possibility of an undefeated right trumping the duty should help us set aside all worries about any unjustified interference in a person's negative liberty. There may be another set of borderline cases, where it is not easy to characterize the putative duty-bearer as, for example, an employer.[34] Even in these cases, the real question is often whether it is appropriate to impose the antidiscrimination duty on the defendant, which in turn is partly an inquiry into whether their character is sufficiently public.

The difficulty that lies at the borderline does not detract from the soundness of the claim that the duty-bearers in discrimination law tend to gravitate towards the public end of the public-private spectrum. For this reason, they normally have a weaker interest in negative freedom when acting in their capacity as employers, landlords, or providers of goods or services. As a result, the imposition of the antidiscrimination duty—which serves an essential freedom-enhancing purpose, allows for justification, and may be defeated if our assumption concerning the weak

[32] Jeremy Waldron, 'A Right to Do Wrong' (1981) 92 Ethics 21; Larry Alexander, 'What Makes Wrongful Discrimination Wrong? Biases, Preferences, Stereotypes and Proxies' (1992) 141 University of Pennsylvania Law Review 149, 210ff; Matt Cavanagh, *Against Equality of Opportunity* (Oxford University Press 2002) 174.
[33] *Bull v Hall* [2013] UKSC 73; *Eweida v United Kingdom* [2013] ECHR 37; *Re Same-Sex Marriage* [2004] 3 SCR 698. In most jurisdictions, the doctrine fails to make the necessary distinction between the right to freedom of religion and the right to be free from religious discrimination, causing much confusion.
[34] *Jivraj v Hashwani* [2011] UKSC 40.

negative liberty turns out to be untrue—is legitimate. The unidirectionality of the duty, ie its non-application to tenants and consumers, should
also make sense now. I do not, as a typical end-state consumer (ie a consumer who buys to consume, as opposed to a trader who buys to sell
or a manufacturer who buys to add value), set myself up to serve the
public generally. There may be reasons, based on the power and influence they wield, to impose the antidiscrimination duty on certain specific
consumers. The state or a multi-chain supermarket—in their capacity as
consumers of goods—may be good examples. But the general claim is
that tenants and consumers are not common callers, and therefore have a
stronger interest in their negative freedom than landlords, retailers, and
service-providers. They do not possess any power comparable to that of
employers either. Employees, though, are in a curious position. Although
they do not possess sufficient power against the employer, in relation
to other employees, they may wield significant power (especially since
most work-forces are organized hierarchically). This power over one's colleagues is derived from the power of the employer. Discrimination law
deals with this problem by recognizing that employees act as agents of
their employers, and therefore their discriminatory acts may be attrib-
utable to the employer. This essentially imposes an obligation on the
employer not only to refrain from discriminating, but also to ensure that
his employees are protected from discrimination by other employees.
Given the long-standing recognition of vicarious liability in labour law,
this is hardly exceptional and follows from the unique quasi-public character of the employer.

In this section, I have argued that the antidiscrimination duty is
imposed on bodies which are sufficiently public—namely the state, charities, employers, landlords, and common providers of goods and services.
The argument should not be taken to suggest that there is no difference
between the state on the one hand, and these non-statute bodies on the
other. The state is paradigmatically public to a degree that is unrivalled in
contemporary societies. There are many duties which may appropriately be
imposed only on the state (and, possibly, bodies that perform functions of
the state and therefore act as its instrumentality). The non-state duty-bearers do not lose all their claims to negative liberty simply because they are
somewhat public. Unlike the state, for example, they may not legitimately
be required to act rationally or proportionately in all circumstances. Only
non-state actors may sometimes be *permitted* to engage in unjustified discrimination. I have made the modest claim that imposing a wrong-sensitive
antidiscrimination duty on this group of duty-bearers is legitimate because
of their *weaker* (but not empty) claim to negative liberty.

7.2 Gatekeepers of Opportunities

The second, overlapping, rationale for (unidirectionally) imposing the anti-discrimination duties on the state, employers, landlords, and providers of goods and services alone is that these groups have the most control over our access to the three basic goods that discrimination law seeks to distribute. Recall that these goods include negative freedom, an adequate range of valuable opportunities, and self-respect. Recall also that although we need secured access to enough of these goods, what is enough depends on what others have. Although a sufficiency requirement, our access to these basic goods is sensitive to relative deprivation. Which is why relative group disadvantage seriously disrupts our efforts to access them. Any effort to ameliorate relative group disadvantage must therefore secure these goods to members of protected groups. Imposing the antidiscrimination duty on those who affect our enjoyment of these basic goods the most is therefore eminently sensible. The duty-bearers control access to the most valuable opportunities in our societies. Their conduct often impacts our ability to have self-respect. And some of them can constrain our negative liberty significantly. To put this in proportionality terms, the duty is only imposed when it is necessary to do so to achieve the broader objective of discrimination law.

The application of this second rationale throws up the same selection as the first one. The reasons for imposing the duty on the state are the strongest, followed by the employer, followed by landlords, retailers, and other service-providers. Like the public-ness rationale, it does not provide sufficient reasons to impose the duty on persons generally, or on employees, tenants, or consumers, qua their personhood, employment, tenancy, or consumption, respectively. Let us begin by considering the state.

The modern regulatory welfare state determines our access to basic goods like no other state in the past. Among contemporary institutions, its influence is typically unparalleled. It plays a large role in creating an environment which determines which opportunities we end up with. Not only that, it remains one of the major sources for the deprivation of, as well as the protection of, negative liberty. We have also noticed that what the state expresses matters a good deal more to our self-esteem than many other bodies and persons. Given its potentially comprehensive control over the lives of its subjects, discrimination by the state has particularly egregious consequences for relative group disadvantage. It is no surprise that most democratic constitutions today constrain it with the antidiscrimination duty. Unlike other persons who bear the duty only in specific capacities, the state carries its burden all the time, doing anything it does. Given its enormous control over the conditions that make basic goods available, this is just as well.

Let us consider employers next. Employment is easily the most important of valuable opportunities. As the main source of livelihood for most people, employment is *the* enabling opportunity. Unless we have accumulated considerable wealth, we need to be gainfully employed in order to access all those valuable opportunities that are available for a price. For many people, their work-place is also the space where they make friends, and access other non-economic opportunities. Unemployment benefits, even under the most generous welfare regimes, are unlikely to compass very much else after securing one's biological needs such as access to food, shelter, and clothing. Moreover, employment provides a means for participation in one's community as a valued and productive member. Without secure employment, not only is one deprived of most valuable opportunities, but one is also likely to lack self-respect. Although an individual employer's refusal to hire me will not typically have a significant impact on my access to basic goods, if enough employers refuse, the prospect of my societal exclusion becomes real.[35] Thus, collectively, employers have a substantial influence over our ability to lead a good life.

From what has just been said, it may seem that the antidiscrimination duty is relevant only to the hiring and dismissal stages of employment. As long as I am hired or fired without discrimination, it may seem that my access to employment remains unimpeded by the relative disadvantage of my group. This is not true. Discrimination can take other forms, and can affect a person during the course of the employment as well. Harassment at the workplace can make the employment very difficult, and may lead to the loss of self-respect. Continued or serious discriminatory behaviour may force one to give up on the job 'voluntarily'. Even if one decides to stick it out, many of the softer benefits that employment brings will be lost to a person who suffers in a discriminatory workplace. It is also irrelevant whether the employer herself discriminates, or merely tolerates the discriminatory conduct of another employee—in either case she is making my ability to continue to work very difficult.

Other duty-bearers—landlords and providers of goods and services—control our access to basic goods to a lesser degree, but significantly enough

---

[35] Hugh Collins, 'Discrimination, Equality and Social Inclusion' (2003) 66 The Modern Law Review 16, 29.

to be of concern. Landlords in particular can, in many contexts, have an impact comparable to employers. In many Indian cities, Muslims face considerable discrimination in the housing sector. Whole neighbourhoods become unavailable because no landlord will let to those encumbered with a 'Muslim-sounding' name.[36] These tend to be the upscale districts with better schools, hospitals, and transport facilities. Widespread discrimination by landlords can therefore seriously impede one's access to civic amenities. One may be forced to travel long distances to work, or to perform a less desirable job. For this reason, housing discrimination can affect one's access to employment as well. The impact of residential segregation on self-esteem is also likely to be considerable.

Our interaction with retailers and service-providers is less substantial, but not irrelevant. As with other duty-bearers, their concerted action can no doubt be very damaging. But even the isolated refusal by a corner-shop to sell or a restaurant to serve impedes our freedom and our self-esteem.[37] Because of the history of protected groups, refusing to serve their members is a powerful expressive act which brands them as second-class citizens. This is especially the case when such refusal comes from those providers who have set up shop to serve the public generally. In singling out members of protected groups to exclude from their service, the expressive message is a powerful one. Hellman recognizes the gravity of its impact by characterizing it as 'humiliation'.[38] Thus, even when providers discriminate in an isolated case, they can have a serious effect on our access to one of the basic goods—self-respect. When they act collectively, the problem is much worse.

Collective action by employers, landlords, and providers is facilitated by the fact that many of them organize themselves into trade bodies, exchange social, political, and economic information and adopt similar behaviour patterns. Housing associations in Indian cities have been known to pressurize those members who would like to sell or let to Muslims to refrain from doing so.[39] These trade and business associations can act like cartels, preventing competitively rational non-discrimination through collective peer pressure. Employers, landlords, retailers, and service-providers are all likely to be members of collective trade associations.

---

[36] Indefensibly, discrimination by private landlords is legal in India: *Zoroastrian Co-operative Housing Society v District Registrar* AIR 2005 SC 2306.

[37] See Sophia Moreau, 'What is Discrimination?' (2010) 38 Philosophy and Public Affairs 143.

[38] Deborah Hellman, *When is Discrimination Wrong?* (Harvard University Press 2008).

[39] 'Not Allowed to Sell Her Flat to a Muslim, Pune Woman Takes on Entire Society' *The Indian Express* (Pune, 3 April 2008) <http://archive.indianexpress.com/news/not-allowed-to-sell-her-flat-to-a-muslim-pune-woman-takes-on-entire--society-/291804/> accessed 4 November 2014.

These organizational structures, directly or indirectly, have the potential to translate eccentric individual discrimination into devastating collective embargo against protected groups.

Employees, tenants, and end-state consumers tend to wield far less control over the access to the basic goods by others in comparison to the duty-bearers. Their numbers tend to be very large, and often approximate the population of a state. This makes any meaningful genuinely representative association—as tenants and consumers—difficult. Historically, trade unions have been very powerful in certain countries, although their power has been in steady decline. But that is not a problem for unidirectionality—as associations providing a service for their members, trade unions, or consumer forums may also bear the antidiscrimination duty. Unidirectionality only requires that as *individual* tenants or consumers, they do not share the antidiscrimination burden. Employees sometimes do, with respect to their co-employees, as has already been explained, since they are agents of their employers. Imposing the duty on individual tenants or consumers, in most cases, is likely to make little difference to relative group disadvantage, but could have serious implications for the negative liberty of these individuals. For this reason, discrimination law leaves them out of its fold.

7.3 Conclusion

The antidiscrimination duty, unlike the duty of care in negligence, is not imposed universally. Despite the concern with relative group disadvantage, they are not imposed on dominant groups (qua dominant groups) either—the liberty costs and expressive dangers are too high.

Instead, the duties are typically imposed on the state, on employers, on landlords, and on providers of goods and services. We have seen that there are two overlapping reasons that explain why this is justified. These persons have a weaker claim to negative liberty (when acting in these capacities), and they usually possess a significant ability to affect our access to the basic goods, the want of which underlies relative group disadvantage. The duty is imposed unidirectionally—employees, tenants, and consumers, when acting in these capacities (rather than, say, as representatives of their employer) do not usually bear the duty. This is because they tend to have a stronger claim to negative liberty, and usually lack the ability to seriously affect anyone's access to the basic goods. The puzzling distribution of the antidiscrimination duty makes sense, after all.

It is true that public-ness and control over opportunities are both features determined by a multiplicity of factors, and admit to degrees. The law, on the other hand, tends to draw sharp lines. This is the price we pay for reaping the benefits of certainty, in the hope that even when legal generalizations impose the duty on a person who should fall on the other side of the dividing line, the possibility of justification will avoid onerosity.

8

Affirmative Action

Part III of this book has dealt so far with the design of the duties that discrimination law imposes, seeking to explain and justify the scope of the antidiscrimination duty and its imposition on selected persons. It is now time to turn to what is arguably the most controversial feature of discrimination law: affirmative action. Our starting point should be to revisit some classifications drawn in Chapter 3.[1] First, we are concerned only with non-remedial affirmative action measures. Remedial measures, it was noted, were simply responses to make up for past discrimination: they were a reaction to some historical wrong. Non-remedial measures, on the other hand, are wrong-insensitive—the person adopting the measure need not herself have done anything wrongful. This is the case even when a non-remedial affirmative action measure is undertaken to fulfil a mandatory legal duty—there is no requirement of prior exacerbation of relative group disadvantage by the duty-bearer, nor that she made a person suffer for his membership of a normatively irrelevant or valuable group. Second, as there is no requirement of wrongfulness, there are normally no direct 'victims' in whom a reflex right may be generated.[2] For this reason, the duty is typically non-rights-generating. There may be exceptional cases when the beneficiaries of an affirmative action measure are individually identifiable—for example, if an employer had a duty to provide special training to all his *dalit* employees. In that case, the beneficiaries are not an amorphous group. Each *dalit* employee may then be invested with a right. On the other hand, when the measure simply seeks to encourage black candidates to apply, it is not clear that any particular person has a 'right'.[3]

---

[1] See Chapter 3, section 3.3.5.

[2] See the paragraph immediately preceding section 3.4 in Chapter 3. One could, of course, still speak of the right of *a group* to affirmative action when there is a duty on the state to undertake such measures. See *National Legal Services Authority v Union of India* 2014 (5) SCALE 1 [54], [88].

[3] Notice that affirmative action duties may or may not be action-regarding, in that they may or may not attach to something previously done. This is in contrast to antidiscrimination duty, which is necessarily action-regarding.

Affirmative Action

We also learned in Chapter 3, section 3.3.5, that affirmative action measures can be classified into three overlapping sets. In the first set, affirmative
action measures can be divided on the basis of the tools employed. These tools
may be distributive (eg tie-break rules, job quotas) or facilitative (eg reporting requirements). The strength of these tools may vary. A tie-break rule is a
weaker distributive measure than a quota. In the second overlapping set, we
classified these measures based on the degree of their sensitivity to protected
grounds. Tracking the difference between direct and indirect discrimination,
affirmative action measures may be direct or indirect. In the final set, we
organized measures according to whether they were voluntary, contractual,
or mandatory. Jurisdictions under investigation (usually) permit or encourage the use of affirmative action measures, (sometimes) require them to be
adopted by contract,[4] and (rarely) impose mandatory requirements to do so.
Assuming that the contract was not unfair, I will include contractually mandated measures and measures adopted in response to incentives from the state
(such as tax-breaks) within the scope of *voluntary* measures. Any understanding of affirmative action measures must do justice to these various possibilities. Section 8.1 below will define the scope of these provisions, so that we can
determine which deserve to be called affirmative action measures. I will show
that an affirmative action measure is best understood as *a measure designed
to benefit any members of one or more protected group(s) qua such membership.*

Section 8.2 will discuss the legitimacy of affirmative action measures.
These measures are essential for eliminating relative group disadvantage.
The antidiscrimination duty, even when effectively implemented, is likely
to make but little impression upon relative group disadvantage, and at best
prevent its exacerbation. The reason is simple. In order to make its imposition legitimate in a liberal state, the duty had to be action-regarding and
wrong-sensitive, and limited to a small set of duty-bearers. What is more,
the enforcement of the duty depends largely on voluntary compliance or
on claims by victims who have the resources to fund litigation. Given these
limitations, its impact on abiding, pervasive, and substantial advantage gaps
between groups is likely to be small. This does not, of course, make the duty
pointless. It plays an important role in seeking to ensure that this advantage
gap does not widen. Group dominance is self-reinforcing. If the duty just

---

[4] For a general discussion on the use of state contracts to achieve social justice goals, see
Christopher McCrudden, *Buying Social Justice: Equality, Government Procurement, and Legal
Change* (Oxford University Press 2007).

manages to resist its expansionary pressures, it would be successful. But that merely maintains the status quo, which is freedom-inhibiting, even as it prevents it from worsening. Unravelling relative group disadvantage will take more than successful internalization of the antidiscrimination duty by its bearers. It calls for a good deal of affirmative action.

Being wrong-insensitive, however, affirmative action measures raise particular legitimacy concerns. It is helpful to distinguish between the legitimacy of the voluntary adoption of an affirmative action measure and the legitimacy of its mandatory imposition by the state. The latter is rare, and implicates the interests of the person administering the measure in a way that the former does not. Furthermore, affirmative action by state institutions raise special concerns, which also need to be addressed separately. For the sake of clarity, section 8.2 will consider the various relevant interests involved separately: namely the interests of the beneficiaries, the interests of the administrator of the measure, the interests of adversely affected members of cognate groups, and the public interest. In this section, I will argue that the legitimacy of a measure requires a contextual evaluation of the measure adopted. Even so, some general claims can be made about measures that are likely to be more legitimate than others.

8.1 A Definition

Let us begin by defining what affirmative action measures are. An affirmative action measure is *a measure designed to benefit any members of one or more protected group(s) qua such membership*. Recall that protected groups are groups defined by normatively irrelevant or valuable personal characteristics whose members suffer significant, abiding, and pervasive relative disadvantage, in comparison with members of other groups defined by the same characteristic (ie their cognate groups). This definition clarifies several features of affirmative action measures which are worth noting.

First, their characterization as measures that are *designed* captures several aspects of affirmative action. The term connotes that these measures are intentional. In fact, securing some benefit to members of protected groups must be the main purpose of the measure. Many measures may incidentally secure these same benefits. A measure seeking to reduce poverty in the first place may end up benefiting black people, *dalits*, or women. But because this wasn't its primary objective, it will not count as an affirmative action measure. On the other hand, indirect affirmative action measures are correctly characterized if they satisfy the design requirement (among others), even if the protected ground is not a direct axis of benefit distribution.[5]

Second, 'design' also entails the requirement that there should be a *reasonable* prospect that the measure will be successful to a degree. A measure whose design makes it unlikely that it will achieve at least some of its stated objectives does not merit the label. Distinguish such measures from those which do benefit its target group, but whose costs (especially expressive costs) are so high that they end up doing net harm. This latter set of measures fall within the remit of affirmative action—they are simply unwise or unjustified affirmative action measures. Simply put, in order to qualify as an affirmative action measure, it must be designed to bring some *gross* benefit to the intended beneficiary, even if a final analysis shows that it actually ended up causing a *net* harm to them.

The third feature of the definition is that the measure must seek to achieve its purpose by *benefiting* members of protected groups. Relative group disadvantage could, of course, be reduced by burdening members of cognate groups too. We have already seen that the law no longer insists on proof of comparative adverse effect to prove discrimination. One implication of a non-comparative approach is that levelling down the benefits afforded to the dominant group does not automatically mitigate the charge of discrimination.[6] Only pushing those lower down the scale upwards may close the advantage gap. It is true that, when limited, diverting certain resources to members of protected groups may deny these resources to members of cognate groups. But this is an incidental consequence of the operation of the measure, not something the measure *seeks* as an objective. A measure that burdens members of dominant groups when such burdens are not a necessary consequence of extending certain benefits to disadvantaged groups is not an affirmative action measure. If this was not the case, all affirmative action measures would qualify as collateral discrimination.

Fourth, the measure could (politically, socio-culturally, or materially) *benefit* its target group immediately by distributing the benefit itself (distributive measures), or remotely by creating a facilitative environment where such benefits are more likely to accrue (facilitative measures). The benefit may be tangible (a job) or expressive (encouragement to apply).[7] Recall from Chapter 3

---

[5] Daniel Sabbagh, 'The Rise of Indirect Affirmative Action: Converging Strategies for Promoting "Diversity" in Selective Institutions of Higher Education in the United States and France' (2011) 63 World Politics 470.

[6] See Chapter 6, section 6.2.3.

[7] William Carter, 'Affirmative Action as Government Speech' (2011) 59 UCLA Law Review 2.

that affirmative action measures employ a very wide range of tools, including interventions that seek to increase transparency or influence the behaviour of the intended beneficiaries, persons who control access to scarce resources, or policy-makers.[8] Most distributive measures target the behaviour of those who control access to scarce resources (including state institutions). Measures could be strongly distributive (when group membership is the predominant factor determining the distribution) or weakly distributive (when group membership plays a more limited role). Quotas are the paradigm examples of strong distributive measures. Facilitative measures could take many forms. Transparency measures, which typically require the reporting of group-based makeup of a workplace, facilitate the benefiting of disadvantaged groups by shaming particularly non-diverse enterprises. Access initiatives encouraging members of protected groups to apply to a university are also facilitative, whereas preferences in the admission process will be distributive. Facilitative measures also include 'mainstreaming': positive duties requiring duty-bearers to consider the impact of their policies on protected groups.[9] We will realize later in this chapter that both distributive and facilitative measures can be direct or indirect—the two sets of distinctions cut across each other rather than mapping onto each other.

Fifth, the benefits must be designed to reach *any members* of one or more protected groups. It is not required that all members of such a group derive benefit; even a single beneficiary could suffice. A preference for female candidates for a job where there is only one vacancy could also count as an affirmative action measure. Nor is it required that all the beneficiaries belong to a protected group. Most indirect affirmative action measures tend to benefit members of dominant groups too. For example, a policy that guarantees university places to the top 10 per cent of every high school class, adopted with the objective of increasing the access of black students to universities in a context where high schools are highly segregated along racial lines, will count as an affirmative action measure even though many—possibly even a majority—of its beneficiaries may belong to dominant groups. There is no doubt a point at which the number of beneficiaries belonging to protected groups is so small that we can no longer say the measure is *designed* to benefit them.

Sixth, the measure may be designed to benefit members of *one or more* protected groups. Most affirmative action measures tend to target a single disadvantaged group. However, intersectional disadvantage against, say, *dalit* women, may necessitate tailor-made tools that address the specific patterns of disadvantage they may face. Of course, a measure designed to benefit women

---

[8] See Chapter 3, section 3.3.5.   [9] UK Equality Act 2010, s 149.

may incidentally also benefit *dalits*. The point here is that there is no reason to avoid characterizing measures designed to benefit *dalit* women in particular as affirmative action measures.

Seventh, the measures must benefit members of *protected groups*. Universal welfare schemes are not affirmative action measures. Measures that exclusively or primarily benefit dominant groups are paradigmatically discriminatory, and do not qualify for characterization as affirmative action measures.[10] There is some difficulty in determining whether groups such as whites in South Africa—lacking electoral clout but economically and socially advantaged—could be legitimate beneficiaries of an affirmative action measure.[11] Because the different modes of disadvantage flow into one another, whether a group is relatively disadvantaged is to be judged holistically and not in one single dimension. Remember also that the threshold required is high—the disadvantage must be substantial, abiding, and pervasive.

Finally, the measure should be designed such that it seeks to benefit members of protected groups *qua their membership of these groups*. An affirmative action measure benefiting women must do so because, *as women*, they belong to a protected group. The fact that their group membership is relevant to their disadvantage must inform the design of the measure. In short, affirmative action measures primarily target the reduction of relative disadvantage of *protected groups*. This is what distinguishes them from poverty alleviation measures, general welfare measures, or policies to enforce social rights.

When wisely designed, the impact of affirmative action measures should be to reduce relative group disadvantage, which we know from Chapter 5 is a great impediment to securing access to certain basic goods. In fact, given the limitations of the antidiscrimination duty, they are essential in the fight against such disadvantage. As such, our default normative position ought to be that these measures are desirable. This presupposition is no doubt subject to the legitimacy condition of proportionality, which requires a highly contextualized, evidence-based assessment and balancing of all the relevant interests involved.

There are those, however, who argue for a default suspicion of affirmative action measures. They argue that affirmative action constitutes *reverse* discrimination, and is therefore ethically suspect. This view is largely informed

---

[10] In a socially dynamic scenario, previously disadvantaged groups can become dominant over time. This requires constant evaluation of underlying factual presumptions and regular review of all affirmative action policies. See generally, Rakesh Basant and Gitanjali Sen, 'Who Participates in Higher Education in India? Rethinking the Role of Affirmative Action' (2010) XLV Economic and Political Weekly 62.

[11] See *Minister of Finance v Heerden* 2004 (6) SA 121.

by the lay, motive-based, model of discrimination, one that is hostile to all actions based on protected grounds. We rejected this model in favour of the victim-centred, group-based, legal model. People who characterize affirmative action as 'reverse' discrimination tend to demand that a very heavy justificatory burden must be discharged before a measure is accepted (that is, if they concede that these measures ought not to be categorically prohibited). The US courts have, by and large, adopted this position;[12] all the other jurisdictions have, on the whole, rejected it decisively.[13] As with many other issues in discrimination law, the outlying American position on affirmative action is wrong.

Technically, it is true that affirmative action measures will often satisfy the requirements of collateral discrimination. Even though they are not *designed* to harm members of dominant groups, under conditions of resource constraint they may have adverse effects on such members, and such effect correlates with their group membership. If the measure is designed to benefit a group that, along with its cognate, satisfies the expressive clause, the only remaining question will be whether the measure is justified.

Given that most jurisdictions subject affirmative action measures to a justification test anyway, whether they constitute 'reverse' discrimination may look like a pedantic quibble. But this debate involves more than mere hair-splitting. One of the difficulties with characterizing affirmative action as 'reverse' discrimination is that its intentional character immediately attracts the high justification threshold reserved for especially culpable discriminatory measures. The implied moral equivalence between affirmative action and malicious or intentional direct discrimination is dangerous sophistry.

Even if this standard-of-review problem is overcome, expressive ramifications follow from the manner in which the measures are characterized. Given the negative connotations that the term 'discrimination' has come to acquire in most societies, reverse discrimination invites suspicion and censure. It also lends itself to insidious slogans. Affirmative action has come to acquire a similarly negative expressive currency in the United States, but elsewhere it often has neutral or sometimes even positive connotations. It is not a term that captures what these measures are really doing, and taken literally is rather sterile. But most people understand what it means. Given the moral imperative that drives affirmative action measures, we should reject

---

[12] The United States Supreme Court subjects racial affirmative action measures to strict scrutiny: *Gratz v Bollinger* 539 US 244 (2003) 270.

[13] *Ashoka Thakur v Union of India* (2008) 6 SCC 1 [52]; [16]; *R v Kapp* [2008] 2 SCR 483 [37]–[40].

characterizing them as reverse discrimination. Most states, recognizing this, make explicit exceptions in their antidiscrimination rules to clarify that proportionate affirmative action measures do not constitute discrimination. The issue of characterization laid to rest, we can now turn to their legitimacy.

8.2 Legitimacy of Affirmative Action Measures

The main controversy around affirmative action concerns its justifiability. Determining whether a measure is justifiable requires a proportionate consideration of all the relevant interests involved. Most affirmative action measures engage the interests of four sets of persons: the targeted beneficiaries, the person supposed to undertake the measures (for want of a better term, I shall call her 'the administrator'), members of dominant groups who may be affected by it, and the state representing the public interest.

8.2.1 Interests of the Beneficiaries

The *raison d'être* of affirmative action measures is to benefit members of protected groups. If a measure is likely to result in a net harm to these groups rather than a net gain, it will have no leg to stand on. Whether there will be a net gain for the protected group(s) in question is, of course, an empirical one, and a notoriously difficult one. This is because any such investigation will need to consider not only the tangible costs and benefits of the measure, but also its expressive impact, which is often significant but difficult to quantify.

An affirmative action measure may hold two diametrically opposed expressive implications for a disadvantaged group (and the same measure can simultaneously hold both these implications). On the one hand, it may send a message that the relative disadvantage (and consequent injustice) faced by the protected group has been acknowledged. It can mark the beginning of the process of recovery for the group, thereby boosting the self-worth of its members. This impact may be particularly strong when the messenger is the state. On the other hand, affirmative action measures, especially when they are used too pervasively and for too long, can be interpreted as suggesting that members of the beneficiary group are not good enough to make it in the world without extra help. Such perceptions can congeal into or fortify a negative stereotype that members of the group are lazy or unintelligent.

Smarter design can sometimes reduce the costs of the measure for the beneficiary group. Universal measures which can reap comparative benefits do not single out protected groups in the same way that affirmative action measures do. Facilitative measures are encouraging and empowering. But, because the beneficiaries eventually pass the same selection criteria as everyone else, they do not stigmatize them to the same extent. Weak distributive measures (such as those that use caste only as one of many factors in the eventual distribution) also incur less expressive costs than strong distributive measures (such as quotas). Indirect measures also have a similar advantage over direct ones.

It follows that, in general, strongly distributive direct affirmative action measures should be used as a last resort because they are more likely to imply that the beneficiary group is somehow lacking in talent or industry. The exception is when the advantage gap between the groups is a result of egregious historical injustice, such as slavery, apartheid, or the caste-system. In these cases, strongly distributive measures could signify a society's acknowledgement of the grievousness of these past injustices.

Even when the balance of benefits favours strongly distributive measures, they must be designed very carefully. In singling out (and marking) members of protected groups, carelessly designed measures sometimes end up creating segregated institutions (special schools for disabled children) or de facto segregation within existing institutions (*dalit* students alone attending 'remedial' English-language classes). Segregation is inimical to cohesion and solidarity, and usually wrong for that reason alone. But often, the parallel spaces it creates compare poorly with the 'ordinary' spaces accessed by non-beneficiaries. Often, even those members of target groups who do not need these 'special' spaces end up with access only to these less-good niches.[14] This is another reason why direct, strongly distributive, measures need serious consideration.

So far, we have considered the interests of a disadvantaged group as a monolithic phenomenon. We know from the eccentric distribution condition encountered way back in Chapter 2 that discrimination law does not necessarily (or even usually) prioritize the interests of those individuals, within relatively disadvantaged groups, who have the most limited access to the basic goods.[15] The distribution pattern is, by and large, group-oriented rather than individual-oriented. This does not mean that a priority for those most in need, when it can be achieved without undermining the integrity of discrimination law, will not be welcome.

---

[14] Often, these sub-standard, segregated, settings become a cause of intersectional discrimination. In *Horváth v Hungary* (2013) 57 EHRR 31, for example, 42 per cent of children in Hungarian special schools for disabled students were Roma, who constituted about 8 per cent of the population [7]. Only 0.4–0.6 per cent of the students from special schools had the opportunity to access mainstream secondary education [8].

[15] See Chapter 2, section 2.5: the *duty-imposing norm* must be designed such that it is likely to distribute the non-remote tangible benefits in question to some, but not all, members of the intended beneficiary group.

The eccentric distribution condition largely corresponds to the design of the action-regarding antidiscrimination duty, which is borne by select duty-bearers. It is difficult to tailor this wrong-sensitive duty on a needs-based prioritarian model at an individual level. Incorporating the group disadvantage dimension while retaining its wrong-sensitivity was hard enough. Affirmative action, however, is different. It is wrong-insensitive. There is, therefore, greater scope for at least some affirmative action measures to respond simultaneously to relative group disadvantage as well as to those most in need within a protected group at the same time. Minus the requirement of establishing prior wrongdoing, there is simply greater elbow-room in designing the measures, which makes this possible.

The possibility of intra-group prioritization has, unsurprisingly, been explored most deeply in India—given that it has the longest experience with affirmative action measures. In what has come to be known as the 'creamy-layer' exclusion, the benefits of certain types of affirmative action measures for 'socially and educationally backward classes' are denied to the relatively well-to-do sections within a relatively disadvantaged group.[16] This is, of course, only one way of weaving in some degree of priority of the worst-off.

There are, of course, practical limitations to the extent to which prioritization is possible. Especially with respect to affirmative action measures at higher-echelon positions requiring specialized skills, the pool of eligible candidates belonging to protected groups is likely to be small, and drawn from the more advantaged sections ('the creamy layer') of these disadvantaged groups. Excluding the creamy layer from accessing affirmative action benefits sometimes effectively kills the measure itself. Assuming that even benefiting the creamy layer has some implications for the benefit of the group as a whole, prioritizing the interests of the worst-off is desirable only where it is possible. It should not become a tool for emasculating affirmative action measures or for pitting one section of a disadvantaged group against another.

So long as these caveats are borne in mind, intra-group prioritization of affirmative action measures is a good thing. Benefiting the most disadvantaged members of relatively disadvantaged groups is likely to be the best way to deal with both individual and group disadvantage simultaneously. Thus, a well-designed affirmative action measure will accrue a net benefit to its target protected group, and will prioritize its worst-off members where possible.

---

[16] *Indra Sawhney v Union of India* AIR 1993 SC 477 [86]. The metaphor alludes to the layer of cream that floats to the top when boiled milk begins to cool down, with a consistency different enough from the remaining milk to be easily separable.

To conclude this section, we can say that short-term, facilitative, or weakly distributive, and prioritarian measures are more likely to accrue a greater net benefit to the target beneficiary groups. Given their complexity, even the best design can result in insufficient impact or unintended consequences.[17] It is essential that the impact of affirmative action measures remains under constant review and the measures open to necessary revisions. Even when the target group accrues a net benefit, a measure may be so burdensome to others that it should not be undertaken. We will examine these other interests now.

8.2.2 Interests of the Administrator

Having looked at the interests of the intended beneficiary, we should consider those of the administrator of an affirmative action measure. Measures that are voluntary—even if undertaken in response to a legal incentive such as a tax break or undertaken towards the performance of a contractual obligation—are less controversial. The reason should be obvious: the non-coercive nature of the measures eliminates our concern regarding the negative freedom of the administrator.

The negative freedom of the administrator is most significantly affected if the measure has to be undertaken pursuant to a legal mandate. This is rare in discrimination law—we know that the selected jurisdictions tend not to impose mandatory affirmative action duties on private persons. This is just as well. Such duties, when mandatorily imposed, have a significant impact on the negative liberty of the administrator. This is only in part because of the expense that they have to incur. We know that even the antidiscrimination duty can be expensive, especially with respect to accommodative costs. On the other hand, certain facilitative affirmative action measures may accrue negligible monetary costs. Installing wheelchair-accessible ramps is typically more expensive than holding an access event to encourage applications from women candidates. What makes these duties particularly burdensome is their wrong-insensitive nature. Recall our assumption that a wrong-sensitive duty is less deleterious to personal liberty than wrong-insensitive ones.

It is true, of course, that when the costs of a measure are particularly high, mandating it is even more intrusive. It is important, however, that its costs on the administrator are computed properly. Often, affirmative action

---

[17] Aimee Chin and Nishith Prakash, 'The Redistributive Effects of Political Reservations for Minorities: Evidence from India' (2011) 96 Journal of Development Economics 265; Rohini Pande, 'Can Mandated Political Representation Increase Policy Influence for Disadvantaged Minorities? Theory and Evidence from India' (2003) 93 The American Economic Review 1132.

entails modified eligibility criteria that are easier for members of protected groups to satisfy. Such changes have been attacked, often too quickly, for being unmeritocratic. To be sure, some administrators (especially employers) have an interest in meritocratic selection. Even so, from a non-state administrator's viewpoint,[18] the merit argument has bite only when the affirmative action duty is imposed mandatorily. Only in such cases is it important to interrogate the true nature of a merit-based objection, and the real costs that affirmative action measures which institute new eligibility conditions impose on the employer.

In some cases, the older eligibility criteria simply mask a dominant norm (such as a requirement to work inflexible hours which impacts women's ability to take up employment) that leads to reduced access by disadvantaged groups. Such cases ought not to be characterized as affirmative action. They are more appropriately described as cases involving indirect discrimination, where *remedial* affirmative action measures have become necessary to undo the harm inflicted by discrimination. This will usually be the case only when the offending norm is changed so that its adverse effect is negated—in our example, the modification would introduce the possibility of flexible working hours, at least for those with caring responsibilities. Since the justification clause allows for the preservation of those criteria which are genuinely required to select meritorious candidates, there is no impact on meritocracy in these cases. In some cases, however, remedial affirmative action could be unrelated to the offending rule: an employer who has historically refused to hire *dalits* may now be forced to take measures to encourage their participation in the workforce. In this case, merely getting rid of the offending rule may not be seen as an adequate remedy—its negation may require further action. What is common to cases involving remedial affirmative action is that they all involve some historical or continuing wrongdoing by the duty-bearer. Just like the failure to provide reasonable accommodation, these really are cases of wrongful discrimination rather than wrong-insensitive affirmative action.

A truly non-remedial mandatory affirmative action duty is different because of its wrong-insensitive character. Even so, when it requires a change in the eligibility criteria for selection, we should not automatically assume that there is a dilution of the requirement of merit. Even the most demanding affirmative action measures, such as mandatory quotas, may be compatible with the requirements of merit. This will be especially the case when it is not simply an aggregate of individual talents that informs the overall

---

[18] There are some remaining concerns when state institutions undertake such measures, concerns that we will deal with in section 8.2.4.

efficiency of a firm or legitimacy of a public institution, but also the diversity within its workforce. In such cases, the identity of individual members does become a legitimate merit-related concern. An applicant who is likely to make the work-place more diverse is, in this respect, better. Merit is not simply a matter of how talented an individual is in the abstract, but rather it is a measure of the contribution they can make to an institution. Where institutional diversity is desirable, whether for productivity, goodwill, creativity, or legitimacy reasons, the identity of a candidate is relevant for reasons of merit. The US Supreme Court has, for example, upheld an affirmative action policy that sought to 'achieve that diversity which has the potential to enrich everyone's education and thus make a law school class stronger than the sum of its parts'.[19]

This discussion complicates our understanding of the net cost of an affirmative action measure to its administrator. The impact of an affirmative action measure on meritocracy in any institution is a complex empirical question. Much depends on the particular context. We cannot start with an a priori assumption that there is a supposed tension between affirmative action and merit. Any evaluation of the actual costs of a mandatory, even if genuinely wrong-insensitive, affirmative action duty should therefore be based on a contextual consideration of all relevant factors. Having said that, since we are speaking of the coercive enforcement of a wrong-insensitive duty, the bar for its legitimacy is quite high—even if it eventually ends up benefiting the duty-bearer. It is one thing to interrogate whether merit has indeed taken a hit by an affirmative action measure, quite another to coercively require a private person to hire more meritoriously. Precisely for this reason, voluntary measures ought not to be impeached on the ground that they will reduce the efficiency of the firm concerned.

Measures designed to address problems with institutional culture lie between remedial and non-remedial affirmative action. In these cases, the exclusion of disadvantaged groups takes place not because of detrimental rules but due to a more inchoate institutional culture. It is difficult to establish *wrongdoing* in these cases, but we cannot confidently deny its existence either. The problem is one of epistemic limitations, and is often manifested in societies where relative group disadvantage is particularly deep and entrenched. Racial disadvantage in South Africa and caste disadvantage in India may be good examples. In these exceptional cases, the imposition of a weak or facilitative, if mandatory, affirmative action duty even on non-state administrators may be proportionate, and therefore legitimate.

---

[19] *Grutter v Bollinger* 539 US 306 (2003) 315.

Before we move on to consider the interests of non-beneficiaries who are adversely affected by a measure, notice that when a non-mandatory measure is challenged by such a person, the claimant seeks to restrict the administrator's negative freedom in undertaking the measure. This is the flip side of our concern for her negative freedom—just as we need to consider the impact of a coercive affirmative action duty on her negative liberty, we also need to account for the liberty costs of disallowing her from undertaking a non-coerced measure. This liberty interest, as always, will give way to a sufficiently strong third-party interest in the measure not being undertaken. But because it is often overlooked in affirmative action debates, it bears mentioning.

Bearing the negative freedom of a non-state administrator in mind, mandatory affirmative action duties may be imposed only in very exceptional circumstances. We can also conclude that when assessing the impact of a measure on the efficiency of a workforce, our inquiry should be holistic. We should consider not just the particular talents of an individual worker, but also the overall efficiency of the workforce, which may be informed (among other things) by the diversity of its composition.

8.2.3 Interests of Those Adversely Affected

We can now turn to the most controversial of the interests involved: those of a person who is adversely affected by the measure, one who is not a direct beneficiary of the measure, nor its administrator, nor a state institution. She typically belongs to an expressively salient group that is a cognate of the one whose members are likely to benefit from the measure. What is the nature of the interest that such a person has in an affirmative action measure?

To consider the issue more concretely, let us consider the case of a businesswoman, Estha, who screens applicants on the basis of their performance on an examination. She invites the top ten overall scorers on this examination to an interview, along with the top five *dalit* scorers from the remaining candidates. Let us imagine that Rahel, a non-*dalit* applicant, is ranked 12th overall. To avoid distraction, let us also assume that Estha has set this system up voluntarily rather than in response to any legal duty. Does Rahel have a claim to be interviewed? We are not interested in any argument that relies on what is good for Estha's business—that is primarily her concern, not Rahel's.

Rahel's claim could be based on any of three possible lines of argument: legitimate expectations, meritocratic appointment, or non-discrimination. He may insist that he should get an interview on some legitimate expectations type claim: by instituting the test, Estha has indicated the parameters by which she judges the candidates, at least at the screening stage. In doing so, she has created a legitimate expectation in persons like Rahel that everyone selected for the interview will be judged based on this common parameter.

This claim based on legitimate expectations is the weakest of all three. To begin with, it is unlikely that legitimate expectations are available against non-state bodies. It is a ground for challenging the administrative action of state bodies and has typically had a negligible reach beyond state institutions, especially when compared to the much wider application of antidiscrimination norms to quasi-public bodies. The extension of administrative law norms, like respect for legitimate expectations, much beyond the state and its instrumentalities is unlikely to be a justifiable intrusion into negative liberty. Even if such a claim could stand against Estha, it is doubtful that her actions could have given rise to these expectations in Rahel legitimately.[20] The design of her screening policy was clear and public. He cannot rely on one part of the selection policy to base his expectations upon. He would have any claim to legitimate expectations only if he ranked amongst the top ten candidates.

The second possible argument is a meritocratic one. Rahel may claim, based on the test, that he is better qualified than candidates who were selected for the interview. In other words, he is more deserving of an interview call and should, for that reason, get one. Estha's refusal to interview him, on this account, is irrational.[21] In section 8.2.2, I acknowledged that the administrator (in this case, Estha) has a genuine interest in the overall efficiency of her workforce, which is a function of the merit of her individual employees as well as other possible factors, such as the diversity of her workforce. When a mandatory affirmative action measure makes her work-place less meritocratic, she incurs a cost that must be accounted for. When the administrator is a state institution, there may even be a general public interest in ensuring that public servants are meritorious. However, claims of merit loss are often made by third parties to challenge even non-mandatory (ie voluntary or at least consensual) affirmative action measures. What interest does Rahel have in the efficiency of Estha's workforce or the merit of her workers?[22]

---

[20] See generally, Richard Arneson, 'What is Wrongful Discrimination?' (2006) 43 San Diego Law Review 775, 785.

[21] For a forceful articulation of a moral right to meritorious treatment, see Donal Nolan, 'A Right to Meritorius Treatment' in Conor Gearty and Adam Tomkins (eds), *Understanding Human Rights* (Pinter 1996).

[22] For a defence of the idea that merit-based claims are derived from considerations of efficiency rather than desert, see Norman Daniels, 'Merit and Meritocracy' (1978) 7 Philosophy and Public Affairs 206.

If there was a general legal duty on Estha to act rationally, or even a specific legal duty to only employ the most talented people, Rahel may have
a case. But Estha has no such duty in law. It is doubtful whether she has
a moral duty to do so either. At best, she may have reasons of prudence or
self-interest. Like legitimate expectations, a duty to act rationally is usually
only imposed on the state and institutions that closely resemble the state
or carry out its functions. Even if we have a moral claim to rational treatment generally (which itself is unlikely),[23] the law is typically (and correctly,
because of liberty constraints) reluctant to enforce this claim against bodies
other than the state. Even with respect to state institutions, it is hardly clear
that a preference for the less advantaged is in some sense 'irrational'. There is
no reason for Rahel to assume that the examination is the real test for merit
and the separate rule for *dalits* an exception to it. We have already seen that
merit of the overall workforce may well be concerned with the diversity of its
composition. The argument is not confined to employment. Diversity may
be of value in educational and residential settings too. As with much else in
affirmative action, the issue is empirical rather than conceptual.

The third argument is the strongest of the three claims. The argument is
that it is unfair to apply different screening thresholds to *dalit* and non-*dalit*
students, because doing so makes him suffer merely for belonging to a group
whose membership is not immoral. This claim tracks cases of collateral
discrimination.[24] The argument, put simply, is that the affirmative action
measure satisfies all clauses in the definition of collateral discrimination
apart from the justification clause, and is for that reason at least prima facie
discriminatory.

In the debate on its characterization, we learnt that most jurisdictions create a special exception for affirmative action measures: these measures are
deemed to be non-discriminatory, rather than as instances of 'reverse' discrimination. The main reason for doing so is that characterizing them as
discriminatory invites the moral opprobrium that normally attaches to the
term, and makes one predisposed to oppose affirmative action. In reality,
however, this is largely a terminological debate. Most jurisdictions require
affirmative action measures to satisfy a justification requirement. Even
if they did amount to prima facie collateral discrimination, a very similar
inquiry under the justification clause will be conducted anyway. Typically,

---

[23] Judith Thomson, 'Preferential Hiring' (1973) 2 Philosophy and Public Affairs 364, 369: 'no
perfect stranger has a right to be given a benefit which is yours to dispose of; no perfect stranger
even has a right to be given an equal chance at getting a benefit which is yours to dispose of'.

[24] See Chapter 6, section 6.5.

the judicial standard of review applied when determining the validity of an affirmative action measure is deferential (except, as ever, in the United States). Recall our discussion on the connection between blameworthiness based on the mens rea of the discriminator and the relevant standard of review from Chapter 6.[25] A deferential approach to affirmative action acknowledges the benign purpose that informs these measures—to reduce the liberty-denying advantage gap between groups. So, doctrinally, it makes little difference whether affirmative action measures are tested as instances of collateral discrimination—either approach should lead to a deferential investigation into any underlying justification. Our refusal to accept the label 'reverse discrimination' for affirmative action is for semantic and political reasons, not doctrinal reasons. This does not mean that all acts of collateral discrimination amount to affirmative action. A programme of conscription for men but not women amounts to collateral discrimination, but cannot be characterized as an affirmative action measure designed to benefit women.

The upshot is this. Only this third claim of Rahel's packs any punch. It is a claim that he has been discriminated against. It is a weak claim, because it is based on collateral rather than paradigmatic discrimination. Paradigmatic discrimination entails two types of wrongs: a systemic wrong of exacerbating relative group disadvantage, and a particular wrong of making the victims suffer because of their belonging to a group whose membership should not make a difference to our live chances. Collateral discrimination readily entails the particular street-level wrongdoing. It is wrongful at the systemic level only because discriminating against members of a dominant group may have expressive repercussions which may also worsen the situation of the disadvantaged group. What is clear is that the concern of discrimination law is primarily focussed on the relatively disadvantaged group.

With this background, it should be easy to see where Rahel's discrimination claim is headed. Collateral discrimination is prima facie wrong because of our assumption that, when the expressive clause is satisfied, it worsens relative group disadvantage. When this assumption is disproved, it is likely that collateral discrimination will be justifiable. But collaterally discriminatory measures are not designed to benefit disadvantaged groups. Affirmative action measures, on the other hand, are. Thus, the main question with respect to Rahel's discrimination claim is whether there is a non-discriminatory or less discriminatory means to secure comparable benefit.

This is essentially a requirement of necessity and minimum impairment. Given our assumption that collateral discrimination incurs expressive costs, if

---

[25] See Chapter 6, section 6.6.4.

the benefits of affirmative action can be garnered through other means, they ought to be preferred. In addition, other things being equal, measures which have a lower adverse impact on the members of dominant groups ought to be preferred over those which have a greater impact. In general, therefore, universalist welfare measures are better than those targeted at protected groups if they can achieve a comparable reduction in relative group disadvantage. Given that many members of relatively disadvantaged groups are also more likely to face *absolute* disadvantage, universalist welfare measures such as a guarantee of minimum wages, universal education, universal health care, universal food security, and universal pension benefits can play a significant role in reducing the advantage gap between groups. These measures are often expensive, but are required in any case to secure to us the most basic of the basic goods required to satisfy our biological needs. That they serve to secure the other basic goods as well (by reducing the advantage gap somewhat) gives them a special normative urgency. Universalist measures will not constitute even prima facie collateral discrimination.

Where an extension of universal benefits is not feasible, indirect affirmative action measures are generally preferable to direct affirmative action measures. Indirect measures, we have seen, make a non-protected ground their axis of distribution, when such a ground is a reasonably good proxy for a protected ground. If *dalit* applicants are significantly more likely not to have a parent who went to university than members of other caste or religious groups in India, distributing a benefit on the basis of whether a parent went to university is preferable to doing so directly on the basis of caste.[26] If Estha had used this as a criterion in the screening process, Rahel may still have suffered because of his group membership (assuming his parents are university graduates). But he would not have suffered *only* because of his group membership, but also because his group was relatively privileged in having disproportionately fewer members whose parents did not go to university. The extent of wrong suffered by him is less. Incidentally, the example also highlights the fact that indirect measures may be better at benefiting multiple protected groups and intersectional groups, which often suffer similar types of disadvantage. It is quite possible that not just *dalits*, but certain religious minorities are also disproportionately more likely to have parents who did not go to university. The alternative measure could benefit not just *dalits*, but also Muslims, and even *dalit*-Muslims!

---

[26] Given the very small number of candidates that Estha interviews (15), the connection between *dalits* and candidates whose parents do not have a university education has to be very close for the latter to be an adequate proxy for the former. This may or may not be the case, but we will assume it to be so for our example. When the measure targets very large numbers (eg for state employment), the connection can be weaker and still secure the desired indirect benefit to *dalits*.

Finally, it would also be preferable to have facilitative rather than distributive measures in place, if they could deliver comparable outcomes. Suppose that instead of the measure she did adopt, Estha had identified talented *dalits* from the pool of potential applicants, encouraged them to apply, and perhaps even trained them in the skills that the screening examination tests. She could then simply screen the top 15 candidates without a special rule preferring *dalit* candidates, and could still end up with a pool which has some *dalit* representation. Facilitative measures are not necessarily zero-sum in the same way that distributive measures are. They do not give the beneficiaries any advantage over others in the actual selection. Rahel would have run the same race as everyone else and would have fewer reasons to complain. It is true that indirect and facilitative measures have their limitations. But when they can deliver significant (even if somewhat lower) benefits to the protected group and the administrator, they ought to be preferred.

Even a justified affirmative action measure can have the effect—though not the design—of making Rahel suffer because of his group membership. This is unfortunate, but not a wrong that is, in itself, sufficient to constitute discrimination. Without its expressive implications, this would be no worse than a refusal to hire a person because his name begins with the letter 'W'. Discrimination law offers such a person no protection.[27] What is more, an affirmative action measure is morally superior because it is at least necessary to serve a valuable goal (of reducing relative group disadvantage) unlike the hypothetical regime, where the harm to the unfortunate Mr Wimble is simply gratuitous. Rahel's interest in not being made to suffer because of his group membership is genuine, but without the accompaniment of the systemic goal of reducing relative group disadvantage, is simply not weighty enough to hold sway.

Bearing the interests of members of dominant groups in mind, we can say that if they deliver comparable benefits, universal welfare measures are preferable to affirmative action measures, indirect measures are better than direct ones, and facilitative means should be explored before distributive measures are adopted.

8.2.4 Public Interest

So far we have considered the interests of the beneficiaries, the administrators, and third parties. Now we can consider if the public interest engaged by

---

[27] Unless, of course, there is a correlation with group disadvantage. See Yasmine Seale, 'Q v. K' (*LRB Blog*, 2013) <http://www.lrb.co.uk/blog/2013/10/16/yasmine-seale/q-v-k/> accessed 5 November 2014.

affirmative action measures impose further constraints. Our starting point is the acknowledgement that there is a strong public interest in reducing abiding, pervasive, and substantial relative group disadvantage. Insofar as affirmative action measures serve this objective, they are eminently desirable. We also know from Chapter 7 that relative group disadvantage is a problem not only because of the impact it has on a protected group's access to basic goods. The democratic legitimacy of public institutions is also seriously compromised if certain groups are systematically excluded.[28] This lends special weight to the importance of measures that make state institutions more representative of its populations. It is not surprising then that so many of these measures focus on increasing diversity in public employment directly, or on making access routes such as higher education more diverse. Any problems that affirmative action measures pose for the public interest should be evaluated in the light of these compelling gains.

There are two specific public interest concerns that need addressing here. The first relates to the special considerations that apply to affirmative action by state institutions. The second involves the expressive costs that affirmative action measures can sometimes incur, and the public interest in minimizing these costs.

Let us begin with the first of these interests. The state is special. Unlike the more private duty-bearers, it does not merely carry the burden of the antidiscrimination duty. It also has a general duty to act rationally, and to respect legitimate expectations. This has implications for how the interests of third parties are accounted for when an affirmative action measure is undertaken by the state. Let us modify slightly the example involving Rahel to understand these implications. Imagine that, rather than Estha, the measure with a lower score threshold for screening *dalit* candidates was adopted by a state institution. Unlike Estha, who did not have any duty to uphold Rahel's legitimate expectations or treat him rationally, the state does. In our specific example, this would not make a real difference because we concluded that Rahel did not have any legitimate expectation to get an interview, and Estha may not have acted irrationally. But under other circumstances, this may not be so.

In the decision of the US Supreme Court in *Ricci*, the city of New Haven had administered a test for selecting firefighters, which it later worried had a disproportionate adverse effect on racial minorities. As a result, it decided to set aside the results and conduct a new test. One of the relevant considerations for the majority, in this otherwise controversial judgment, was that the

---

[28] See Chapter 7, section 7.1.

examination 'create[d] legitimate expectations on the part of those who took the tests.... some of the firefighters here invested substantial time, money and personal commitment in preparing for the tests'.[29] The case involves remedial affirmative action, not our main concern in this chapter. But it does highlight an important constraint that legitimate expectations impose on state policy: once the state announces a particular policy and others rely on it to their detriment, it becomes difficult for the state to change course. Of course, when the need for a modification is sufficiently weighty, legitimate expectations may be overridden. But in the normal course of affairs, the state must respect any legitimate expectations its actions may give rise to and live with the consequences. This underlines the importance of good design, and all the thought and research that should go into predicting the possible outcome of any particular policy. The task is not easy, which only makes it even more important that any measure is adopted after due deliberation.

The state also has a duty to treat persons rationally, in addition to duties such as non-discrimination. Unlike private persons, it cannot refuse to hire someone simply because his name starts with the letter 'W'. It cannot refuse an interview to Rahel on a whim either. There must be good reasons to do so. Refusing him an interview while granting it to those who scored less than him in the screening test calls for an explanation. In our example, there were good reasons that justify this: a holistic conception of merit, the importance of diversity in state institutions, and the need to reduce relative group disadvantage. In fact, no *justified* affirmative action measure is irrational. Whatever we may think of the rationality with respect to private persons, the state is essentially an other-regarding institution whose conception of rationality cannot be based on self-interest alone. Although the state does have a special duty to act rationally, in the context we are concerned with, this duty tracks the legitimacy concerns we have been discussing in this chapter.

The next important public interest in affirmative action measures is to keep their expressive costs to a minimum. We have already discussed the expressive implications of affirmative action measures for its intended beneficiaries. There are other expressive implications which are pertinent to the public interest more generally when the measure implicates expressively salient grounds such as race, religion, and caste. These implications are stronger when the administrator of the measure is the state.

On the positive side, taking affirmative action measures, and their subsequent success in making the composition of the officialdom more diverse, can send a message that public institutions are genuinely representative and

---

[29] *Ricci v DeStefano* 557 US 557 (2009) 583–4.

participative. Although more diverse public institutions are good in themselves, the messages they send are also key to their perceived legitimacy. A democracy will remain imperfect if any section of the society feels that it is excluded from its governance. Affirmative action, by visibly making the state more diverse, gives us all a stake in its success.

The flip side of affirmative action is its potential to express a negative message: that the interests of the dominant group do not count, or that they do not count as much as that of the protected group. Persistent and festering resentment among its dominant groups can be very dangerous for any society, possibly resulting in 'balkanization' and other dire and unforeseen consequences.[30]

The apparent partisanship of affirmative action is even more pronounced than that of the antidiscrimination duty. Discrimination law is partisan, but in favour of *whichever group happens to suffer from relative group disadvantage*. It is *not* partisan in the sense that it values the interests of black people, *dalits*, or women any more than it does those of white people, *brahmins*, or men. In fact, 'prioritarian' is a better description of this disadvantage-centric approach than 'partisan'. Ambiguous terms like 'race-consciousness' make it difficult for us to distinguish between sectarian partisanship and need-based prioritarianism.[31] Unlike partisan measures, there is no desire behind an affirmative action measure to hurt the dominant group—if there was, it would probably amount to collateral discrimination.

The fact that dominant groups so frequently misinterpret this as an identity-based partisanship intrinsic to discrimination law is, in part, a discursive failure. Politicians, judges, and scholars are all to blame for failing to consistently explain the true nature of the prioritarianism in discrimination law. The relative novelty of discrimination law generally, and of affirmative action (at least outside India) in particular, partly explains why it seems to cause more resentment in more people than the more demanding, wrong-insensitive, prioritarian duty imposed by progressive taxation.

An important aspect of this discursive failure is a failure to emphasize that almost all of us are potential beneficiaries of discrimination law. As

---

[30] Reva Siegal, 'From Colorblindness to Antibalkanization: An Emerging Ground of Decision in Race Equality Cases' (2011) 120 The Yale Law Journal 1278; Thomas Sowell, *Affirmative Action around the World: An Empirical Study* (Yale University Press 2004) 92. See also, Chapter 6, section 6.5.

[31] It is unsurprising that the term has so much currency in the United States, where the distinction is the most blurred. *Ricci v DeStefano* 557 US 557 (2009) is but one example of a failure to tell partisanship from prioritarianism.

discrimination law has expanded from its early days when the focus was on single grounds, to a stage when we acknowledge a whole range of protected groups, the number of persons who fall within one or the other protected group is likely to be quite a substantial chunk of any population. Most of us currently benefit from its protection. Those of us who are not are protected *potentially* when we become older, or if we become disabled. It is surprising that so many still believe such a regime to be narrowly partisan.

Unfortunate as it is, the fact of the matter is that affirmative action is seen as unfairly partisan by many. This imposes a great burden, mainly on the state, to attempt to minimize its expressive cost. Transparency of reasons, solid evidence, and smart design will go some way towards securing this objective. It is essential that affirmative action measures are politically defended as prioritarian rather than partisan. Because they are viewed with suspicion, all efforts must be made to clarify the sincerity of motive. The beneficiaries must be identified according to solid sociological research rather than rule-of-thumb assumptions. In fact, Indian law insists on a report from a fact-finding commission as a precondition to the characterization of any group as 'educationally and socially backward' (a status which makes it eligible for affirmative action).[32]

Better regulatory design can help too. Certain types of measures are likely to lead to less resentment among dominant groups than others. Universalist measures, indirect measures, facilitative measures, or weak distributive measures are likely to have lower expressive costs in this regard too. A caveat is necessary at this stage. Indirect affirmative measures are preferable because they do not directly use a protected ground as their axis of distribution. But their expressive costs are likely to be lower for the dominant group only if the chosen axis of distribution has a distributive rationale independent of the benefits it brings to the protected group. Let us return to our modified example, where Estha selected the top five candidates whose parents had not gone to university rather than selecting the top five *dalit* candidates (alongside the top ten of the remaining candidates). I claimed that this modified measure was less harmful to Rahel. It follows that it is also likely to cause less resentment among the dominant groups, and is therefore less detrimental to the public interest in a cohesive society.

But this will be the case only if the measure is not seen as manipulative: ie doing surreptitiously what is too controversial to do overtly. Let it be clear that a preference for indirect affirmative action is not in fact manipulative. If the costs it imposes on a third person are lower than direct

---

[32] National Commission for Backward Classes Act 1993, s 9; Constitution of India, art 340.

affirmative action, as the preceding section argued is indeed the case, there is a genuine reason to prefer them. But there remains a danger that they may be *viewed* as if they are manipulative, if the chosen axis of distribution (parental university qualifications) is nothing more than a smoke-screen for the expressively salient characteristic (caste). In our example, this is not the case. Whether one's parents have been to university is one indicator of disadvantage in its own right. What is more, it is a factor whose causal connection with the consequent disadvantage is more transparent (educated parents are more likely to educate their children, who are more likely to have better life chances). Even without its disproportionate benefits to *dalits*, the measure would have made sense. Compare this to another alternative, where the distribution was based on whether one was a meat-eater or a vegetarian. Assuming that 'lower' castes are more likely to be meat-eaters than 'higher' ones, this distributive measure could also have tracked caste-based distribution. Here, however, the direct axis of distribution—food preference—does not have an obvious causal connection with disadvantage. It is unlikely that this second alternative measure is going to reap the expressive benefits that the first one could.

What follows is that the direct axis of distribution of a universalist or indirect measure must be capable of bearing some justificatory burden independent of its implications for the protected group. This will be the case when the actual axis of distribution has an obvious and independent causal connection with disadvantage. An added benefit of this sort of indirect measure is that it also has an in-built, intra-group priority for the less advantaged *dalits* (whose parents did not go to university) over the more advantaged ones (whose parents did).

Finally, affirmative action measures have to be dynamic, and respond to changing social realities. If a previously disadvantaged group stops being so, affirmative action measures benefiting it will indeed become unjustified discrimination. A failure to end measures which have achieved their purpose makes them partisan rather than prioritarian. Because the continued application of these measures creates a group with vested interests, ending them politically when the time is ripe can be difficult. Even so, the fact remains that only a measure designed to benefit members of *protected groups* counts as an affirmative action measure.

Despite all these caveats and precautions, the mere fact that a carefully designed affirmative action measure is *motivated* by the desire to help relatively disadvantaged groups may cause some resentment. Unfortunate as this is, it is inevitable if we are to take the project of securing access to basic goods for all seriously. In fact, unless we discount this pernicious reaction, the entire foundation of discrimination law becomes shaky. It is wise to avoid expressive costs where possible, even if they are unjustifiably incurred. When the overall goal is as important and as pressing as the one that discrimination law pursues, certain unavoidable and unwarranted expressive costs just have to be accepted.

8.3 Conclusion

In this chapter, I have argued that affirmative action is best understood as *a measure designed to benefit any members of one or more protected group(s) qua such membership.* I have also concluded that:

i. Affirmative action measures must accrue a *net* benefit to members of protected groups.

ii. They should not be imposed mandatorily on non-state bodies, unless there are exceptional and compelling reasons for doing so.

iii. When their impact on merit is in question, merit should be evaluated holistically.

iv. They should be defended as prioritarian rather than partisan.

v. The choice of their beneficiaries should be backed by solid empirical evidence.

vi. The measures should be regularly reviewed to assess their impact and revised or repealed in light of emerging social dynamics.

We have also noted that when they have comparable benefits and are equally feasible,

vii. Affirmative action measures should have an in-built priority for the worst-off members of these groups where possible.

viii. Universalist measures are preferable to affirmative action measures.

ix. Facilitative measures are better than distributive ones.

x. Weak distributive measures are preferable to strong distributive ones.

xi. Indirect measures are better than direct ones, provided that the direct axis of distribution underlying any indirect measure has an independent and obvious causal connection with the disadvantage being addressed.

A few general comments can be made with respect to these suggestions. First, they highlight how fact-sensitive the viability of any affirmative action measure is. The debate has been mired too deeply in ideology, with very little reliance on sociological data. That must change. Second, the first comment highlights the institutional limitations of courts in engaging with affirmative action in any meaningful way. The design, framework, defence, and execution of affirmative action measures are primarily political rather than adjudicative tasks.[33] This is especially the case given the importance of expressive implications of these measures, which judges are particularly ill-equipped to assess. This is not an argument against any judicial role in this regard: instead, it is only a cause for caution while determining what such role should be. Third, affirmative action, especially for potentially national groups, is treacherous territory. The possibility of balkanization and consequent violence is borne out all too emphatically by the historical record. A good deal of care and caution is warranted.

---

[33] See generally, Cass Sunstein, 'The Anticaste Principle' (1994) 92 Michigan Law Review 2410, 2439ff.

PART IV

CONCLUSION

9

The Vindication of Discrimination Law

I will give you a Talisman... Recall the face of the poorest and the weakest man whom you may have seen, and ask yourself, if the step you contemplate is going to be of any use to him... Will it restore him to a control over his own life and destiny? In other words, will it lead to *swaraj*...?[1]

Generations of Indian schoolchildren have faced up to this epigraphic injunction from MK Gandhi in their textbooks. Because it seeks to bring freedom (*swaraj*) to society's underdogs, discrimination law should meet his approval. We have now reached the point where we are able to sum up the discussion in this book. Part I, comprising Chapters 2 and 3, dealt with the issue of the definition and scope of discrimination law. Chapter 2 showed that for a duty-imposing legal norm to be characterized as a norm of discrimination law, it must satisfy the following four necessary conditions, which, taken together, are also sufficient:

The Personal Grounds Condition: *The duty-imposing norm in question must require some connection between the act or omission prohibited or mandated by the norm on the one hand and certain attributes or characteristics that persons have, called 'grounds', on the other.*

The Cognate Groups Condition: *A protected ground must be capable of classifying persons into more than one class of persons, loosely called 'groups'.*

The Relative Disadvantage Condition: *Of all groups defined by a given universal order ground, members of at least one group must be significantly more likely to suffer abiding, pervasive, and substantial disadvantage than the members of at least one other cognate group.*

---

[1] Pyarelal Nayyar, *Mahatma Gandhi: The Last Phase*, vol 2 (Navajivan 1958) 65. *Swaraj* is a complicated ideal, and may be roughly translated as self-rule, freedom, or autonomy. It was a key slogan in the Indian anti-colonial struggle.

The Eccentric Distribution Condition: *The duty-imposing norm must be designed such that it is likely to distribute the non-remote tangible benefits in question to some, but not all, members of the intended beneficiary group.*

Overall, Chapter 3 presented the architecture of the practice of discrimination law in the selected jurisdictions. Here, we learnt that in order to define the protectorate of discrimination law, a *ground* must: (i) be a personal characteristic that classifies persons into groups with a significant advantage gap between them; and (ii) it must either be immutable or it must constitute a fundamental choice. We also saw that relatively disadvantaged groups are typically offered greater protection than their cognates—in other words, the protection of the law was largely asymmetric.

Chapter 3 also told us that discrimination law does not impose its burdens universally, nor does it impose them on advantaged groups. Instead, its burdens are imposed unidirectionally on the state against its citizens, on employers against their employees, on landlords against their tenants, and on providers of goods and services against their consumers.

Finally, Chapter 3 explained the various tools used by the law: the prohibition on direct and indirect discrimination and on ground-sensitive harassment, provision for reasonable accommodation, and for affirmative action. It clarified the interconnections between these tools (for example, that reasonable accommodation is best understood as a *remedy* for discrimination, rather than as a primary wrong). Affirmative action measures were classified based on three different overlapping criteria as distributive or facilitative, direct or indirect, and voluntary or mandatory.

Part II explored the purposive question: what is the general justifying aim—the *point*, if you will—of discrimination law? Towards this end, Chapter 4 provides an account of positive liberty, claiming that even liberty is necessarily comparative (although not in the same way that equality is comparative). It explained that in order to live a good life, we need secured access to at least four basic goods: (i) a set of goods which will adequately satisfy one's biological needs; (ii) negative freedom, ie freedom from unjustified interference by others in one's person, projects, possessions, relationships, and affairs; (iii) an adequate range of valuable opportunities to choose from; and (iv) an appropriate level of self-respect. Sufficient and secured access to these goods make a person free and enable her to seek a good life. We learnt that while these goods promote liberty, how much of each we are entitled to is a relative and contextual judgment rather than an absolute and insular one.

Chapter 5 claimed that discrimination law seeks to reduce (and ultimately remove) any significant advantage gap between a protected group (defined by an immutable or valuable ground) and its cognate groups. It applied the normative framework outlined in Chapter 4 to argue that the pursuit of this goal helps secure the final three of the four basic goods a person needs to freely pursue a good life—this is because membership of a relatively disadvantaged group is a serious impediment to our freedom. The chapter argued, against egalitarianism, that the relatively modest goal of discrimination law can, at best, be little more than lip-service to the ideal of strict equality.

Part III dealt with the distributive concerns in the law: who bears the duties and who benefits from them? Chapter 6 provided a conceptual restatement of the antidiscrimination duty (which entails the prohibition on direct and indirect discrimination and ground-sensitive harassment, and provision for reasonable accommodation). The duty has two aspects: the paradigmatic duty protects members of disadvantaged groups, while the collateral duty protects those of advantaged groups. The following definitions were defended:

An action φ by a duty-bearer x is/will be paradigmatically discriminatory if and only if,

(i) *φ has/will have a non-remote adverse effect ε on a set of person(s) V (the adverse effect clause); and*

(ii) *V is/will be constituted entirely or disproportionately by persons who are (or are perceived to be or are closely associated with) members of a protected group P (the group membership clause); and*

(iii) *there is a correlation between a person's membership of V and her (actual or perceived, or her associate's) membership of P (the correlation clause); and*

(iv) *φ-ing lacks adequate justification (the justification clause).*

An action φ by a duty-bearer x is collaterally discriminatory if and only if,

(i) *φ has/will have a non-remote adverse effect ε on a set of person(s) V (the adverse effect clause); and*

(ii) *V is/will be constituted entirely or disproportionately by persons who are (or are perceived to be or are closely associated with) members of a group C that is a cognate of a protected group P (the group membership clause); and*

(iii) *there is a correlation between a person's membership of V and her (actual or perceived, or her associate's) membership of C (the correlation clause); and*

(iv) *memberships of groups P and C have expressive salience (the expressive clause); and*

(v) *φ-ing lacks adequate justification (the justification clause).*

We learnt that the *antidiscrimination duty* on x is to not φ. It was shown that a discriminatory act involves two wrongs: it exacerbates relative group disadvantage; and it makes a person suffer for their membership of a normatively irrelevant or valuable group.

Chapter 7 explained that the liberty cost of imposing the antidiscrimination duty universally, or only on members of advantaged groups, or bi-directionally would be too high. The law imposes the duty only on persons who have a (relatively) public character and are optimally placed to make a sufficient difference to relative group disadvantage.

Chapter 8 defined affirmative action as a measure designed to benefit any members of one or more protected group(s) qua such membership. It specified a number of conditions under which such measures may be legitimate—for example, it was shown that these measures must be prioritarian rather than partisan, flexible, evidence-led, and frequently reviewed. We also learnt that it is desirable to minimize their expressive costs; to avoid imposing them mandatorily; and to prefer indirect, facilitative, or weak measures to direct, distributive, or strong ones. That said, it was recognized that the antidiscrimination duty, on its own, cannot close the advantage gap between groups—shrewdly designed affirmative action measures are essential for securing freedom to the members of protected groups.

9.1 Significance and Implications

These conclusions are significant. I will highlight five reasons why this is the case. First, they avoid many of the pathologies afflicting established scholarship. In particular, the separation of the purposive and the distributive questions, and the consequent distinction between systemic and particular concerns, cuts through much existing confusion. We also have better tools to resolve enduring debates concerning symmetry and comparisons: we now know that discrimination law is much more asymmetric and comparative at the systemic level than it is at the particular (or manifest) level.

Second, our findings highlight the fact that discrimination law's regulation is contingent on socially dynamic factors. A group is protected only if it suffers relative disadvantage, a status that changes over time and space. The desirability of an affirmative action measure depends on its design as well as its (continuing) impact on the various interests involved, which will be different in different contexts. This underlines a special political and academic challenge. The legitimacy of the law depends not just on its underlying normative foundation but also on its assumptions about a complex, dynamic, and contested set of social facts. This calls for robust and reliable sociological and economic data—social scientists have their task cut out for them.

The third significant implication relates to the role of alternative values, especially equality. I admitted that a successful discrimination law would make a society more equal, but that this would only be a by-product of seeking freedom. Lawyers tend to call discrimination law 'equality law'. This equivalence either overestimates the potential of discrimination law or underestimates the demands of equality. Champions of equality need not only address sceptical doubts about its desirability in the first place, but also propose a system of laws its genuine pursuit would require. While we recognize that the aspiration of discrimination law does not seek true equality, it is also important to highlight what the egalitarians got right: their intuition that *relative* disadvantage is key to understanding discrimination law is correct. If this intuition were sufficient to make one an egalitarian, this would be an egalitarian account of discrimination law.

In fact, advocates of dignity and rationality also hit several marks. Dignitarians understood that discrimination law is not about material disadvantage alone—its systemic concern with socio-cultural disadvantage and its hostility at the particular level to expressive injuries would have been difficult to establish without recourse to the discourse on the significance of dignity. Even as rationality failed to explain why discrimination was prohibited in the first place, its (limited) role in justifying discrimination and affirmative action is recognized in the law. All of these impulses are founded on the basis of some truth—all I have shown is that they are but pieces in a larger jigsaw, founded upon a capacious appreciation of human freedom.

Fourth, we have seen that discrimination law is prioritarian rather than partisan. It prioritizes the interests of the disadvantaged, but does not commit itself to benefiting any particular group as such. We are all actual or potential beneficiaries. This insight allows us to transcend the narrow confines of identity politics. It goads us to build coalitions with (rather than compete with) others who are deprived as we are, and to forge a fellowship of the disadvantaged.

Finally, and perhaps most importantly, I have shown that the effects-based legal understanding of discrimination is superior to the intention-based lay approach. This has clear implications for the current debate on the nature and shape of discrimination law, in the United States in particular. But the implications of this finding extend wider. This is an area where law has shown moral leadership, and society would do well to follow. This is certainly not a call for our social understanding of what discrimination is to mirror the understanding in law. The law of a liberal state works under certain constraints, often allowing us to commit moral wrongs. Right moral intuitions are likely to be more demanding than the law: we would certainly do well to consider the effect of inviting Muslim friends to a lunch party during

Ramadan, even if the law has nothing to do with it. But the book does highlight the need to narrow the gap between the lay and the legal models, mostly through the lay model moving towards the legal one.

9.2 Possibilities

Some concerns, that were tangential to my project, could be developed further. Four significant ones bear mention. Meta-theoretical concerns have acquired considerable currency in *general* jurisprudence—what methodology should someone interested in exploring the nature of law generally adopt? Whose point of view is relevant? Can general jurisprudence be a purely descriptive exercise? These questions have invited much attention from scholars recently.[2] This book is an exercise in *particular* jurisprudence—it theorizes not about law generally, but about a specific area of law. I have made certain meta-theoretical assumptions—sometimes defended, often not—as any such work must. Chapter 2, especially, spent some time thinking about the basis on which we demarcate law into different 'areas', and the legitimacy of their definition as this or that area of law. Tort lawyers, labour lawyers, and others have suffered similar existential angst.[3] It will be helpful to think more generally about the reason why we classify law in this way, the various bases upon which we make the classification, whether the classifications made by practice and by the academy map onto one another, and whether there are any implications of such classifications. Thinking generally about particular jurisprudence—its methodology, possible points of view, the influence of other jurisprudential commitments—is fertile ground for future scholarship.

The second issue that received only tangential treatment in this book is the demands that liberalism makes on a state. Chapter 4 developed a basic goods-focussed approach to liberty, and argued—perhaps counterintuitively—that our positive freedom depends on what others have. The relative, contextual, perfectionist vision of freedom is admittedly contestable, and needs more detailed exploration than what Chapter 4 was able to undertake.

Third, the insights of this book concern discrimination law at a high level of generality. They have implications for a number of more specific concerns,

---

[2] For examples, see Ronald Dworkin, 'Hart's Postscript and the Character of Political Philosophy' (2004) 24 Oxford Journal of Legal Studies 1; Julie Dickson, *Evaluation and Legal Theory* (Hart 2001).

[3] John Gardner, 'What is Tort Law For? Part 1: The Place of Corrective Justice' (2011) 30 Law and Philosophy 1; Hugh Collins, 'Labour Law as a Vocation' (1989) 105 Law Quarterly Review 468.

which have not been borne out clearly in the discussion. Further work is needed to consider and clarify how our conclusions impact these specific concerns. To take one example, we focussed on only the very general features of protected grounds. We know, however, that these grounds also differ in significant respects. The conclusions of the book are relevant to, but do not determine, whether the law should treat certain grounds (such as religion) differently, and if so, in what ways should that difference manifest itself.

Finally, the project is a product of the dataset I chose. Insights from other jurisdictions, or rival understandings of the practice in the selected jurisdictions, will no doubt put pressure on the claims I have made. There may even be countries that have sought to address the problem of relative group disadvantage through tools entirely distinct from (and, perhaps, more effective than) discrimination law. Considering the questions from other vantage points could highlight the possibilities and stimulate our imagination.

Substantial, pervasive, and abiding advantage gaps between groups whose membership is valuable or at least value-neutral is a serious impediment to human freedom. Discrimination law is a modest step towards realizing this freedom. Ultimately, only when enough of us internalize and pursue the values underpinning discrimination law voluntarily will this aspect of freedom be truly secured.[4] Gandhi knew this: issuing his talisman as he did to individuals, rather than the state.

---

[4] It is important that the norm is internalized even by those who are *permitted* by law to engage in wrongful discrimination, especially in private contexts. Even though the law does not directly regulate this conduct, it can make desirable structural interventions. See generally, Elizabeth Emens, 'Intimate Discrimination: The State's Role in the Accidents of Sex and Love' (2009) 122 Harvard Law Review 1307.

Bibliography

Abram M, 'Affirmative Action: Fair Shakers and Social Engineers' (1986) 99 Harvard Law Review 1312

Albertyn C and Goldblatt B, 'The Decriminalisation of Gay Sexual Offences: The National Coalition for Gay and Lesbian Equality and Another v The Minister of Justice and Others, 1998 (6) BCLR 726 (W)' (1998) 14 South African Journal of Human Rights 416

Alexander L, 'What Makes Wrongful Discrimination Wrong? Biases, Preferences, Stereotypes and Proxies' (1992) 141 University of Pennsylvania Law Review 149

Alexy R, *A Theory of Constitutional Rights* (Rivers J tr, Oxford University Press 2002)

Ambedkar B, *Annihilatin of Caste* (Verso 2014)

Anderson B, *Imagined Communities: Reflections on the Origin and the Spread of Nationalism* (revised edn, Verso 2006)

Anderson E, 'Recent Thinking about Sexual Harassment: A Review Essay' (2006) 34 Philosophy and Public Affairs 284

Anderson M, *Islamic Law and the Colonial Encounter in British India* (Grabels 1996)

Areheart B, 'The Anticlassification Turn in Employment Discrimination Law' (2011–12) 63 Alabama Law Review 955

Aristotle, *The Nicomachean Ethics* (Ross D tr, Oxford University Press 2009)

Arneson R, 'What is Wrongful Discrimination?' (2006) 43 San Diego Law Review 775

Arneson R, 'Discrimination, Disparate Impact, and Theories of Justice' in Deborah Hellman and Sophia Moreau (eds) *Philosophical Foundations of Discrimination Law* (Oxford University Press 2013)

Avins A, 'What is a Place of "Public" Accommodation?' (1968) 52 Marquette Law Review 1

Bagenstos S, '"Rational Discrimination", Accommodation, and the Politics of (Disability) Civil Rights' (2003) 89 Virginia Law Review 825

Bagenstos S, 'Implicit Bias, "Science," and Antidiscrimination Law' (2007) 1 Harvard Law and Policy Review 477

Bamforth N, *Sexuality, Morals and Justice* (Cassell 1997)

Bamforth N, 'The Public Law–Private Law Distinction: A Comparative and Philosophical Approach' in Leyland P and Woods T (eds), *Administrative Law Facing the Future: Old Constraints and New Horizons* (Blackstone 1997)

Bamforth N, 'The Application of the Human Rights Act 1998 to Public Authorities and Private Bodies' (1999) 58 Cambridge Law Journal 159

Bamforth N, 'Conceptions of Anti-Discrimination Law' (2004) 24 Oxford Journal of Legal Studies 693

Bamforth N, O'Cinneide C, and Malik M, *Discrimination Law: Theory and Context* (Sweet & Maxwell 2008)

Basant R and Sen G, 'Who Participates in Higher Education in India? Rethinking the Role of Affirmative Action' (2010) XLV Economic and Political Weekly 62

Becker G, *The Economics of Discrimination* (2nd edn, University of Chicago Press 1971)

Berlin I, *Liberty: Incorporating Four Essays on Liberty* (Hardy H ed, Oxford University Press 2002)

Birks P, *Unjust Enrichment* (2nd edn, Oxford University Press 2005)

Black C, 'The Lawfulness of the Segregation Decisions' (1960) 69 The Yale Law Journal 421

Brake D, 'When Equality Leaves Everyone Worse Off: The Problem of Levelling Down in Equality Law' (2004) 46 William and Mary Law Review 513

Brest P, 'In Defense of the Antidiscrimination Principle' (1976) 90 Harvard Law Review 1

Brontsema R, 'A Queer Revolution: Reconceptualizing the Debate over Linguistic Reclamation' (2004) 17 Colorado Research in Linguistics 1

Butler J, *Gender Trouble: Feminism and the Subversion of Identity* (10th anniversary edn, Routledge 1999)

Carter W, 'Affirmative Action as Government Speech' (2011) 59 UCLA Law Review 2

Cartwright J, 'Remoteness of Damage in Contract and Tort: A Reconsideration' (1996) 55 Cambridge Law Review 488

Cavanagh M, *Against Equality of Opportunity* (Oxford University Press 2002)

Chin A and Prakash N, 'The Redistributive Effects of Political Reservations for Minorities: Evidence from India' (2011) 96 Journal of Development Economics 265

Choudhry S, 'Distribution vs. Recognition: The Case of Anti-Discrimination Laws' (2000) 9 George Mason Law Review 145

Choudhry S, 'How to Do Comparative Constitutional Law in India: Naz Foundation, Same Sex Rights, and Dialogical Interpretation' in Khilnani S, Raghavan V, and Arun Thiruvengadam (eds), *Comparative Constitutionalism in South Asia* (Oxford University Press 2010)

Collins H, 'Labour Law as a Vocation' (1989) 105 Law Quarterly Review 468

Collins H, 'Discrimination, Equality and Social Inclusion' (2003) 66 The Modern Law Review 16

Collins H, 'Social Inclusion: A Better Approach to Equality Issues?' (2004–2005) 14 Transnational Law and Contemporary Problems 897

Collins H, 'The Vanishing Freedom to Choose a Contractual Partner' (2013) 76 Law and Contemporary Problems 71

Crenshaw K, 'Demarginalising the Intersection of Race and Sex: A Black Feminist Critique of Antidiscrimination Doctrine, Feminist Theory and Antiracist Politics' [1989] The University of Chicago Legal Forum 139

Crisp R, 'Equality, Priority and Compassion' (2003) 113 Ethics 745

Cunningham C, Dorsey DE Jr, Bowen J et al., 'Rethinking Equality in the Global Society' (1997) 75 Washington University Law Quarterly 1561

Daniels N, 'Merit and Meritocracy' (1978) 7 Philosophy and Public Affairs 206

Darwall S, 'Two Kinds of Respect' (1977) 88 Ethics 36

di Torella E, 'No Sex Please: We're Insurers' (2013) 38 European Law Review 638

Dickson J, *Evaluation and Legal Theory* (Hart 2001)

Dillon R, 'Respect' Stanford Encyclopaedia of Philosophy <http://plato.stanford.edu/entries/respect/> accessed 27 October 2014

Dirks N, *Castes of Mind: Colonialism and the Making of Modern India* (Princeton University Press 2001)

Doyle O, 'Direct Discrimination, Indirect Discrimination and Autonomy' (2007) 27 Oxford Journal of Legal Studies 537

Dupré C, 'Human Dignity in Europe: A Foundational Constitutional Principle' (2013) 19 European Public Law 319

Dworkin G, *The Theory and Practice of Autonomy* (Cambridge University Press 1998)

Dworkin R, 'Hart's Postscript and the Character of Political Philosophy' (2004) 24 Oxford Journal of Legal Studies 1

Eidelson B, 'Treating People as Individuals' in Hellman D and Moreau S (eds), *Philosophical Foundations of Discrimination Law* (Oxford University Press 2013)

Ely J, *Democracy and Distrust: A Theory of Judicial Review* (Harvard University Press 1980)

Emens E, 'Integrating Accommodation' (2007–2008) 156 University of Pennsylvania Law Review 839

Emens E, 'Intimate Discrimination: The State's Role in the Accidents of Sex and Love' (2009) 122 Harvard Law Review 1307

Epstein R, *Forbidden Grounds: The Case Against Employment Discrimination Laws* (Harvard University Press 1992)

Eyer K, 'Marriage This Term: On Liberty and the "New Equal Protection"' (2012) 60 UCLA Law Review Discourse 2

Fallon R and Weiler P, '*Firefighters v. Stotts*: Conflicting Models of Racial Justice' [1984] The Supreme Court Review 1

Finnis J, *Natural Law and Natural Rights* (Clarendon Press 1980)

Finnis J, 'Directly Discriminatory Decisions: A Missed Opportunity' (2010) 126 Law Quarterly Review 491

Fishkin J, *Bottlenecks: A New Theory of Equal Opportunity* (Oxford University Press 2014)

Fiss O, 'The Fate of an Idea Whose Time has Come: Anti-Discrimination Law in the Second Decade after *Brown* v. *Board of Education*' (1974) 41 University of Chicago Law Review 742

Fiss O, 'Groups and the Equal Protection Clause' (1976) 5 Philosophy and Public Affairs 107

Ford R, 'Bias in the Air: Rethinking Employment Discrimination Law' (2014) 66 Stanford Law Review 1381

Frankfurt H, 'Equality as a Moral Ideal' (1987) 98 Ethics 21

Frankfurt H, 'Equality and Respect' (1997) 64 Social Research 3

Franklin C, 'The Anti-Stereotyping Principle in Constitutional Sex Discrimination Law' (2010) 20 New York University Law Review 101

Fredman S, 'Equality: A New Generation?' (2001) 30 Industrial Law Journal 145

Fredman S, *Discrimination Law* (Oxford University Press 2002)

Fredman S, 'Women at Work: The Broken Promise of Flexicurity' (2004) 33 Industrial Law Journal 299

Fredman S, *Discrimination Law* (2nd edn, Oxford University Press 2011)

Fredman S, 'Addressing Disparate Impact: Indirect Discrimination and the Public Sector Equality Duty' (2014) 43 Industrial Law Journal 349

Freeman A, 'Legitimizing Racial Discrimination Through Antidiscrimination Law: A Critical Review of Supreme Court Doctrine' (1978) 62 Minnesota Law Review 1049

Fuller L, 'The Forms and Limits of Adjudication' (1978) 92 Harvard Law Review 353

Galanter M, 'Who are the Other Backward Classes?: An Introduction to a Constitutional Puzzle' (1978) 13 Economic and Political Weekly 1812

Galanter M, *Competing Equalities: Law and the Backward Classes in India* (University of California Press 1984)

Gardner J, 'Liberals and Unlawful Discrimination' (1989) 9 Oxford Journal of Legal Studies 1

Gardner J, 'On the Ground of Her Sex(uality)' (1998) 18 Oxford Journal of Legal Studies 167

Gardner J, 'Obligations and Outcomes in the Law of Torts' in Cane P (ed), *Relating to Responsibility: Essays for Tony Honoré on his Eightieth Birthday* (Hart 2001)

Gardner J, 'What is Tort Law For? Part 1: The Place of Corrective Justice' (2011) 30 Law and Philosophy 1

Gardner J, 'What is Tort Law For? Part 2: The Place of Distributive Justice' in Oberdiek J (ed), *Philosophical Foundations of the Law of Torts* (Oxford University Press 2014)

Gibson D, 'Analogous Grounds for Discrimination Under the Canadian Charter: Too Much Ado About Next to Nothing' (1991) 29 Alberta Law Review 772

Goldberg S, 'Equality Without Tiers' (2004) 77 Southern California Law Review 481

Goldberg S, 'Marriage as Monopoly: History, Tradition, Incrementalism, and the Marriage/Civil Union Distinction' (2009) 41 Connecticut Law Review 1397

Goldberg S, 'Discrimination by Comparison' (2011) 120 Yale Law Journal 728

Gotanda N, 'A Critique of "Our Constitution is Color-Blind"' (1991) 44 Stanford Law Review 1

Green L, 'Rights of Exit' (1998) 4 Legal Theory 165

Green L, 'Two Worries about Respect for Persons' (2010) 120 Ethics 212

Green L, 'Sex-Neutral Marriage' [2011] Current Legal Problems 1

Green L, 'Should Law Improve Morality?' (2013) 7 Criminal Law and Philosophy 473

Hare R, 'Ethical Theory and Utilitarianism' in Lewis H (ed), *Contemporary British Philosophy* (George Allen & Unwin 1976)

Hart HLA, 'Prolegomenon to the Principles of Punishment' (1959–60) 60 Proceedings of the Aristotelian Society 1

Hart HLA, *Law, Liberty and Morality* (Oxford University Press 1963)

Hart HLA and Honoré T, *Causation in the Law* (2nd edn, Clarendon Press 1985)

Havelková B, 'Gender in Law Under and After State Socialism: The Example of the Czech Republic' (DPhil thesis, University of Oxford 2013)

Hellman D, *When is Discrimination Wrong?* (Harvard University Press 2008)

Hellman D and Moreau S, *Philosophical Foundations of Discrimination Law* (Oxford University Press 2013)

Hepple B, 'The European Legacy of *Brown v. Board of Education*' [2006] University of Illinois Law Review 605

Holmes E, 'Anti-Discrimination Rights Without Equality' (2005) 68 Modern Law Review 175

Hunt M, 'The "Horizontal Effect" of the Human Rights Act' [1998] Public Law 423

The Indian Express, 'Not Allowed to Sell Her Flat to a Muslim, Pune Woman Takes on Entire Sicoety' *The Indian Express* (Pune, 3 April 2008) <http://archive. indianexpress.com/news/not-allowed-to-sell-her-flat-to-a-muslim-pune-woman-takes-on-entire-society-1291804/> accessed 4 November 2014

Issacharoff S and Nelson J, 'Discrimination with a Difference: Can Employment Discrimination Law Accommodate the Americans with Disability Act?' (2000–1) 79 North Carolina Law Review 308

Jolls C, 'Antidiscrimination and Accommodation' (2001) 115 Harvard Law Review 642

Kahn-Freund O, *Kahn-Freund's Labour and the Law* (Davies P and Freedland M eds, 3rd edn, Stevens 1983)

Kang J, 'The Burdens of Manliness' (2010) 33 Harvard Journal of Law and Gender 477

Kannabiran K, *Tools of Justice: Non-Discrimination and the Indian Constitution* (Routledge 2012)

Karlan P and Rutherglen G, 'Disabilities, Discrimination, and Reasonable Accommodation' (1996) 46 Duke Law Journal 1

Kelsen H, *The Pure Theory of Law* (Knight M tr, University of California Press 1967)

Kennedy D, 'Form and Substance in Private Law Adjudication' (1976) 89 Harvard Law Review 1658

Kessler L, 'The Attachment Gap: Employment Discrimination Law, Women's Cultural Caregiving, and the Limits of Economic and Liberal Legal Theory' (2001) 34 University of Michigan Journal of Law Reform 371

Khaitan T, 'Beyond Reasonableness: A Rigorous Standard of Review for Article 15 Infringement' (2008) 50 Journal of the Indian Law Institute 177

Khaitan T, 'Transcending Reservations: A Paradigm Shift in the Debate on Equality' [20 September 2008] Economic and Political Weekly 8

Khaitan T, 'Reading *Swaraj* into Article 15: A New Deal for all Minorities' (2009) 2 NUJS Law Review 419

Khaitan T, 'Dignity as an Expressive Norm: Neither Vacuous Nor a Panacea' (2012) 32 Oxford Journal of Legal Studies 1

Khaitan T, 'Prelude to a Theory of Discrimination Law' in Hellman D and Moreau S (eds), *Philosophical Foundations of Discrimination Law* (Oxford University Press 2013)

Kline B, 'The Origin of the Rule Against Unjust Discrimination' (1917–18) 66 University of Pennsylvania Law Review 123

Kline B, 'The Scope of the Rule Against Unjust Discrimination by Public Servants' (1919) 67 University of Pennsylvania Law Review 109

Kristen E, 'Addressing the Problem of Weight Discrimination in Employment' (2002) 90 California Law Review 57

Lacey N, 'Legislation Against Sex Discrimination: Questions from a Feminist Perspective' (1987) 14 Journal of Law and Society 411

Lawrence C, 'The Id, the Ego, and Equal Protection: Reckoning with Unconscious Racism' (1987) 39 Stanford Law Review 317

Leigh I, Marcus A, Dobosh P, and Allen T, 'Deaf/Hearing Cultural Identity Paradigms: Modifications of the Deaf Identity Development Scale' (1998) 3 Journal of Deaf Studies and Deaf Education 329

Lessard H, 'Dollars Versus [Equality] Rights: Money and the Limits on Distributive Justice' (2012) 58 Supreme Court Law Review (2d) 299

Lester A, 'Equality and United Kingdom Law: Past, Present and Future' [2001] Public Law 77

Lewis P, 'Pregnant Workers and Sex Discrimination: The Limits of Purposive Non-Comparative Methodology' (Spring 2000) The International Journal of Comparative Labour Law and Industrial Relations 55

Lippert-Rasmussen K, 'The Badness of Discrimination' (2006) 9 Ethical Theory and Moral Practice 167

Lippert-Rasmussen K, 'Discrimination and Equality' in Marmor A (ed), *Routledge Companion to Philosophy of Law* (Routledge 2012)

Lippert-Rasmussen K, *Born Free and Equal? A Philosophical Inquiry into the Nature of Discrimination* (Oxford University Press 2014)

MacKinnon C, 'Toward a Renewed Equal Rights Amendment: Now More than Ever' (2014) 37 Harvard Journal of Law and Gender 569

Mandal B, *Report of the Second Backward Classes Commission (First Part)* (Second Backward Classes Commission 1980)

Margalit A, *The Decent Society* (Harvard University Press 1996)

Massey S, 'Is Self-Respect a Moral or a Psychological Concept' (1983) 93 Ethics 246

McAllister D, 'Section 15—The Unpredictability of the *Law* Test' (2003) 15 National Journal of Constitutional Law 35

McColgan A, 'Cracking the Comparator Problem: Discrimination, "Equal Treatment" and the Role of Comparisons' (2006) 6 European Human Rights Law Review 650

McConnachie C, 'Human Dignity, "Unfair Discrimination" and Guidance' (2014) 34 Oxford Journal of Legal Studies 609

McCrudden C, 'Institutional Discrimination' (1982) 2 Oxford Journal of Legal Studies 303

McCrudden C, 'Introduction' in McCrudden C (ed), *Anti-Discrimination Law* (Dartmouth 1991)

McCrudden C, 'A Common Law of Human Rights?: Transnational Judicial Conversations on Constitutional Rights' (2000) 20 Oxford Journal of Legal Studies 499

McCrudden C, 'Theorising European Equality Law' in Costello C and Barry E (eds), *Equality in Diversity: the New Equality Directives* (Irish Centre for European Law 2003)

McCrudden C, 'Introduction' in McCrudden C (ed), *Anti-Discrimination Law* (2nd edn, Ashgate 2004)

McCrudden C, *Buying Social Justice: Equality, Government Procurement, and Legal Change* (Oxford University Press 2007)

McCrudden C, 'A Comparative Taxonomy of "Positive Action" and "Affirmative Action" Policies' in Schulze R (ed), *Non-Discrimination in European Private Law* (Mohr Siebeck 2011)

McCrudden C, 'Dignity and the Challenge to Liberty: Reading Andras Sajo's Constitutional Sentiments' in Renata Uitz (ed), *Freedom and its Enemies: The Tragedy of Liberty* (Eleven international 2015)

McCrudden C, Muttarak R, Hamill H, and Heath A, 'Affirmative Action Without Quotas in Northern Ireland' (2009) 4 The Equal Rights Review 7

Meenan H (ed), *Equality Law in an Enlarged European Union: Understanding the Article 13 Directives* (Cambridge University Press 2007)

Mehta P, *The Burden of Democracy* (Penguin 2003)

Michelman F, 'Foreword: On Protecting the Poor Through the Fourteenth Amendment' (1969) 83 Harvard Law Review 7

Mill J, *On Liberty* (JW Parker & Son 1859)

Moon G and Allen R, 'Dignity Discourse in Discrimination Law: A Better Route to Equality?' [2006] European Human Rights Law Review 610

Moreau S, 'What is Discrimination?' (2010) 38 Philosophy and Public Affairs 143

Morris A, 'On the Normative Foundations of Indirect Discrimination Law: Understanding the Competing Models of Discrimination Law as Aristotelian Forms of Justice' (1995) 15 Oxford Journal of Legal Studies 199

Nayar P, *Mahatma Gandhi: The Last Phase*, vol 2 (Navejivan 1958)

Nolan D, 'A Right to Meritorius Treatment' in Gearty C and Tomkins A (eds), *Understanding Human Rights* (Pinter 1996)

Numhauser-Henning A and Laulom S, *Harrassment Related to Sex and Sexual Harrassment Law in 33 European Countries: Discrimination versus Dignity* (European Commission 2012)

Nussbaum M, *Women and Human Development: The Capabilities Approach* (Cambridge University Press 2000)

Nussbaum M, *Frontiers of Justice: Disability, Nationality, Species Membership* (Harvard University Press 2006)

Nussbaum M, 'Perfectionist Liberalism and Political Liberalism' (2011) 39 Philosophy and Public Affairs 3

O'Cinneide C, 'Positive Duties and Gender Equality' (2005) 8 International Journal of Discrimination and the Law 91

O'Cinneide C, 'The Uncertain Foundations of Contemporary Anti-Discrimination Law' (2011) 11 International Journal of Discrimination and the Law 7

O'Connell R, 'The Role of Dignity in Equality Law: Lessons from Canada and South Africa' (2008) 6 International Journal of Constitutional Law 267

Owen D, *Philosophical Foundations of Tort Law* (Clarendon Press 1995)

Pande R, 'Can Mandated Political Representation Increase Policy Influence for Disadvantaged Minorities? Theory and Evidence from India' (2003) 93 The American Economic Review 1132

Parfit D, 'Equality and Priority' (1997) 10 Ratio 202

Pettit P, 'Freedom as Antipower' (1996) 106 Ethics 576

Pettit P, *Republicanism: A Theory of Freedom and Government* (Oxford University Press 1999)

Pikkety T, *The Capital in the Twenty-First Century* (Harvard University Press 2014)

Plato, *Republic* (Waterfield R tr, Oxford University Press 1994)

Posner R, 'An Economic Analysis of Sex Discrimination Laws' (1989) 56 University of Chicago Law Review 1311

Post R, Appiah A, Butler J, Grey T, and Siegel R, *Prejudicial Appearances: The Logic of American Antidiscrimination Law* (Duke University Press 2001)

Rawls J, 'Two Concepts of Rules' (1955) 64 The Philosophical Review 3

Rawls J, *Political Liberalism* (Columbia University Press 1993)

Rawls J, *A Theory of Justice* (Oxford University Press 1999)

Raz J, 'Legal Principles and the Limits of Law' (1972) 81 The Yale Law Journal 823

Raz J, 'The Rule of Law and its Virtue' (1977) 93 The Law Quarterly Review 195

Raz J, *The Morality of Freedom* (Clarendon Press 1986)

Raz J, 'Facing Up: A Reply' (1989) 62 Southern California Law Review 1153

Raz J, *Value, Respect, and Attachment* (Cambridge University Press 2001)

Raz J, *The Authority of Law* (2nd edn, Oxford University Press 2009)

Réaume D, 'Harm and Fault in Discrimination Law' (2001) 2 Theoretical Inquiries in Law 349

Réaume D, 'Discrimination and Dignity' (2003) 63 Louisiana Law Review 645

Réaume D, 'Dignity, Equality and Comparison' in Hellman D and Moreau S (eds), *Philosophical Foundations of Discrimination Law* (Oxford University Press 2013)

Rousseau J-J, *A Discourse upon the Origin and Foundation of the Inequality among Mankind* (R & J Dodsley 1761)

Rutherglen G, 'Concrete or Abstract Conceptions of Discrimination' in Hellman D and Moreau S (eds), *Philosophical Foundations of Discrimination Law* (Oxford University Press 2013)

Sabbagh D, 'The Rise of Indirect Affirmative Action: Converging Strategies for Promoting "Diversity" in Selective Institutions of Higher Education in the United States and France' (2011) 63 World Politics 470

Schauer F, *Profiles, Probabilities and Stereotypes* (Harvard University Press 2003)

Seale Y, 'Q v. K' (LRB Blog, 2013) <http://www.lrb.co.uk/blog/2013/10/16/yasmine-seale/q-v-k> accessed 5 November 2014

Segall S, 'What's so Bad about Discrimination' (2012) 24 Utilitas 82

Segev Re, 'Making Sense of Discrimination' (2014) 27 Ratio Juris 47

Sen A, *Inequality Reexamined* (Clarendon Press 1992)

Shapiro M, 'Enforcing Respect: Liberalism, Perfectionism, and Antidiscrimination Law' (DPhil thesis, University of Oxford 2012)

Shin P, 'The Substantive Principle of Equal Treatment' (2009) 15 Legal Theory 149

Shin P, 'Liability for Unconscious Discrimination? A Thought Experiment in the Theory of Employment Discrimination Law' (2010) 62 Hastings Law Journal 67

Shin P, 'Is There a Unitary Concept of Discrimination?' in Hellman D and Moreau S (eds), *Philosophical Foundations of Discrimination Law* (Oxford University Press 2013)

Shue H, *Basic Rights: Subsistence, Affluence, and US Foreign Policy* (Princeton University Press 1980)

Siegel R, 'From Colorblindness to Antibalkanization: An Emerging Ground of Decision in Race Equality Cases' (2011) 120 The Yale Law Journal 1278

Sikka S, 'Untouchable Cultures: Memory, Power and the Construction of *Dalit* Selfhood' (2012) 19 Identities: Global Studies in Culture and Power 43

Silvers A and Stein M, 'An Equality Paradigm for Preventing Genetic Discrimination' (2002) 55 Vanderbilt Law Review 1341

Simpson B, *A History of the Common Law of Contract: The Rise of the Action of Assumpsit* (2nd edn, Clarendon Press 1987)

Somek A, *Engineering Equality: An Essay on European Anti-Discrimination Law* (Oxford University Press 2011)

Sowell T, *Affirmative Action around the World: An Empirical Study* (Yale University Press 2004)

Suk J, 'Quotas and Consequences: A Transnational Re-Evaluation' in Hellman D and Moreau S (eds), *Philosophical Foundations of Discrimination Law* (Oxford University Press 2013)

Sunstein C, 'The Anticaste Principle' (1994) 92 Michigan Law Review 2410

Sunstein C and Thaler R, *Nudge: Improving Decisions about Health, Wealth and Happiness* (Yale University Press 2008)

Szigeti T, 'Stereotyping as Direct Discrimination?' Oxford Human Rights Law Blog <http://ohrb.law.ox.ac.uk/?p=3803? accessed 22 September 2014

Tatum B, '*Why are all the Black Kids Sitting Together in the Cafeteria?' and Other Conversations about Race* (Basic Books 1997)

Thiruvengadam A, 'In Pursuit of "The Common Illumination of our House": Trans-Judicial Influence and the Origins of PIL Jurisprudence in South Asia' (2008) 2 Indian Journal of Constitutional Law 67

Thomson J, 'Preferential Hiring' (1973) 2 Philosophy and Public Affairs 364

Thoreau H, *Walden and Other Writings* (Bantam Books 1981)

Timmer A, 'Towards an Anti-Stereotyping Approach for the European Court of Human Rights' (2011) 11 Human Rights Law Review 707

US Census Bureau, *Statistical Abstracts of the United States* (US Census Bureau 2011)

Waddington L, 'Reasonable Accommodation: Time to Extend the Duty to Accommodate Beyond Disability?' (2011) 36 NTM|NJCM-Bulletin 186

Walby S, Armstrong J, and Humphreys L, *Review of Equality Statistics (UK Equality and Human Rights Commission)* (UK Equality and Human Rights Commission 2008)

Waldron J, 'A Right to Do Wrong' (1981) 92 Ethics 21

Waldron J, 'Dignity and Rank' in Waldron J and Dan-Cohen M (eds) *Dignity, Rank, and Rights* (Oxford University Press 2012)

Weber M, *From Max Weber: Essays in Sociology* (Gerth H and Mills W trs, Routledge & Kegan Paul 1970)

Westen P, 'The Empty Idea of Equality' (1982) 95 Harvard Law Review 537

White S, 'Freedom of Association and the Right to Exclude' (1997) 5 The Journal of Political Philosophy 373

Wilkinson R and Pickett K, *The Spirit Level: Why Equality is Better for Everyone* (Penguin 2010)

Williams B, 'The Idea of Equality' in Laslett P and Runciman W (eds), *Philosophy, Politics and Society* (second series edn, Blackwell 1962)

Williams B, 'What has Philosophy to Learn from Tort Law?' in Owen D (ed), *Philosophical Foundations of Tort Law* (Clarendon Press 1995)

Wintemute R, *Sexual Orientation and Human Rights: The United States Constitution, the European Convention, and the Canadian Charter* (Clarendon Press 1995)

Wolff R, *In Defense of Anarchism* (Harper & Row 1970)

Yoshino K, 'Assimilationist Bias in Equal Protection: The Visibility Presumption and the Case of "Don't Ask, Don't Tell"' (1998) 108 Yale Law Journal 485

Yoshino K, 'Covering' (2001–2002) 111 Yale Law Journal 769

Yoshino K, *Covering: The Hidden Assault on Our Civil Liberties* (Random House 2007)

Yoshino K, 'The New Equal Protection' (2011) 124 Harvard Law Review 747

Index

affirmative action 16, 27–9, 68, 80f,
164–5, 215f
  direct and indirect 84–5, 216, 232, 237–8
  facilitative and distributive 83–4, 216,
222f, 233
  justification 222f
  mandatory and voluntary 85–6, 216
  merit 226–7, 229–30
  positive duties 84
asymmetry (*see* groups: asymmetry)

basic goods (*see also* freedom; well-being)
  negative freedom 98f, 123–4,
  priority 40, 97, 107–8, 113–14, 129, 132,
179, 223–4, 236–8, 247
  relative access 97, 104–7, 110–12
  secured access 95–7, 100–1, 108, 122
  self-respect 108f, 126–8 (*see also*
expressivism)
  social forms 103–7
  sufficiency 97, 104, 110, 114
  valuable opportunities 102f, 124–6, 133,
209f
benefits and burdens 148f, 191, 218–19, 222f
  (*see also* duties; duty-bearers)
  costs of antidiscrimination 186f, 195f
  eccentric distribution of 38–41, 120,
129–30, 192, 223–4
  expressive and tangible 39–41,
149–53, 192, 218–19 (*see also*
expressivism)
  third-party interests 191–2, 228f

comparators (*see also* basic goods: priority,
basic goods: relative access, equality)
7, 34–5, 71–5, 92, 113f, 132, 151–3, 218
comparative law 11–17, 46–9

dignity (*see* expressivism)
disadvantage 34–7
  material 54–6, 123–6
  political 52–3, 123
  relative group disadvantage (*see also* groups:
asymmetry) 31–8, 51f, 117f, 152,
155–156, 167f, 175–180, 191,
216–217, 220

socio-cultural, expressive 53–4, 126f, 176
  (*see also* expressivism)
discrimination (*see also* benefits and burdens)
  collateral discrimination 145–6, 155, 171f,
221, 230–2
  direct discrimination 69f, 87, 143–4, 156f,
163–4, 183f
  indirect discrimination 73f, 87, 143–4,
156f, 163–4, 170, 183f
  justification 73, 75, 79, 80, 180f, 195f
  lay and legal models 1–4, 37–8, 144,
160f, 247
  mens rea, requirement of (*see also*
discrimination: lay & legal
models) 69f, 79–80, 166–7, 183f
  paradigmatic discrimination
  (*see also* disadvantage: relative
group disadvantage, groups:
asymmetry) 145, 171f, 231
  remedy for 76–9, 81–2, 226–7
  wrongfulness of 144, 155–6, 167f, 183f,
197, 217
discrimination law
  norms, coherence of 23–5, 42, 118–19
  origins 45–7
  theoretical foundation of 4–9, 243f
    pluralism 9–11, 247
    purposive and distributive
questions 9–11, 91, 117–18, 135,
143, 155–6, 246
duties 67f
  action-regarding and non-action-regarding
69, 74, 143–4, 146–8
  comprehensive 66
  positive and negative 86–7
  rights-generating and
non-rights-generating 86–7, 143
  unidirectional 65–6, 199–200, 212
  universal 39–41, 120, 198, 232, 237–9
  wrong-sensitive and wrong-insensitive (*see*
discrimination, wrongfulness of)
duty-bearers 62f, 186f, 195f, 225f
  employers 204–5, 210
  public-private divide 62f, 201f, 233f
  sellers and service-providers 205–6,
210–11

equality 6–8, 31, 68, 113f, 130f, 247
(*see also* basic goods: self-respect;
benefits and burdens: expressive and
tangible; disadvantage: relative group
disadvantage, socio-cultural, expressive;
groups: expressive salience of)
levelling-down objection 133, 153–4
expressivism 7–8, 32, 53–4, 222–3,
236–9, 247 (*see also* basic goods: self-
respect; benefits and burdens: expressive
and tangible; disadvantage: socio-
cultural, expressive; groups: expressive
salience of)

freedom, liberty 7–8, 91f, 130f, 181–2,
203f, 225, 228 (*see also* basic goods;
well-being)
perfectionism 93–5, 104, 134f

grounds 27–30, 45, 49
immutable and fundamental
grounds 50, 56–60
intersectionality 69, 137, 162–3, 219
irrelevance
normative 56f, 93–5, 134f (*see also*
freedom: perfectionism)
descriptive 134, 168, 188
protected grounds 49, 56, 119
universal and particular order 29–30,
57, 136
groups 3, 31f, 50f, 119–21, 154f
assimilation 58–60, 71, 99–100
asymmetry 34, 61–2, 120, 172f
cognate groups (*see also* discrimination:
collateral discrimination) 29–30, 119,
122, 145–6, 171f
expressive salience of 171f (*see also*
expressivism)
potentially national and non-national
groups 173–6
protected groups 31, 50f, 119, 145–6,
155–6, 220 (*see also* discrimination:
paradigmatic discrimination)

relative disadvantage of (*see* disadvantage:
relative group disadvantage)

harassment 29, 49, 79–80, 150–1, 159, 171,
182, 184, 210

identity (*see* expressivism)
immutability (*see* grounds: immutable and
fundamental grounds)
intersectionality (*see* grounds: intersectionality)

justification (*see* affirmative
action: justification;
discrimination: justification;
duty-bearers)

opportunities (*see* basic goods: valuable
opportunities)

priority (*see* basic goods: priority)
perfectionism (*see* freedom: perfectionism)
prejudice (*see* disadvantage: socio-cultural,
expressive)
protectorate (*see* grounds; groups)

rationality (*see also* grounds: descriptive
irrelevance) 229–30, 235, 247
reasonable accommodation, reasonable
adjustment 28, 39, 48–9, 76f, 86, 143, 196
relative group disadvantage (*see*
disadvantage: relative group
disadvantage)
remedies (*see* discrimination: remedy for)

security (*see* basic goods: secured access)
self-respect (*see* basic goods: self-respect)
stereotypes, proxies (*see*
disadvantage: socio-cultural, expressive)
sufficiency (*see* basic goods: sufficiency)
symmetry (*see* groups: asymmetry)

well-being 91f (*see also* basic goods; freedom,
liberty)

Printed and bound by CPI Group (UK) Ltd, Croydon, CR0 4YY

Newport Community
Learning & Libraries